TEACHING LEARNING IN THE PRESCHOOL

A DIALOGUE APPROACH

Revised Edition

Marion Blank

BROOKLINE
BOOKS

Library of Congress Cataloging in Publication Data

Blank, Marion.
   Teaching learning in the preschool.

   Bibliography: p.
   Includes index.
   1. Slow learning children — Education (Preschool)
2. Interaction analysis in education.   3. Concept
learning.   I. Title.
LC4661.B553   1983   372′.21   83-16884
ISBN 0-914797-06-9
Second printing, February 1988.

First edition published by Charles E. Merrill Publishing Co.

For Donna and Jonathan

Published by
Brookline Books, Inc.
P.O. Box 1046
Cambridge, MA 02238

Printed in the United States of America at McNaughton & Gunn, Inc.

Preface

Education, particularly special education, has been assigned the great responsibility of enhancing the course of a child's development. A major tool for accomplishing this ambitious goal is dialogue. We have long taken for granted that teachers and children speak with one another but, until recently, relatively little effort has been directed at understanding precisely what takes place during this exchange. This book, originally written a decade ago, represents an effort to highlight some of the intricacy and power of dialogue. When dialogue is moving effectively, both teacher and child learn from each other and benefit from the exchange. When it is not moving effectively, the interchange is one of pain and frustration for both. For the teacher, it means failure in their assigned task of enhancing the child's development. For the child, it means not only the torment of confusion and failure, but also a lost opportunity to profit from the material which the teacher has so carefully planned and organized.

Given the complexities of dialogue, it is not surprising that the system does not always succeed. However, success or failure will appear as though it were a chance phenomenon as long as the system remains unanalyzed. If the dialogue is to achieve its potential it is essential that we gain a fuller understanding of the forces at play when teachers and children are speaking to one another. Even more, we must begin to control these forces so that the likelihood of success increases for both teacher and child.

Unfortunately, our conscious understanding of language is limited by the concepts of language that researchers have formulated. The extent to which we are bound by available concepts is clearly evident in the text that follows. At the time it was written, the focus of psychological and psycholinguistic research was on syntactic and semantic themes (i.e., the structures that children use in their speech, the concepts they express, etc.). I had a definite, but rather ill-defined, sense of discomfort with these constructs. The discomfort arose because they were not central to the problems I observed in the classroom. Repeated observations of teacher-child talk could not be adequately defined by constructs from either a syntactic or semantic frame of reference. The central issue seemed to be one of communication.

My discomfort was registered most directly by my placing the word *dialogue* in the title. I hoped this word would convey the essential core of the book, the theme that "the teaching of the adult" and "the learning of the child" could no longer be separated and compartmentalized — if both teaching and learning are to occur, an effective dialogue has to take place. At the time the book was written, the state of the art was such that the outline of a dialogue approach could be offered in only an incomplete and elementary form. Fortunately, the past decade has been notable for the dramatic growth in our understanding of dialogue or, as it is more commonly termed, pragmatics. Inevitably with these new developments my own thinking has altered in a number of ways. Nevertheless, many of the ideas in this volume continue to be relevant and it is for this reason that this book is being reissued in its original form. In order to help the reader place past and current viewpoints in perspective, an epilogue is offered at the conclusion of this volume. Its purpose is to highlight the continuities and differences between the ideas written a decade ago and the ideas that I hold today. Change in thinking always adds complexity to an area, but it is also a sign of the remarkable vitality that marks the field of language development and makes it such an exciting area in which to work.

Acknowledgements

Many people have played an influential role in the development of the ideas in this book. These include my former colleagues in the Department of Psychiatry at Albert Einstein College of Medicine; in particular, Wagner Bridger whose extensive grasp of behavioral sciences constantly stimulated my thinking, Frances Solomon, whose insight into young children's behavior made me aware of the need to make theoretical ideas accord with practical realities, and Sibylle Escalona under whose tutelage I became keenly aware of the affective and cognitive interrelationships in children's functioning.

Along with working in the environment created by these people, I was most fortunate to receive a Career Development Award (Grant No. 5 KO2 MH10749) from the National Institute of Mental Health. This program, initially under the leadership of the late Bert Boothe and now directed by Mary Haworth, has and continues to offer an unparalleled opportunity for investigators to devote themselves fully to research. I shall always be grateful to the committee governing these awards for the opportunity and support they have given to me. I am also indebted to many of the faculty of the School of Education at the Hebrew University in Jerusalem for their help and encouragement during much of the initial writing of the manuscript. These include, in particular, Seymour Fox, Zev Klein, and Carl Frankenstein.

I also feel great appreciation for some of the central experiences earlier in my training. I had the privilege of being a student at the City College of New York during the time that Kenneth Clark was waging his historical battle for desegregation and so the drive for equality became for me not simply an abstraction but a living reality. I have no doubt that the tutorial basis of education at Cambridge University, where I took graduate studies, heavily influenced the ideas I subsequently developed. It was there too that I came into contact with an encouraging supervisor, Derek Russell Davis, who imbued me with his unshakeable belief in the modifiability of man and in the significance of the environment in affecting a child's development.

With this training, I then began to conduct experimental work on children's learning and the role of language in the young child's thinking. Much of this work was supported by the National Institute of Mental Health (Grant No. 5 RO1 MH08498, Grant No. 1 RO3 MH17904, Grant No. 2 M6418 and Grant No. MH07322), The Grant Foundation, The Ford Foundation, and the Soundview Throggs Neck Community Mental Health Center of the Albert Einstein College of Medicine. The work was carried out for the most part in day-care centers sponsored by Division of Day Care in the City of New York and in public schools operated by the Board of Education of this city. These centers, under the guidance of their devoted and gracious directors, offered the space and cooperation which were essential to the conduct of the research.

I wish to thank, too, the dedicated staff who helped me carry out the research; they include Laura Berlin, Frances Goldenberg, Barry Fritz, and Roger Zeeman. In addition, I would like to express my gratitude to Marilyn Tartaglia, Nina Cioffi, and Merrilly Calabrese for their endless patience in typing and retyping the drafts of the manuscript and to Frances Solomon, Sue Rose and Ellen Rossman for their careful reading and helpful comments of these drafts. My appreciation goes also to the Society for Research in Child Development for permission to reprint material from my article "Problems in the Teaching of Young Children," Monograph Series No. 9 (1970): 2-20; to Allyn and Bacon for permission to reprint material from my article "The Wrong Response: Is It to

Be Ignored, Prevented, or Treated," in *The Preschool in Action: Early Childhood Programs* (Boston: Allyn and Bacon, Inc., 1972), pp. 36-58. Copyright © 1972 by Allyn and Bacon; to the Society for Research in Child Development for permission to reprint sections from Frances Solomon and my article "How Shall the Disadvantaged Child Be Taught" in *Child Development* 40 (1969): 52-59; and to Random House to reprint excerpts from their Beginner Book *Are You My Mother?* by P. D. Eastman (New York: Random House, 1960). Copyright © 1960 by Random House, Inc.

Support for research comes from colleagues and agencies; support for the erratic home schedules that occur during such a period comes from a loving family. Therefore, I would like to give an award for tolerance to my husband, Martin, and my children, Donna and Jonathan, for their endless patience and to Blanche Harris who kept the household running smoothly during this time.

MARION BLANK

Contents

part 1

The Enhancement of Teacher-Child Interchange

chapter 1

Formulating the Problem

The problem is clear: many children are not learning in school. This failure is reported in many major technological countries (Gahagan & Gahagan, 1971; de Vries, 1972; Smilansky, 1967) and is most severe among what has been termed the "culture of poverty" (Lewis, 1966) — a phrase that has appeared under various guises as "the disadvantaged," "the deprived," "the minorities," and "the lower class." Learning problems are by no means confined to these groups — as society has begun to examine itself more critically, these problems have been shown to be far more widespread than was realized (Silberman, 1970).

The prevalence of school failure makes its recognition inescapable. A solution, however, is far less certain. The variables in the school situation are numerous and, depending upon one's perspective, each is a possible candidate for change. Hence, the proposed solutions range from rather conservative ones which call for revisions in materials to radical ones which call for the elimination of compulsory schooling (Illich, 1971).[1] In such a

---

[1]An alternative approach is gaining increasing prominence on the educational scene. For example, some current interpretations emphasize that uniformly poor academic achievement is a result, not of any difficulty in the child but of a cultural clash between the

complex and controversial situation, it seems clear that there can be no simple, single solution. Nevertheless, this should not detract from the search for an answer or, perhaps more accurately, a set of answers. While the path is far from certain, the search may lead both to reducing failure and to providing insight into such vital issues as "What enhances a child's learning?" and "What are the qualities of good teaching?"

It is from this perspective that I wish to describe a specialized teaching program that I have developed for children of preschool age. Given our current incomplete knowledge, it contains much that is speculative and uncertain but, in spite of these limitations, it is beginning to offer some striking insights into the principles that govern an effective learning-teaching situation. Before describing the program itself, it is necessary to spend some time considering the issues which underlie both the form and content of the program.

THE CENTRAL ISSUES

The program described here has been developed around the following issues:

1. The analysis of the child's functioning
2. The educational objectives deriving from this analysis

---

child and the school. The child is said to have a different motivational system, a different language, and a different set of values from that of the school which is oriented toward maintaining traditional "middle-class" standards (see Valentine, 1971; Houston, 1970; Labov, 1965; Baratz & Baratz, 1970). The presence of cultural differences is undeniable, but it is such a complex issue that it is uncertain at this point as to what contribution its recognition will make. The intricacy of the problem is reflected in the varied solutions which stem from this interpretation. Some recommendations based upon this approach suggest that schools develop programs more in accord with the child's life style (e.g., teaching in dialect — Baratz & Shuy, 1969). Although this approach has intuitive appeal, to my knowledge, no full curricula have been developed with this orientation. Therefore, to date it remains a theoretical ideal rather than a working model. Much more radical suggestions have also been proposed. These include the elimination of compulsory schools since they are deemed to be restrictive, artificial institutions that are destructive to learning (Illich, 1971). In this view, decisions about educational goals are to be left solely to the discretion of the child and family. Not only is this so antithetical to our present system as to be almost beyond realization but also it does little to handle the problem currently facing us — the development of an effective system that will achieve literacy for all.

3. The contents and methods necessary to attain these objectives

While these issues play a role in all teaching systems, the emphasis that they receive varies according to the system being developed. Thus, in many educational programs, particularly those for children who are functioning well, the basic goal is to transmit a body of knowledge that is not easily acquired without planned instruction. The teaching of literacy and mathematics is a case in point: the logical starting point is the content to be taught (i.e., the particular aspects of reading or mathematics that one wishes the student to learn). The analysis of the child's functioning plays a relatively minor role in program development. For example, in teaching literacy, the schools essentially rely on letting nature do the work; that is, they assume that by six years of age children will be sufficiently advanced developmentally to be ready to learn. This is not to deny the adjustments that are made for children according to the relative skills that they display. The children's level of functioning, however, is secondary; the primary focus is on the material to be taught.

Specialized programs for poorly functioning children are generally guided by a different set of considerations — considerations which lead to a reversal of priorities (Gray & Klaus, 1965; Weikart & Weigerink, 1968; Kamii, 1970; Deutsch & Deutsch, 1967; Bereiter & Engelmann, 1966). In these cases, the educational effort is mounted because of the child's generally weak performance. In the case of intervention programs for those of preschool age, the weak performance is generally not displayed in classroom performance because the demands at that age are limited. Rather the weak performance is displayed through tests that correlate with later school success (e.g., a poor oral vocabulary score is likely to mean later difficulties in written language). This situation means that the primary focus of the intervention effort is the student's initial level of functioning. The goal is not to teach traditional subject matter but to alter the child's mode of intellectual functioning so that general learning is facilitated and future failure is prevented or at least minimized. Content arises only as it may foster changes in the overall level of functioning. Therefore, the first step in the teaching effort is devoted to examining the reasons that underlie the child's difficulties in the school setting.

DEFINING THE CHILDREN'S DIFFICULTIES

Those who have followed early intervention efforts will be familiar with the amount of time and energy that has been directed toward defining the cause of the children's difficulties (i.e., the relative contribution of heredity vs. environment). While this debate continues unresolved, another issue exists which, although less compelling, is in fact of far greater relevance to education. This other issue is the limited knowledge we possess about the nature of children's difficulties. The problem exists largely because of the range and complexity of the behavior that is reflective of failure. Even at the preschool age, children who are later likely to fail in school show poor performance on such varied tasks as discrimination of sounds, categorization, analysis of complex visual patterns, recall of stories, and perceptual-motor representation (Stambak, 1951; Siegel et al., 1966; Deutsch, 1966; Birch & Belmont, 1964; John, 1963; Mattick, 1965; deHirsch et al., 1966; Blank, Weider, & Bridger, 1968; Blank & Frank, 1971; Blank, Higgins, & Bridger, 1971).

The predisposition we have to compartmentalize skills into different domains results in a strong pull to treat this disparate array of poor test performances as the composite result of many specific difficulties. This orientation is clearly evident in the Individual Educational Profiles (IEPs) that are a common feature of special education programs: poor performance on a set of visual tests will lead to suggestions for visual training, on a set of auditory tests to suggestions for auditory training, on a set of language tests to suggestions for language training, etc. This discrete skills orientation is so prevalent that it begins to feel both "right" and "natural."

This approach, however, is beset by difficulties. One set of problems stems from purely practical matters. As our knowledge of behavior becomes more sophisticated, an ever-increasing number of tests is created. The area of language is a case in point. The number of tests, both informal and formal, now available to the psychologist and educator is becoming overwhelming. Given what we already know, the administration of these tests to poorly functioning children is bound to yield low-level performance. When each index of poor performance is taken as a sign of a particular deficiency requiring remediation, the therapeutic situation becomes intolerable. Not only does the number of demands placed upon the educational system become unrealistically great, but also the remediation effort becomes a set of disjointed tasks.

Many of these problems can be overcome if one abandons the view of discrete skills and instead interprets the child's performance as reflecting a global quality of failure on school related tasks. Almost any test which correlates with school performance, regardless of its content (spatial, linguistic, memory, auditory, etc.), will reveal lower levels of functioning in children who are likely to fail in the classroom setting. I believe that the global quality of the failure is the central factor that must be explained if we are to make progress in educating the poorly functioning child.

THE CHILD'S MENTAL SET

In trying to understand the global quality of failure of the poorly functioning child, it is useful to take the seemingly paradoxical step of viewing the opposite side of the coin; namely, to examine the global success that marks the performance of the well functioning child. Regardless of the test that is used, these children tend to display high levels of performance. The success that they display on a wide variety of tests suggests that they have a generalized internal mental set which transcends the specific content of any test. With this set, the child can analyze both novel and familiar tasks in a way that permits him to recognize which skills are relevant at the moment. For example, after taking her first formal test—a reading readiness test—a five-year-old, upon returning to her classroom, reported to her teacher, "I had to work with letters today. Like I had to put a big A with a little a, and a big B with a little b." She then paused and independently corrected herself. "It wasn't exactly like that. That would have been too easy. They mixed the letters all up. First there was a G and then a D and then an M."

The child's remarks showed that she was familiar with the

content being tested. But her comment was indicative of far more than familiarity. She was saying, in effect, that she had recognized that there was a design in the seemingly independent terms. This recognition was not solely a function of the information available in the environment at that moment. It was also a function of the child's internal mental set — a set that led her to go beyond the specific content of the test and discern the unstated, but nevertheless highly meaningful, relationships that it contained.

The example just offered is derived from a test setting. The observation of children, however, indicates that this behavior is not limited to this setting. It is a major characteristic present in the spontaneous comments and question-asking that are the hallmark of the well functioning preschool child. Isaacs, in her studies of behavior of children in her nursery school (1930), has given extensive coverage to this behavior, but all who work with children are familiar with it. It is expressed in comments such as a child (a) remarking, upon encountering a dark ditch, "Now I know where the night hides itself," or (b) asking, when in conversation with his parents, "Daddy, when you were little, were you a boy or a girl?" (Chukovsky, 1963).

It may seem strange to use these quotes as evidence of the child's intellectual skills because these examples, though delightful, reflect the misconceptions of reality that Piaget has so forcefully brought to our attention (e.g., when the child talks about the "night hiding itself," he is treating the night as if it had the capacity to perform the purposeful actions that animate beings can perform). Consequently, the behavior can easily be interpreted as a sign not of the child's skill but of his failure to grasp certain concepts.

Such an interpretation, however, overlooks the fact that a considerable amount of mental effort has been expended in just formulating the question. Further, the effort was expended even though there was no demand for such a question to be formulated. The child has independently taken upon himself the task of figuring out a design through which the parts of his world can be related, in much the same way as the child who took the reading test sought to figure out its rationale. He is attempting to bring order to events around him — not because it is essential for adaptation but rather for the pleasure of intellectual understanding. For example, in the second anecdote above the child is pondering nonpresent events (i.e., his parent as a child) even though he has not directly experienced these events.

The child may continue to confuse the issue he is thinking about for a long time since he is groping with highly complicated phenomena, both cognitively and emotionally. The failure to reach a rapid resolution does not detract from the obvious striving for mastery that is being displayed. His ideas may be naive or contradictory, but they are a constantly present sign of his "stubborn determination . . . to bring at least illusory order into his limited and fragmentary knowledge of the world. Let the child at first establish associations in a haphazard and spontaneous way; let him apply false analogies. Just the same, the desire to answer for himself the questions — What for? Why? In what way? — is a most important aspect of his psychological development. This research for causal relationships is the basis of culture; it is the guarantee of the progress of human thought and no matter how often the child stumbles when he takes his first intellectual steps (and he stumbles literally at every such step!) he is following the right road" (Chukovsky, 1963, p. 24).

This self-imposed urge for understanding that characterizes well functioning children has been seen by many investigators as the key to higher-level intellectual functioning and has been variously designated as *reflectivity* (Kagan et al., 1963), *attention* (Duetsch, 1966), *conceptual representation* (Werner, 1957), *field independence* (Witkin et al., 1954), and the *abstract attitude* (Goldstein, 1959). While such high-level terms are used commonly, it may be somewhat surprising to have them raised in the context of a discussion on the preschool child. Not only are they associated with the achievements of the mature mind, but also it is evident that, at least in their traditional usage, they are beyond the young child's capabilities. It may even seem like an intrusion upon the naivete of childhood to expect anything approximating this level of functioning. But, as I have attempted to show in the examples above, the precursors of these behaviors are available. Because these are the precursors and not the final product, I feel that, of all the various terms for higher-level performance, the designation "abstract attitude" is perhaps the most useful shorthand.

Admittedly, this term has many weaknesses. It is often

discredited scientifically because it is so imprecise that it can be molded to fit such different groups as the the brain-damaged, the schizophrenic, and the mentally retarded. Such vagueness makes it difficult to accept any hypothesis based on the abstract attitude since it is almost impossible to pinpoint the particular characteristics it is supposed to define. (For a fuller discussion, see Brown, 1958, Chapter VIII.)

Despite these shortcomings, this term has the value of capturing the self-initiated aspect of the well functioning child's intellectual activity. The definition, as put forth by Goldstein, is imbued with this quality because the emphasis throughout his work is on factors such as the ability to assume a definite mental set, to shift reflectively from one aspect of a situation to another, to voluntarily evoke previous experiences, and to keep in mind various aspects of a task. These characteristics do not refer to specific skills, but rather to the set one has in approaching information. It is a set that is characterized by spontaneity in that it comes into play only if the individual, whether an adult or a child, elects to use it.

This spontaneity goes far beyond the easy, free-flowing responsiveness that is usually associated with this word. It reflects instead the set that is adopted when one actively seeks to maximize understanding of the world. As such, the term abstract attitude may be most apt for the well functioning child. In contrast to the thinking of the mature adult, the child does not possess the *ability* to reason abstractly but instead the *motivation* and *quest* to do so.

THE ABSTRACT ATTITUDE AND THE SCHOOL SETTING

For those who value a certain range of intellectual skills, possession of an abstract attitude would seem to be inherently useful. It would allow one to seek a richer and deeper interpretation of a variety of situations. For example, imagine a five-year-old seeing a large ship in a river. If that child does not possess a self-initiated search for meaning, the ship is simply a ship; that is, a large, moving, attractive object in the water. However, if the child possesses the abstract attitude, the ship is likely to trigger a variety of reactions including questions such as "Heavy things sink. That ship is heavy, why isn't it sinking?" Parents of well functioning preschoolers are familiar with having to answer this and other intricate questions asked by their offspring. Although this type of intellectual curiosity has great appeal to many, it is important to recognize that it is not essential to the situation. The child whose concept of the ship is confined to simply "seeing a ship" may have a less rich mental life than the other child, but this difference need not have any significant effect on the child's functioning in the setting.

In other situations, the presence or absence of the abstract attitude plays a far more critical role. One such situation is the school. In the case of the ship, the child had no need to deal actively with the material he was confronting. In the case of the school, however, the child must do precisely that — he is consistently asked to grapple with an endless number of imposed tasks, whether the tasks be in the form of a workbook, a computer program, or verbal demands by the teacher. Despite their varying forms (a question by a teacher, a blank to be completed in a workbook, a key to be pressed on a computer console), the tasks in school are ones which the adult community has deemed the child ought to master. As such, unlike the example of the ship, the children's ability to comprehend fully and grapple actively with the material becomes critical. To the degree that they can mobilize their intellectual efforts, their performance will be judged as effective; to the degree that they cannot or will not mobilize these efforts, their performance will be judged as ineffective.

This interpretation of the situation has important consequences for any intervention effort. The child who possesses the abstract attitude will freely and spontaneously elect to use it — he does not require the imposed tasks of the school to reflect about a wide variety of situations. On the other hand, the child who does not possess the abstract attitude will not readily initiate analytic and reflective skills — he is highly dependent upon the school setting for application of such skills.

Ironically, the need for teaching does not insure that the poorly functioning child will eagerly take advantage of the teaching experience when it is offered. In fact, he is likely to show avoidance of this situation (Silberman, 1970). For the older child, the avoidance is due in part to the uninspiring way in which much of education is packaged. However, this factor is not as central to the nursery school age because preschools are generally marked by a much freer and happier atmosphere than are schools for older children. Nevertheless, the poorly functioning child still withdraws from the school experience, even at the preschool age (Mattick, 1965).

THE ROLE OF MOTIVATION

The reason for the child's disengagement can be found in the emotional reactions that inevitably accompany difficulties in any sphere. When a person's mastery of a given area is not well developed, he is made uncomfortable in situations demanding that behavior. It is the most natural of human responses to avoid anxiety-provoking situations. Limitations in the abstract attitude, therefore, have profound implications for they can lead the child to avoid the cognitively-loaded situations where self-directed questioning and observation would be most useful. This means that the intervention setting, which the adult sees as helpful, may be viewed by the child as a place where he is required to do all the things he feels least capable of doing.[2] Not only must he listen to information that is confusing, but also he will be asked to answer questions that he does not understand. From his point of view, he only stands to lose since his weaknesses are bound to be exposed.

With time the tension between the teacher and the child grows to be so severe that it has been described in the following terms. "The child is in an asymmetrical situation where anything he says can literally be held against him. He has learned a number of devices to avoid saying anything in this situation, and he works very hard to achieve this end" (Labov, 1969, p. 6). In other words, the child devotes his efforts to removing himself from the educational

---

[2]This discussion is relevant to the recent concerted efforts to develop cognitive skills through structured preschool programs. In the past, much less emphasis was placed by nursery schools on such directed training and therefore one might be tempted to revert to the unpressured atmosphere. While this would have the advantage of reducing the child's anxiety since the stress would be lessened, it would have the serious disadvantage of abandoning cognitive growth as a goal of early education.

situation by calling upon the defenses he possesses against stress, including withdrawal, anger, resistance, and denial.

The child need not be consciously aware of his anxiety. His experience is simply that people — even people he may like — are demanding something from him, and he does not understand what that something is. This feeling is sufficient cause for anxiety in any person; in fact, its lack of specificity can be sufficient cause for massive anxiety in certain situations. While the anxiety need not be at a conscious level, in both my own experience and that of others (Mattick, 1965), it is often explicit by kindergarten age. Common reactions to cognitive demands are "I can't," "I'm dumb," "I'm stupid," and "I don't know how to do things."

The natural immaturity of the young means that all children will experience some discomfort in learning since so many situations are beyond their ken. The possession of the abstract attitude, however, helps to protect the well functioning child since his encounters with failure will be fewer. In addition, when they do occur the impact can be lessened because the child's relatively advanced cognitive skills permit him to establish correspondingly more sophisticated defenses. For example, one bright preschooler feigned the ability to read.[3] When asked to prove his nonexistent skill, he quickly gave as an alibi the apology that he could not comply because he had "forgotten his glasses" (Chukovsky, 1963).

THE OBJECTIVES FOR THE PRESCHOOL CHILD

This discussion on the abstract attitude has focused almost exclusively on its importance in the school environment. This emphasis is intentional, since present methods do not permit us to say whether the abstract attitude is of value in tasks that occur in school alone or whether it is of use in meeting the more general demands of everyday life. A reliable answer is impossible because any systematized attempt to assess the abstract attitude almost

---

[3]As with all defenses, these behaviors may be overused and ultimately serve to prevent learning. This is particularly likely if the initially well functioning child feels himself pressured to deal with situations that he finds overly complex. In the normal course of events, however, the occasional use of cognition to hide ignorance serves the child well.

always requires the imposition of an externally imposed task (i.e., a test). By definition, such a test conveys some of the school-like atmosphere. Recently linguists have begun to develop techniques for assessing children under the more "natural" conditions of their home environment (Labov et al., 1965). If these techniques are developed further, it may be feasible to study the spontaneous, self-generated attempts at reasoning and thinking that the poorly functioning child displays in the nonacademic setting. Until such time, however, speculations about the importance of the abstract attitude must be confined to the school situation. At this point, the most that can be reasonably concluded is that the abstract attitude is central to academic achievements and that weaknesses in this sphere are present in children who function poorly in school.

The question that logically arises is: What are the educational goals derived from this analysis? The issue of educational goals forces us to confront another of the many controversial topics in education. Unfortunately, a specific solution does not automatically flow from a diagnosis. As in medicine, a choice of actions can be offered even when there is agreement as to the nature of the problem. Indeed, diversity of opinion is an outstanding characteristic of the educational scene. For example, we now know that an enriched preschool experience, such as the Headstart program, need not show marked or lasting gains. Many use such findings to suggest even earlier intervention (Gordon, 1969; Schaefer, 1969); others use these same findings to "advocate forgetting about preschool programs and concentrate instead on improving the later educational programs" (Caldwell as quoted by Silberman, 1970).

Other examples of diverse opinions can readily be found. For instance, among investigators who agree on the importance of cognitive performance in school, some stress the need to develop these skills in poorly functioning children (Kamii, 1970; Siegel et al., 1966; Karnes et al., 1970). Others, however, are experimenting with the idea of redesigning academic tasks so that the same skills (i.e., reading) will be achieved under situations that reduce the "conceptual and problem-solving difficulties of school learning" (Bereiter, 1970) — in other words, rather than enhance the cognitive functioning of the children, limit the cognitive demands of the task.

These contrasting views can serve to benefit education, for as programs based on varied approaches develop, they may begin to yield some of the knowledge that is so badly needed. It may even be found that some of the seemingly conflicting proposals are in fact complementary. For example, the reduction of complexity through programmed learning may help to improve performance in skill areas such as reading, while the retention of complexity might be useful for the development of problem solving and logical thinking. At this stage in our knowledge, it is essential that work proceed along all avenues so as to ascertain the relative effectiveness of these different ideas. But any particular investigator would be lost if he attempted all possible approaches. Therefore, each must elect his own guiding philosophy.

My own training and experience has led me to believe that it would be most fruitful to attempt to enhance the cognitive repertoire of the child at the preschool period with the goal of helping him develop the self-imposed search for meaning that is so vital to strategies of thinking and information processing. While there are many reasons for this conclusion, two seem paramount. The first has to do with a phenomenon noted earlier — the resistance and anxiety that increasingly become associated with the school setting. Under this tense atmosphere, learning is made extraordinarily difficult. Thus, to leave the child until school age without any formal efforts to facilitate his performance is to set the stakes against the child's future success.

A second factor militating for early intervention is the quality of the behavior subsumed under the term abstract attitude — in particular, the self-initiated urge for mastery and understanding. If this attitude can be inspired within the poorly functioning child, his learning will not be so tightly confined to specific situations where demands are placed upon him. Instead, he will feel the internal press to grapple with cognitive problems, thus maximizing the learning he will obtain.

Neither of these factors means that the enhancement of performance at the preschool age will be sufficient for future academic competence. As with any behavior, it will fall into disrepair if not used. But both factors do indicate that special efforts in the early years cannot be easily bypassed without serious risk. It was on the basis of ideas such as these that the goal of the teaching program became the fostering of the abstract attitude in the preschool child.

A CHANGE IN STRUCTURE

With the goal established, we now confront the third factor set out at the beginning of the chapter — the serious practical problem of how is the aim to be achieved? Normally, this question would lead to a focus on content since, as noted earlier, that represents the heart of most educational efforts. This emphasis has characterized many early intervention programs: a Montessori program will offer special equipment designed to develop particular concepts; a Piagetian-based program will offer material leading to the (pre)scientific concepts of space, time, causality, and conservation; a language-based program will offer certain types of linguistic experience; and so on.

In the present instance, content, though vital, does not receive primary consideration. An emphasis on content seems most appropriate when the objectives are the transmission of specific skills (e.g., reading, music, and French). That is not the objective here. Instead, the aims are to alter the child's functioning so that his general academic performance is enhanced. This goal leads the initial focus to be not on content but on format — a format based upon a tutorial method of instruction. In order to see why this structure was selected it is useful to consider the instances of thinking that mark the well functioning child's performance — instances such as "Why does water go out of the way when anything goes in?" Isaacs (1930) in her classic book on intellectual development provides hundreds of anecdotes of a comparable nature.

An implicit but constant factor in a vast percentage of these examples is the presence of an intimate adult-child dialogue. This is not to deny that the child can try out many of his thinking skills on his peers, and even in conversations with himself (see Weir, 1962). Nevertheless, most meaningful, directed, and sustained interchange at the preschool level occurs between the adult and child, and usually, because of our societal structure, it is between the mother and child. This dialogue virtually has to have a qualitatively different nature from any other type of dialogue in which the child engages.

When the young child is by himself or with other children, it is not likely that he will experience objections if he begins to ramble on "meaninglessly," if he changes subjects without any apparent logic, or if his sentences are actually senseless. The adult world, however, can present a wall of reality which greatly modifies this egocentric speech. Even when the mother intuitively knows that the child is incapable of mature thinking, if she herself is predisposed toward a style of interchange characteristic of the abstract attitude, she will react to a youngster as if he were more logical and mature than he is. She corrects his referents ("No, that isn't a table, it's a desk"); she informs him of what is to happen ("Now I'll get lunch ready"); she asks him to clarify his verbal expression ("Now, what do you mean; do you want the doll or the box?") (Ortar & Carmon, 1969). The child is acutely aware of the adult's role and this awareness leads him, in turn, to initiate dialogue with the adult — the person who can provide information, corroboration, and approval (Honig et al., 1970). A basic fact of development is that the child's early thinking system is intimately bound up with this one-to-one relationship (see John & Goldstein, 1964).

Attempts at remediation have recognized this problem since many have been directed toward training mothers to do teaching at home (Levenstein, 1970; Gordon, 1969; Schaefer, 1969). As so often happens in a field as eclectic as compensatory education, this idea has been used in one setting and ignored in another. As a result, programs confined to home training have often adopted this approach; programs established in the school setting generally have disregarded it. Once education was placed in the formal school setting, it seemed only natural and appropriate to turn to the already established structure — the structure in this case being the group-based class. Admittedly, group-based teaching is more economical but serious doubts exist as to its usefulness in helping the young child achieve higher level learning. The limitations of the group structure become evident when one examines the substance that forms the basis of intellectual development.

THE SUBSTANCE OF THE ABSTRACT ATTITUDE

Because of the current wave of interest in intellectual development, there has been strong need to pinpoint precise components of higher level functioning. This has led to a tendency to reduce the child's knowledge to discrete components that somehow make the morass of thinking more manageable. We partition the child's mental world into concepts such as space, time, and number, almost as if bits of information are the critical units in cognition. But, if it is to be meaningful, even the simplest bit of information must be embedded in a larger context. The overriding quality of the abstract attitude is sustained sequential thinking. Just as musical notes attain their full meaning only when heard within a melody, ideas attain their full potential only when embedded in context. This is true even at the elementary level of a simple statement. A sentence like "the car is red" takes on totally different meanings if the immediately preceding event was:

1. A question such as "How did he recognize the car?"
2. A question such as "How is the car different from the other car?"
3. A question such as "What thing outside is red?"

In this example, only a simple two-step interchange was involved. Nevertheless, if the immediately preceding request was not known or understood, the information in the answer is almost meaningless. The question of context becomes increasingly important as chains of events extending into time and space must be understood. To be able to see objects, events, and words as located within their appropriate framework, the child must be able to maintain concentration and evaluate the information that is available to him. The opportunity for the sustained pursuit of an idea is of vital importance; it is critical to the way in which the abstract attitude is acquired.

Neither the child's motivation nor the group's structure is likely to bring about this type of sustained analysis. Thus, as was pointed out earlier, the poorly functioning child has anxiety in the learning situation which leads to a detriment in performance. Such anxiety makes sustained sequential thinking most unlikely.

Even if the poorly functioning child were eager to function in this style, the group situation does not readily allow him to do so. His difficulties in cognition inevitably mean that he will make many wrong responses and attain many incorrect ideas. The teacher might well recognize his difficulty but the constraints of the group situation severly limit her[4] options. For example, imagine a situation where the teacher is reading a story to a small group and she asks a simple question such as "Remember the little boy laughed. What made him laugh? Johnny, you tell us." Should the response be (incorrectly) "His mommy bought ice cream," the most the teacher can do is repeat the request in a supportive way — "No, she didn't buy any ice cream; don't you remember what happened?" — or perhaps give a hint — "Remember something happened in the store when he got there."

If the child at this point repeats his initial incorrect response or offers another incorrect response, the teacher is placed in a difficult position.[5] With her attention confined to only one child, the group becomes restless. Since the group must be saved if the class is to function, what the teacher inevitably must do is to turn to another child for the correct response. In this case, the first child who did not know the information may not have learned it. Even if he attended to the second child's answer, the same difficulties that caused his failure upon the initial asking of the queston may leave him in a confused state as to what the answer actually means. Of course, occasional failure or inattention would be of little concern. It would simply mean that the child might miss a point or two in the course of the day. But should failure or inattention be general, as they are in the poorly functioning child, efforts at teaching in the group setting are rendered useless.

What is perhaps most disconcerting is that the group structure itself allows many of the failures to go undiagnosed. By its very organization it affords the child numerous opportunities to respond appropriately even when he does not possess the desired information. For example, if given the direction to "place the red block on top of the blue one," a child in the group setting can wait to see what the other children do and simply imitate their actions.

---

[4] Because of the overwhelming predominance of women in this field, I find it difficult to refer to the prototypical teacher in any way other than "she." In addition, so as to prevent confusion, the child is generally referred to as "he."

[5] These difficulties refer solely to the cognitive sphere. The group situation has different implications for the child's social and affective behaviors since children with severe cognitive deficiencies can work happily in many noncognitive situations in the nursery school setting. However, such social and affective competence is not sufficient to give the child the skills he needs for cognitive competence.

Of course, the child might listen to the language and associate it with the key features of the performance he just imitated (e.g., "Oh, that's what she meant by top"). This method relies on the hope that the child will avail himself of this opportunity to learn. Nothing inherent in the situation requires him either to heed or to understand the language in order to fulfill the demands placed on him.

It was partly in an effort to overcome these difficulties that the Bereiter and Engelmann program (1966) adopted the controlled structure that they did. Rather than leave learning to the vagaries of the situation, they established a forced-response method in which they had great control over the child's overt behavior. This permitted them to retain the group structure, but only by radically altering its usual character. For example, the child was made to imitate sentences when the teacher made this demand. The lesson would not continue until the child emitted the desired behavior. In this way the material and the teachers could not be ignored.

This forced-response method, however, entails other problems since it treats higher level learning as capable of evolving from a rote system of verbal memorization (e.g., if the child is forced to build up a large enough repertoire of language, it is felt that there will eventually be transfer to more complex learning situations). The issue of transfer has been a long and heated one, in both psychology and education. While proponents can be found across a spectrum of opinions (Ausubel, 1968; Bruner, 1966; Mandler, 1962; Gagne, 1965; Dewey, 1902), there is little substantive knowledge on this complex issue. Therefore, research is vitally needed to determine whether the rote repetition of language eventually will lead to developing the underlying cognitive structures that Bereiter and Englemann wish to foster.

The concept of the abstract attitude outlined above, however, suggests that rote learning may not be the most fruitful path to follow. The ability to process novel cognitive demands is postulated to be a critical feature of the abstract attitude. In fact it is postulated to be the key to the well functioning child's high level of test performance. But any system of memorization, such as the Bereiter-Engelmann program, can do little in this area since it is difficult to use a forced response in novel situations. How can one demand that a child respond when one is not sure the child has the desired information? Instead, in this latter program, almost total reliance is placed on programming the child with the correct information, for only then can one be certain that the child is able to respond appropriately. Ultimately, this training may even hamper the child's development of the abstract attitude since he may be overwhelmed when confronted with new situations where he has not been taught the so-called right response.

With the rejection of the forced-response group method, the one-to-one situation seems to offer the most fruitful means for dealing with the child's difficulties. Here the demands of the group are withdrawn so that the teacher can diagnose and treat difficulties as they occur. For example, if a preschooler is unable to answer a question about a story he has just heard, the teacher can even reread the section which the child missed or misinterpreted. Such review can be deadly in a group setting for it will most certainly lead to boredom among the children who attended to the material at the first reading.

If the need for tutorial instruction is so great, one might ask why the well functioning child should be omitted from such teaching. In effect, he is not: evidence suggests that his parents are supplying this type of interchange throughout the course of his development (Hess & Shipman, 1966; Ortar & Carmon, 1969). The group-based classroom thus offers the opportunity to rehearse the skills which have already been mastered in the home setting. By contrast, many poorly functioning children have had limited access to such interchange. They can only rely on the group setting where adult attention must be diluted, sporadic, and, of necessity, insufficient.

These comments might lead one to conclude that the most effective remediation would be training mothers to deal differently with their children. This possibility has been tried, with apparent success (Levenstein, 1970; Lombard, 1971). This path has not been selected in the present circumstances, however, for it seems an extremely difficult task to influence parents so that they totally reorganize their established ways of relating to their children. Certainly, changes can be made. For example, it is possible to present the mothers with material containing specific tasks and specific information. This, in fact, has been the approach taken in much of the work directed toward parent intervention (e.g., the mothers are told to ask the children to label a particular set of objects, to complete certain puzzles, etc.). While it is of value, such specific teaching material does not appear to achieve the major reorganization of parent-child interaction necessary to foster the abstract attitude. Instead, in the present program hope is placed on using the formal teaching setting but reorganizing it to incorporate the tutorial model.

Thus, from a variety of perspectives — the normal course of adult-child interaction in the home, the "content" of dialogue, and the constraints of the group for the poorly functioning child — I am led to conclude that the child's acquisition of the abstract attitude can best be achieved in a one-to-one exchange. Once the child has acquired firmly established skills in this setting, he can use them in the group situation. He does not learn them in the group setting.

In some ways the emphasis on the one-to-one situation may be misleading when it is raised in the context of talking about education programs. Such programs normally occupy a large part of the child's day. Therefore, when the tutorial concept is put into this framework, there is a tendency to think that the one-to-one method is being proposed as a system to replace the group setting. This would not only be grossly impractical, but also destructive to the child's interests. Life includes far more than the development of the abstract attitude. Even when a child is at an age where the tie to the mother is still paramount, the company of his peers provides him with challenge, excitement, and security. Thus, the group-based class has much to offer the young child. But just as the tutorial method does not negate the advantages of the group, neither do the benefits of the group negate the essential role of tutorial dialogue. One cannot substitute for the other.

Because of their different functions, each of these settings contains its own goals, rules, and methods. One of the most immediately evident differences is the parameter of time — while the young child can remain in the group setting for hours, the gains from the complexity and stimulation of the one-to-one setting are probably optimal only in short periods (e.g., fifteen to twenty minutes per session). Thus, meaningful tutorial sessions need occupy only a small segment of the child's school experience.

These are the considerations that led me to develop a structured tutorial program in which poorly functioning preschool children are individually tutored in short daily sessions. The remainder of the book is directed toward the exposition of this program.

chapter 2

The Language of Dialogue

When I first elected to use the tutorial method and its implied Socratic dialogue, I was unaware of the extent to which the content of the program would later have to be modified. Nevertheless, it was evident from the beginning that the tutorial dialogue, in and of itself, would not produce the desired changes. Everyone has experienced dialogue that is meaningless rather than informative, boring rather than stimulating, unpleasant rather than appealing, and destructive rather than helpful. Therefore, it was essential to define the characteristics that would make the dialogue productive. This task, difficult by itself, was made even more complex by the fact that one participant would always be a poorly functioning preschool child. Thus, unless the teacher knew precisely how to foster meaningful interchange, the tutorial situation might be likely to represent, not dialogue, but merely exposure to an adult verbal model.

Since dialogue is, by definition, bound up with language, it was in this sphere that the search began. Some of the initial formulations seemed to suggest that the poorly functioning child's deficit in the verbal area was so severe that any and all aspects of language should be fostered. Observation of the children, however, proved this to be an indiscriminate generalization. Many

29

of the children would speak freely and at length when with adults and peers. This was in accord with the psycholinguistic research that has emphasized the inherent ability of all children to produce language. Through formulations developed by Chomsky (1957), studies in this comparatively new discipline have revealed that speech is not only available to all normal children, but also that children produce speech of a complex nature (McNeill, 1966; Ervin and Miller, 1963; Brown and Bellugi, 1964). This work has shown that even before three years of age, the child does not simply spout words, but rather produces sequences which have the words placed in a definite pattern. The organization does not follow the rules used by the adult, but it does possess definite rules. Thus, the young child who can say "I no want apple" (Brown and Bellugi, 1964, p. 73) will not say "apple no want I." Even though the same words are involved, the second sentence violates his ordered system and therefore is unacceptable to him. These rule-governed verbal productions hold for all groups of children, including those that have been termed disadvantaged or deprived (Baratz and Shy, 1969; Houston, 1970; Labov, 1969).

There are, admittedly, differences among groups of children. For example, children from minority groups speak dialects that differ from the standard English used by the middle class. In linguistic theory, however, such dialect differences reflect variables in performance (i.e., the form that the language takes) rather than any basic difference in competence (i.e., the speaker's basic knowledge of language) (Smith and Miller, 1966). This work has been vital in showing that a dialect need not be a poorer language; it is a different language but one with a synactic structure of comparable complexity and lawfulness to that of the so-called standard (middle-class) dialect. Thus, educational efforts to alter dialects, just because they are dialects, may change the children's linguistic performance to be more in accordance with what is acceptable to middle-class institutions. Such programs, however, should not be seen as fostering the development of basic linguistic competence, for the child already possesses such competence.

Did this mean, then, that one should conclude that the children had no difficulty in the language sphere? Such a conclusion did not seem justified by observation. Undeniably, the children had many linguistic structures, but frequently they failed to make use of them when cognitive demands were imposed. The critical variable seemed not to be the form of language, but its function. For example, a child might be able to formulate sentences containing the negative when they concerned his own immediate wishes (e.g., "Why can't I watch TV") or a simple statement of refusal (e.g., "It's not my turn"), but be unable to use the negative when it could direct his efforts at problem solving (e.g., "Why won't this work") or when it required careful attention to the ideas of another person (e.g., when asked "Which of these is not like this one").

One might well question the significance of the child's failure. For example, his lack of compliance with a teacher's request might easily be viewed as a legitimate assertion of his own lack of interest in the situation. If this behavior characterized an occasional episode, the interpretation might be valid. Should the failure, however, be characteristic of the child's responses, it would be a most serious sign of his inability or refusal to enter the dialogue situation. It is almost impossible to overestimate the importance of dialogue in learning and hence the disastrous intellectual consequences that can result should such a pattern of nonparticipation emerge. It seems likely that a vast percentage of all higher level learning—whether it be between the individual and his teacher, the individual and a machine, or the individual and a book—is an extension of the principles of dialogue (see Moffett, 1968, pp. 72-83). All these cases share the demand on the individual that he put forth an active effort to adapt himself to the material and ideas available in the outer world. For example, the self-initiated inner dialogue required for later thinking and problem solving is probably the sophisticated development of earlier, more elementary interchanges. Instead of relying on the guidance of an outside person as a child must do (e.g., someone who says "but why do you think that will work?") the more mature individual can now play a dual role—he can both initiate ideas and then independently evaluate and criticize them. Failure to initiate or sustain this involvement, either with oneself or with others, means lost opportunities for developing and enhancing one's thinking. Thus, if the child constantly elects to disengage himself from the learning dialogue, he is following a course that will damage his cognitive development.

This discussion is relevant to the cognitive version of the much discussed difference-deficit model. The difference model interprets the children's poor test performance on higher level tasks (such as analogous reasoning and similarities and differences) to mean that they have different but no less adequate cognitive processes. Because their performance on language-based tasks is almost uniformly poor, these different skills are generally assumed to be in the nonlanguage sphere. If certain of the highest level cognitive skills are fostered solely by language-based dialogue, however, then nonlanguage skills cannot offer equivalent cognitive development.

An intriguing version of the cognitive difference approach has most recently been developed by Olson (1970). He interprets the child's cognitive development as the sum total of his experiences in a variety of "media"—with medium being defined as a sphere of behavior involving decision-making activity. In this way, the sphere of locomotion, prehension, drawing, and language are all media through which the child can gain information about his world. Although each medium makes its own unique demands and yields its own unique information, as Olson himself points out, the two major culture-dependent media are language and drawing. It may be that certain skills of spatial representation such as those involved in drawing are of equal complexity to language skills. Aside from these skills, however, the child's grasp of language is his major entree into the knowledge available from his being human. And the knowledge so gained is not only the community's reservoir of factual information, but also the intricate skills needed for meaningful verbal interchange. Thus, failure to enter freely into dialogue and to initiate dialogue cut the child off from an irreplaceable sphere of human cognition. We are left with the choice of either helping the child to develop these linguistically based skills or of abandoning him to permanent difficulties in the academic environment.

While some aspects of dialogue can exist on a nonverbal level, it is evident that language must play the central role. It is the mode of communication distinctive to human beings and, without it, dialogue is reduced almost to meaninglessness in the cognitive realm. Thus, the central question for education is not whether the child possesses linguistic structures, but whether he can and does summon them to serve him in sustained intellectual interchanges with others and with himself. If he does not, it is the task of education to help him toward this achievement.

Having defined the problem as one of language functioning rather than of language structure, it then becomes necessary to select a framework which would help to delineate the factors that are most central to productive dialogue with the young child. For this purpose, it seems most useful to turn to theorists who emphasize the role of language as the system, *par excellence,* for development of thinking (Vygotsky, 1962; Whorf, 1956; Luria and Yudovich, 1959; Bruner et al., 1956; Myklebust, 1960). Their work demonstrated that language serves a wide variety of cognitive functions, including *communication, categorization,* and *problem solving.* The major difficulty of this approach is in the lack of knowledge about these factors at the preschool age. Headway in analyzing the demands and advantages of dialogue could be achieved only if some understanding could be gained as to how these uses of language might function in early development.

Because of the limited research in this area, only tentative guidelines could be developed. As will be seen from the discussion that follows, these guidelines were not concerned with general language functioning in young children. Rather, in line with the concerns of compensatory education, they were specifically focused on the key differences between well-functioning and poorly functioning children. In particular, two themes are paramount:

1. Does language foster skills, processes, or areas that cannot readily be achieved by other means?
2. Is the poorly functioning child deficient in these aspects of language and, if so, what are the implications for teaching?

The answers to these questions determined in large measure the initial content of the tutorial program. In an effort to show this process more clearly, at the conclusion of each section within this chapter, there will be a short discussion of the practical ideas which were suggested by this particular analysis of language functioning.

LANGUAGE: A MEDIUM OF COMMUNICATION

The phrase tutorial dialogue immediately brings to mind a major function of language—that of intentional communication with others. While most would agree that language serves this role, there would be considerably less agreement as to its importance for the preschool age. There are those who believe that the young child is so immature that the rational communication of information is almost impossible. For example, Piaget has shown the egocentricism of early thinking wherein the young child feels that any phenomenon known to him is also known to others. In this view the child cannot yet assume the perspective necessary if he is to appreciate what the listener needs to know in the particular situation. Thus, meaningful dialogue is seen as nearly impossible.

And should communication prove essential, the child's well-developed sensorimotor skills would seem to provide him with a gesture language sufficient for expressing his needs. For example, as any parent knows, pointing is a tremendously effective communicative device over a wide variety of situations. In fact, "the word, at first, is a conventional substitute for the gesture. . . ." "The only correct translation . . . of any early words, is the pointing gesture" (Vygotsky, 1962, p. 30). This would suggest that the word adds little to what the child already can produce through his sensorimotor repertoire. Does this mean that the child's early language is a superfluous accessory, merely ripening for its use in the later years? Such a conclusion seems precipitous.

THE YOUNG CHILD'S USE OF VERBAL COMMUNICATIONS

The word and the gesture do seem equivalent as long as the situations involve immediately available visual material. For example, pointing to a bottle of milk is probably as effective a request as the words "Could I have a drink?" The removal of the visual component, however, causes a marked change in the efficiency of nonverbal communication, even at the preschool age. For example, as long as three-year-old children are given the simple verbal instructions "Drop the right one" they readily solve a tactual problem which requires a discrimination between two objects (e.g., every time they select a sphere rather than a cube they receive a candy) (Blank, Altman, and Bridger, 1967). Remarkable difficulties are found, however, when it is not possible to give these verbal instructions—the inability being caused by the fact that the children are deaf.

Of course, one might attribute the failure of the deaf to an inability on their part to solve this type of problem. But analysis of the test shows that this is not the case. The trouble resides in the nonverbal transmission of the four words—"drop the right one." In order that these instructions be understood, a series of at least four tasks is required in which visual information is gradually transposed to the tactual level.[1] The training takes about five minutes; communicating the comparable information to the hearing child takes a matter of seconds. While this difference may seem minor in a single situation, it assumes gigantic proportions relative to the many situations in which the young child must deal with nonpresent visual material (i.e., questions of memory, questions about future events, directives to initiate action, interpreting the meaning of information surrounding auditory and tactual events, etc.). If all such information had to be given nonverbally, the process of communication would be stymied.[2] Such blockage might be of little concern if verbal communication were unimportant in early development. The rapid response of the hearing children indicated, however, that even preschool children are acutely attuned to the information available from the verbal world.

Significantly, poorly functioning children have serious difficulties in this aspect of language. For example, Heider, Cazden, and

---

[1] For those readers interested in the procedure, it is as follows. First, the experimenter must model the correct behavior with a pair of visually presented objects (e.g., he holds both objects and then drops the one he wants the child to drop). Significantly, this visual problem is achieved in a single step, reinforcing the observation about the difference between visual and nonvisual learning. Second, the child imitates what the experimenter has done. Third, the visual element is removed so that the child can only hold, and not see, the objects. Fourth, a new tactual task is given (i.e., a different set of objects was used) so that the child can complete a problem without any initial visual clues. When this sequence is completed, the deaf child is able to handle the original test problem as efficiently as the hearing child.

[2] The term nonverbal does not include systems such as the sign language of the deaf. Although there are differences caused by the sensory modality of presentation (tactual-visual vs. auditory-vocal), these systems, nevertheless, have the potential for extreme complexity.

Brown (1968) studied the communication of information among children of different socioeconomic backgrounds. The investigators set up a task in which the children were tested in pairs, with each child having before him an identical set of unusual forms, none of which could be easily labeled. No child could see his partner, however, because they were separated by an opaque screen. The task required that one child describe an object and the second child had to use this description to select the appropriate object. It was found that the lower-class children performed much less well than middle-class children, both in dispensing and in using information about the material. Unexpectedly, though, they functioned more effectively with the descriptions transmitted by middle-class children than they did when the descriptions were transmitted by children who had backgrounds similar to their own. They appeared to need a precise spelling out of information which the middle-class children offered.

Paradoxically, these problems have in some ways been made more apparent by the recent pressure to teach cognitive skills to preschool children (concepts such as form, color, number, etc.). In almost any classroom that one enters, one is likely to find a concept sequence being conducted. One's impression is that the children easily acquire the relevant concepts. For example, as the teacher holds a particular block, the children happily shout out in cadence "red," "round," "big," or whatever word seems appropriate to the stimulus. With further observation, however, it becomes apparent that the children are often at a total loss if the constraints of the particular situation are removed, that is, demands are not explicitly or precisely spelled out. Thus, they might be presented with a novel situation where they must match blocks on the basis of form. No verbalization is required; they must simply put each shape with its identical mate (e.g., a cube with a cube, a sphere with a sphere, etc.). After successfully completing a series of such problems, they may then be asked to describe the objects. Even though they have correctly and consistently worked with the dimension of *form* throughout, in meeting the request to label, they are just as likely to reply "red" or "two" as they are to say "square" or "ball."

In a strict sense, their answer is correct—the objects all are "red." Unfortunately, however, the verbalization is almost meaningless in this context. If words are to carry a message, they must "designate, signal, or specify an intended referent relative to the set of alternatives from which it must be differentiated . . ." (Olson, 1970, p. 264). The word red fails to meet these criteria, for it applies equally to all objects. By contrast the single word ball (or sphere or rounded) does specify a relative characteristic by which the one object may be differentiated from the remaining alternative. What is interesting about the child's response is that it is not caused by his finding form harder to label than color. If he is asked precisely "What form are these?" instead of "What are these?" his response is rapid and appropriate. It is just that without specific externally imposed direction, the poorly functioning child does not readily bring in the verbal label that is most meaningful or useful to the situation.

THE ESSENTIAL ROLE OF IMPLICIT MEANING

When a child performs in this manner, we may well be prone to dismiss it. After all, if we did not state the specific characteristics in which we are interested, it is unreasonable to think that the child should select what we consider the correct one. Given his limited experiences with the nuance of language, we cannot rely on his understanding anything because it is implicitly evident; it must be made explicit. This view implies that implicit meaning is a frill or extra that evolves only in the later years. While this interpretation has the appeal of excusing the young child's failure, it is nevertheless unlikely to be valid.

Analysis of language suggests that implicit meaning is a phenomenon that is basic to adequate language comprehension almost from the very start. Language can never be precise enough to say everything about any piece of material being discussed. The word is not, and cannot be, a total embodiment of the referent—instead, it is an economical "means by which to direct our mental operations, control their course, and channel them towards the solution of the problem confronting us" (Vygotsky, 1962, p. 58). For example, if we are comparing two cars on the basis of size, an explicit statement could encompass such features as "the black one with the convertible top and the tires with white sidewalls . . . that is bigger then the blue one with the. . . ." Not only would this fail to exhaust the possible characteristics that could be mentioned, but it would also actually detract from the message that we would want to convey. It is both more efficient and more meaningful to state tersely "the big one"—with car and all other characteristics being implicitly understood as part of the object to which we are referring (see Olson, 1970 for an extended review of this issue).

If the child cannot freely grasp the intended referent as the occasion demands, he will be unable to enter into a meaningful dialogue, for he will have to have every statement explicated in the most extreme detail. Such explication is antithetical to normal dialogue since the latter is based on the assumption that unstated ideas are permissible because our partners in any conversation have a system of implicit meaning comparable to our own.

As with almost every psychological phenomenon, this expectation can be manipulated, particularly when the situation becomes more complex so that the referent is no longer a concrete, palpable object, but a remote intangible idea. One form of such implicit meaning would be the interpretations that one puts on a speaker's statement. Brown (1958), for example, reviews a series of experiments which showed that adults will attribute totally different meanings to the identical quote according to the person from whom it emanates. Thus, the statement "I hold that a little rebellion now and then is a good thing, and as necessary in the political world as storms are in the physical," when attributed to Jefferson, was interpreted as a "specific reference to the American Revolutionary War." When the same statement was attributed to Lenin, it "seemed to recommend social and economic upheaval, on the model of the Russian Revolution" (p. 320).

These experiments were done to show the distortions attainable through propaganda. Therefore, one might argue that since implicit meaning can be used destructively, it is a skill to be avoided, not fostered. Brown, however, does not interpret the phenomenon as an unthinking "stupid yielding to prestige. . . . The same series of words was involved but not the same proposition. The meaning of any utterance depends on its context and the source of the utterance is highly relevant context" (p. 321). Thus when there is a failure to attend to implicit meaning (as occurs with poorly functioning children in endless situations), a major aspect of linguistic communication is lost.[3]

MISINTERPRETATION OF THE "OBVIOUS"

In any phenomenon as complex as implicit meaning, there is the inevitable possibility that information will be misinterpreted. The poorly functioning child's reliance on explicit messages, however, occurs even in situations which seem (to the adult) to contain no possible ambiguity. For example, in a lesson (to be presented in the next chapter) a four-year-old child looked at some flowers in the corner of the room. The teacher responded to the behavior by asking "Have you seen the flowers?" The child replied, "I saw a beautiful flower outside." The teacher's reaction indicated that she had not anticipated the misinterpretation of such an "obvious" situation.

People who are comfortable with linguistic communication find it ridiculous to phrase the question in the stilted form "Have you seen the flowers *that are here on the table?*" Communication is generally not viewed as a chance to discuss what everyone can see, but rather as a chance to discuss more subtle ideas that are not immediately evident. This luxury cannot be permitted with the young child, in general, and with the poorly functioning child, in particular, for he does not comprehend the implicit meaning that is necessary for discussions that "go beyond the information given" (Bruner, 1957).

In the example of the flowers above, it is significant that the child's difficulty was not caused by a failure in language per se. Her answer was linguistically appropriate. The difficulty arose from the child's failure to relate her statement to the concrete

---

[3] This interpretation may be confusing in light of the research which shows that poorly functioning children rely heavily on implicit referents in their speech productions (e.g., saying "they" about a referent rather than "the boys") (Bernstein, 1961; Osser, in press). This behavior, however, is the mirror image of the phenomenon discussed above; that is, in the comprehension of language the children need explicit detail, while in the production of language, the children fail to give sufficient detail. In both cases, the children are displaying their difficulty in grasping the demands governing the communication of information, in particular, their failure to recognize the needs, sets, and perspective of their partner in the dialogue.

situation. This observation reinforces the idea that well-organized syntactical, phonological, and even lexical formulations can exist independently of any precise relation to reality. The word may initially be a substitute for the gesture; with the poorly functioning child, however, we must insure that he achieves the substitution.

In the desire to avoid any value judgment which might condemn a child's innocent resonse, the type of behavior observed in the flower example can be rationalized as a sign of ability; that is, it can be interpreted as an example of the child's capacity to freely bring in relevant associations rather than being constrained by conventional meaning. Language for rational communication, however, contains the expectation that the hearer will not attribute his own idiosyncratic meaning to words, but will respond to the consensually validated implicit meaning of language. Thus, any attempt to dismiss the significance of the child's behavior may leave him to face the grave consequences of being unable to use the language he has for meaningful interchange.

PROBLEM DIFFICULTY AND THE USE OF VERBAL INFORMATION

Most significant about the "misinterpretation of the obvious" is the extent to which it can occur. For example, in tests of perceptual discrimination, young children are commonly given the instruction "See these two toys. Every time you see them, one of them will be right and you will get candy if you pick it up, the other one will never be right and you will never get candy if you pick it up." As the children nod agreeably, observers unfamiliar with the scene are taken aback with the reaction "You told him everything. There isn't any problem left to solve." These same observers are then stunned to see many children struggle over a number of trials before success is achieved. The difficulty totally disappears if the instructions are altered slightly so that the experimenter points to the item being discussed (e.g., "Every time you see these toys, this one [pointing to it] will have the candy and every time you see this one," etc.) (Blank, 1967). This simple change in procedure eliminates all ambiguity because it does what the child failed to do—it connects the verbalization to the perception.

Young children's difficulty with this visual problem may seem paradoxical in view of the ease with which they could deal with verbal instructions on the tactual problem cited earlier (e.g., "drop the right one"). The contradiction is made more extreme by the fact that young children perform much less well on tactual as opposed to visual problems (Milner and Bryant, 1970). Since they are already in difficulty once they are in the tactual sphere, one would hardly expect them to deal more effectively when the complex verbal dimension is added. Their poorer tactual performance, however, may be precisely the reason for the effectiveness of the verbal information. When the child is given a tactual problem, he knows that he is in strange territory and he grasps at any cues that might be helpful. If verbal information supplies such cues, he will gladly take advantage of it.

Visual information, on the other hand, represents a well-traversed terrain in which the child feels totally in command. Although the feeling may not correspond with reality, its presence causes him to view verbal information as redundant and therefore he fails to heed its message. If the child fails to develop the set of tying language to the visual world (precisely because it is so obvious and secure), he will have to face the consequences of this deficiency later. Although the visual sphere will continue to be a major source of information for the child as he grows older, increased cognitive demands mean that visual information will not be sufficient. Problem-solving questions concerning the visual sphere (e.g., "If I take two of these away, how many will I have left?" "What happened when the milk was added to the flour?" etc.) can be answered only if the child clearly understands the relationship of the verbal question to the visual material. It seems apparent that the child cannot even attempt this type of problem if he has not learned to tie verbal and visual information together in much simpler circumstances.

If these hypotheses are valid, they have significant consequences for preschool education. Because of the emphasis placed on the idea of enrichment, much effort has been directed at providing the child with more, new, and, if possible, relatively abstract information; the concept of enrichment is imbued with this meaning. By contrast, the discussion above suggests a more productive initial effort might be in the development of lessons which permit the child to see, comprehend, and perfect the language he already possesses so that it becomes intimately related to his perceptual world.

Some of the familiar tasks which might be adapted for this purpose are demands which require the child:

1. To analyze his perceptual field in a way whereby the verbal serves as an organizing guide (e.g., "out of all these pictures, find the one with an animal")
2. To attend to less tangible, but nonetheless meaningful, stimuli such as sounds (e.g., "close your eyes and listen—now tell me, which thing made the noise")
3. To use relevant verbal descriptions to characterize his world (e.g., "tell me what the child is doing in the picture")

These requests are so much part of the fabric of everyday existence that it might seem superfluous to have gone through the earlier analysis if all it was to reveal was a restatement of the obvious. But the analysis was vital, not so much in suggesting what should be asked, as in suggesting what should not be asked. Thus, if the child has difficulty in the implicit meaning of language, one must be constantly prepared to bring out the explicit meaning of situations should the child show signs of misinterpretation. This goal is possible only if every question posed can be "brought to life." As a result, one must always stay within verifiable material—verifiable not in the scientific sense, but verifiable in the sense that the child fully perceives the referents. Therefore, questions which refer to the nonpresent (e.g., "What did you do on Sunday?") must be avoided. Even though they would seem, like example 3, to demand relevant verbal descriptions, they actually have a double danger. First, they may encourage the child to ramble on with a potpourri of associations; second, the teacher has no way of knowing what implicit features are being misunderstood or overlooked.

In addition to avoiding the nonverifiable, the teacher must be prepared to change her style of dialogue so as to discuss the simplest of factors that would have been taken as "givens." Just because the adult has said something that appears simple, it does not necessarily mean the child has understood it. As the flower reference was misinterpreted, so too may the child misinterpret other comments that seem to contain no possibility for ambiguity.

This strategy does not mean that the teacher abandon her usual rich speech pattern. For natural conversation, it is vital that the child be exposed to all sorts of language. But when free-flowing conversation is occurring, the teacher must be aware that it may not be fostering the child's grasp of language as a tool for structuring reality. For the latter, the teacher must be prepared to clarify what she would heretofore have assumed was perfectly clear. This means that language must be used with a kind of precision rarely needed in verbal interchange.

THE ROLE OF LANGUAGE IN CONCEPT FORMATION

Children's failure to appreciate the implicit meaning of simple phrases seems related to their well-established difficulty in recognizing the full meaning of explicitly stated words. The child may possess many words and even use them correctly in context without realizing their meaning. We are generally much more willing to acknowledge their difficulty in this regard since, in contrast to the simple sentences, the words are patently complex. Thus, when a four-year-old, in parroting his elders, talks about "atomic energy" or "the world situation," everyone will laugh because they "know" that the child cannot possibly understand the real meaning of the words.

THE CHICKEN AND EGG ENIGMA OF LANGUAGE AND THOUGHT

From an observational point of view, the child's seeming precocity in the verbal realm is a source of charming anecdotes; from a theoretical point of view, it is a source of confusion. Its presence is a clear sign that words can exist without concepts or meaning. We also know from the ability of animals to solve problems involving dimensions such as size and brightness that concepts (at least, concepts at this level) can exist without words (Kohler, 1925; Harlow, 1959). Although both these lines of evidence indicate that language and concepts can lead independent existences, they do not settle the longstanding question as to whether certain concepts can exist only through language. This issue is of more than academic interest; it is critical to preschool education where so much effort is directed at mastering elementary concepts. If certain of these concepts can be achieved only through language, then the question of language skills becomes crucial in teaching.

Unfortunately, methodological difficulties in studying language behavior have barred us from reaching any conclusive findings in this matter. Language can only be assessed through the use of introspective reports, and these are always subject to doubt. For example, a child may honestly be unaware that he used language in his problem solving and report an absence of verbalization. Conversely, a child may not have used verbalization but, upon being questioned, may suddenly "feel sure" that he used it all along. Such false positives and false negatives make it difficult to assess what actually occurred in the child's mind during the course of any problem. Because of these complications, the issue resolves itself into one of belief. Those who believe in the role of language in thinking find it evident that language critically affects concept formation (Vygotsky, 1962; Langer, 1949; Luria, 1957; Whorf, 1956); those who believe that language does not play a major role in thinking find it equally obvious that language (while perhaps an aid) is in no way critical to concept development (Harlow, 1959; Piaget, 1947; Furth, 1969).

A problem of this complexity will obviously not be easily settled. It is apparent, however, that all possibly fruitful avenues have not been explored. For example, in many studies of concept formation, children are commonly tested on problems involving dimensions such as size, shape, color, and brightness. This line of research would seem to be reasonable, for it both reflects the concepts traditionally stressed in the preschool and capitalizes on the well-developed experimental procedures available from animal research in this area (see Blank, 1968b).

The reasonableness, however, is deceptive. The long history of this line of research with animals has clearly indicated that nonverbal organisms can be trained to solve these problems, even though they lack any verbal cues to help them in their endeavors. The major outcome of such research, therefore, will not be to yield evidence about any potentially unique role of language in concept formation. Rather, it merely reinforces the caution against using the same type of problem across different phylogenetic levels if one is concerned with understanding the "distinct modes of intelligence and different neural mechanisms at work in various animals" (Bitterman, 1965, p. 92). If we wish to know how language might affect the thought of the young child, we must develop techniques specifically geared to the child, and not techniques simply carried over from animal research.

BEYOND THE CONFINES OF SPACE

A promising start to this problem seems available if we leave the familiar two- and three-dimensional world of things and enter the somewhat less comfortable world of time. The arrangement of stimuli over time rather than space (e.g., series of flashes of lights as opposed to a group of pictures) appears to make qualitatively different perceptual and cognitive demands. For example, three-year-old children can easily distinguish between one and two circles (or any other spatially organized stimuli) regardless of whether or not they apply language to the situation. These same children, however, cannot differentiate between one and two (sequential) flashes of light if they do not apply the relevant verbal labels (Blank and Bridger, 1964). Their difficulty is quite remarkable. Even when they clearly struggle to understand what is going on, they cannot perceive the difference between the stimuli.

Such ease still does not explain the reason why accurate perception in this sphere is so dependent upon language. Although no firm answer can be given, even a preliminary analysis suggests that temporal stimuli are quite different from the child's usual world of concrete, tangible objects (e.g., books, furniture, toys, food, etc.). Temporal stimuli, like tangible objects, occupy a physical place. The meaning of the temporal stimulus, however, is totally independent of its place. For example, in the two flashes of light, the concept of two is defined not by the light itself, but by the idea that "something went before." This requires that the previously perceived but now absent stimulus (i.e., the first light) be retained and combined with the second light so as to form a meaningful distinctive entity. In the vast percentage of cases, this achievement seems to demand of the child that he resort to a coding system.

After the first element of surprise, one may accept this finding. As in all developmental work, there is the omnipresent hope that the "children will grow out of it." Surprisingly, the poor learner does not "grow out of it." Even at nine years of age, he displays comparable difficulties in coding temporal sequences (Blank and Bridger, 1966, 1967; Blank, Weider, and Bridger, 1968). For example, if told to code the sequence tap, tap, tap—long pause—tap, tap, such a child might say "there were five lights" or "there were a bunch of lights with a stop in the middle." Unlike his well-functioning peer, he does not say "there were five lights with a stop after the third" or "it went 1, 2, 3, stop 4, 5." The poorly functioning child appears to be beset by an inability to take account of both aspects of the task—if he attends to number, he ignores spacing, and, conversely, if he attends to spacing (which is rare), he ignores number. (As will be evident to readers familiar with the classic Piagetian conservation problems, this difficulty is not unlike the difficulty shown by much younger children when confronting relatively complex conceptual situations.)

These results might seem to represent a minor, if nonetheless interesting, demonstration that some concepts are both language-dependent and associated with learning difficulties. The finding assumes, however, potentially great significance when one considers the huge range of concepts that involve temporal components. Many of the young child's major "abstract" concepts contain such components—these include speed ("fast," "slow"), duration ("a long time, a little while ago"), and sequence ("first, before, last," etc.). This latter set of concepts is particularly important for academic learning since it is essential to the reading process (Stambak, 1951; deHirsh et al., 1966).

All young children have problems in learning concepts because they do not know precisely which component of the complex world is being abstracted in the terms "first," "slow," "after," and so on. They have "difficulty in fitting the label to the varying forms of action observed and experienced" (John and Goldstein, 1964, p. 269) (e.g., "how can all these different things and places be called "top?"). It is here that dialogue becomes vital; these concepts can almost never be independently derived by the child. "This fitting process, which consists of selecting the specific connection between word and referent, occurs more easily when there is a variety of verbal interaction with adults. The middle-class child learns by feedback; by being heard, corrected, modified.

. . . The child learns by interacting with an adult teacher who plays an active role in simplifying the various components of word-referent relationships" (ibid. p. 269). In the absence of this dialogue, the poorly functioning child is only confused by the new verbal terms. The words may just add another bit of clutter to his world. Thus, concepts must be introduced in a detailed manner and the teacher must be prepared to explore them intensively with the child.

THE COGNITIVE ADVANTAGES AND DEMANDS OF TEMPORAL CONCEPTS

Again, it may seem as if this line of analysis has led us no further than a restatement of already accepted educational practice, since concepts form the core of many preschool efforts. As in the previous section, however, the analysis is most useful not in indicating positive courses of actions, but in helping us eliminate what may be negative or inappropriate teaching goals. For example, a closer examination of temporal concepts suggests that they are quite different from the concepts that traditionally fall under the rubric of "abstraction" for the preschool child (e.g., oxygen, evaporation, etc.). In temporal concepts, the abstraction is rarely so great as to totally leave the physical reality. That is to say, enough spatially organized cues are available in the initial learning of these concepts so that the child will feel he is grounded in familiar territory. He can point to a real thing that is in the "second place," he can touch a "fast" moving toy car, he can "go behind" the desk, and so forth. Thus, these concepts may be learned on a relatively concrete level before the child is asked to transfer them to truly nontangible referents such as "a long time" and "before we begin."

Contrasted sharply with this situation are the concepts which, from the child's view, have no clear perceptual referents (e.g., "oxygen," "evaporation," "gravity," and "energy"). Perceptual features associated with these latter concepts can be offered, but these features fail to embody the critical attributes of the concept. For example, in teaching oxygen through the classic experiment of placing a glass over a lit candle, what the child perceives is the presence or absence of the flame. Because he never perceives the oxygen itself, this demonstration is beyond the ken of the preschool child whose reality is still bound to sensorimotor experience. Oxygen in this setting may thus become the synonym for "it disappears like magic."

Temporal concepts also differ from the superordinate concepts that have been emphasized in preschool enrichment (i.e., cars, planes, and ships are *vehicles;* a rake, hammer, and shovel are *tools,* etc.). True superordination requires a recognition that a single object can simultaneously be both a member of a major group and a member of a subgroup (e.g., an object can be both a car and a vehicle—but one is not a synonym for the other since vehicles can also include noncars).

As experiments on class inclusion have shown (Piaget, 1952), this is a difficult achievement for the young child, even when he is functioning well (e.g., if asked about a set of wooden beads, some of which are yellow and some brown, "Which are more—the wooden beads or the yellow beads?" the young child will say "The yellow ones" because he is drawn to the larger of the two apparent groups, rather than to the less obvious superordinate). While he can be trained to achieve the correct answer (Kohnstamn, 1963), the introduction of slight variations in procedure easily causes the child to lose any gains he has made (e.g., the experimenter showing doubt, or the use of different materials); with these changes the child readily drops his newly acquired concept (see Kohlberg, 1968). This difficulty is characteristic not only of the poorly functioning preschool child, but also of all preschool children. Their natural developmental limitations appear to place sustained superordinate thinking beyond them.

Some efforts at developing superordinate categories can be effective even at the preschool range, particularly if focused on the precursors of conceptualization rather than on the concept itself. For example, the imitation of new words, without full grasp of meaning, can lead to the later more rapid learning of the concept (see Slobin, 1966). In general, however, superordinate concepts are not the most appropriate means of facilitating abstraction in the preschool age.

Temporal concepts, by contrast, are beset with few of these difficulties. They require flexibility, for the child must shift attention from the whole to some attribute of the whole (e.g., from a row of beads to the *first* bead in the row). Nevertheless, this shift does not require the simultaneous consideration of the part and the whole. Second, temporal concepts can be presented in the tactual and auditory modalities, thus offering a means of fostering abstraction in areas known to be deficient in disadvantaged children (Deutsch, 1966; Blank, 1968a; Lindamood and Lindamood, 1971). Third, the concepts are still tied sufficiently to sensorimotor representation to make them appropriate in age for the preschool child. Fourth, they can extend the child's thinking in the visual sphere, for many temporal concepts require analysis of well-established visual gestalts (e.g., "the *end* of a line," "the *second* in a row"). Since visual perception is secure even in poorly functioning children (Blank and Bridger, 1967) (i.e., the child clearly perceives the row, the line, etc.), these concepts suitably elaborate already established skills, rather than requiring skills that are beyond the child's general level.

It might seem from the discussion that temporal concepts are so central that they should form the core of concept development in intervention programs. This has not been the intent of this section. Rather, the demands and attributes of temporal concepts raise some interesting speculations about the way language may function in the child's acquisition of concepts. If valid, these speculations might have applicability, up or down the hierarchy of difficulty. Thus, the discussion was not meant to be limited to temporal concepts per se, but to show how such concepts might serve as a protype by which to establish guidelines for teaching in this area.

THE CONCEPTS DEMANDED TO MASTER LANGUAGE

The discussion on the relationship between language and concepts reflects the direction traditionally taken by psychology on this question—that is, the focus has been almost solely on whether certain concepts require language. The opposite side of the coin— namely, the concepts needed to master language—has rarely been considered (see Macnamara, 1972). The use of the term concepts in this context may seem somewhat out of place. We are so accustomed to thinking of concepts as descriptive of properties in the real world that it seems strange to apply this term to the tenuous world of language. And, indeed, "linguistic concepts are not characterized in terms of a network of physical properties" (Chomsky, 1967, p. 75). They are concepts nonetheless—albeit concepts which defy measurement by traditional psychological techniques.

It has been left to linguistics and, in particular, to transformational grammar to begin to delineate the conceptual structure underlying language. Through the ingenious analysis of phenomena that are always present, but often unnoticed, linguists under the leadership of Chomsky (1967) have shown that language is a complex system that is based upon unstated, but carefully structured, rules. For example, "Mary hit Alice" has a totally different meaning from "Alice hit Mary"—even though the identical words are involved. Conversely, "Mary hit Alice" and "Alice was hit by Mary" have similar meanings, even though the words are not identical. The ability of the individual to interpret such material (including sentences he has never previously encountered) means that the speaker of a language has operations, rules, or concepts which permit him to produce and evaluate linguistic information. These operations "form part of the technique which a person used for acquiring language; that is, they are part of the conceptual apparatus he uses to specify the form of the language to which he is exposed" (Chomsky, 1967, p. 81).

The cognitive skills needed for mastering the rules of language are almost certain to be important in understanding the thinking of the young child (e.g., by what cognitive processes does the child grasp the rules needed to formulate the negative, the interrogative, etc.). It is partly for this reason that there has been such a burgeoning of interest in psycholinguistics; it is seen as the area that will help fill the vacuum in our knowledge about language development. For example, psycholinguistic research has shown how the child, from early in life, acquires language rules which permit him such behavior as the ability to inflect words correctly so as to indicate number (cup vs. cups), tense (play vs. played), and so on.

Although this research sheds light on a vital area, it does not adequately illuminate our understanding of the cognitive base of language acquisition. In large measure, this is due to the fact that psycholinguistic research has minimized the role of learning in language acquisition; instead, it favors the idea that human beings have a programmed, genetic predisposition to acquire language (the Language Acquisition Device—LAD; see Smith and Miller, 1966). As a result, psycholinguists concentrate their efforts on describing the rules achieved by the child at each stage, but not the cognitive processes that had to be used to achieve these rules. For example, when a child has a rule for forming plurals, many psychological questions remain unanswered as to the cognitive rules that were used by the child for this achievement—must he have some nonverbal concept of number (e.g., a primitive sense of distinguishing one thing in the external world from more than one thing in that world), does he use linguistic contextual cues (e.g., if the word *a* is present, it is a sign not to use the plural), or does he rely on some process of generalization (e.g., every time a number other than one is specified, the plural phoneme is added; sometimes the generalization is overextended as when young children say "foots," "tooths," "sheeps").

LEARNING COMPLEX LINGUISTIC CONCEPTS

Having exphasized the inherent, preprogrammed nature of language acquisition, it is natural that linguistic theory has not focused much effort on the possible cognitive processes underlying language such as those we have just been discussing. Psychological theory, however, must consider such processes since they are vital to understanding how language functioning may be enhanced. Little progress has been made in this area, largely because psychological research on language has generally focused on the study of individual words, and, in particular, on words describing concrete physical properties (e.g., "red," "large," "bright," etc.). There has been little research concerning the acquisition and functioning of more complex linguistic formulations, even though such formulations are of vital importance (e.g., formulations such as why did, because of, if then, etc.).

It is not easy to extrapolate from the findings on single labels to these more complex formulations, for the former relate to circumscribed objects, while the latter refer to a vast array of unbounded situations. It becomes apparent that these differences are critical when we compare a request such as "draw a circle" and a request such as "draw something that is not a circle." While the first request focuses on a single, limited object, the second requires the child to consider a much broader frame of reference. For example, imagine a situation where the child, when asked to "draw something that is *not* a circle," draws a circle. Neither the circle nor the rejection of the circle is sufficient for the correct action to be realized. In an effort to help the child, figures other than a circle (e.g., a square, a triangle, etc.) might be shown. This aid alone may lead to confusion, for the child might believe that he should treat words "not a circle" as a substitute label for these particular other forms. The situation can only be mastered if the child eventually abstracts the desired meaning of the term "not" so that it is independent of any particular object.

The abstraction for a linguistic concept such as "not" is different from the more commonly cited abstraction of the preschool child that is based upon function (e.g., a hat is to wear, a carrot is to eat, and, of course, "a hole is to dig," Krauss, 1952). In these latter cases, a clear action is available to define the referent for the child. No such single guiding function, however, is available with concepts such as "not," "if," "because," "why," and so on. Like the temporal concepts discussed earlier, these subtle terms, which are absolutely vital to effective language functioning, can be adequately grasped only if the child achieves an abstraction that is dependent upon, but beyond, the meaning of any particular stimulus.

One, of course, may try to teach these concepts as if such an underlying similarity existed (see Bereiter and Englemann, 1966). For example, a pencil could be displayed and the child asked to complete the phrase "this is not a _____." This situation can be handled by the child through an understanding rule such as "Say any word other than the label of the object being shown" (e.g., "it is not a couch, plane, table, person," etc.). This rule, however, gravely injures a concept which implicitly contains the idea of a relevant, though unspecified, framework. Thus, if a child were asked "What shouldn't you do if you want to eat now?" he theoretically might say "ride an airplane," "build a table," and so on. An adequate solution, however, must consider the unstated (implicit) premise "What are inappropriate, but possible likely, actions you might take in a situation?" Stated in these terms, the child must evaluate the adequacy of a restricted, but unspecified, set of alternatives. By contrast, stated in the terms "Say anything other than what you see," the child might easily spout wild associations—the very antithesis of the behavior the *not* concept is capable of developing. Significantly, the type of demand involved in the *not* concept appears to be both unique to language and, in turn, to demand unique skills for its mastery.

IMITATION, COMPREHENSION, AND PRODUCTION

This proposition may seem unacceptable since, as Piaget has emphasized, possession of the word does not guarantee possession of the concept. His view might lead to the conclusion that other skills are prerequisite to the grasp of these verbal formulations. For example, the child may not be able to ask the "why" question unless he is first capable of sensing that the relationship between two phenomena is not simply an arbitrary given, but something requiring explanation (e.g., "Why does a car have wheels"). Even if such nonverbal skills are prerequisite, however, what is significant is that they are exercised almost solely with higher level language formulations.

This hypothesis may be relevant to the reversal of the usual comprehension-production sequence in language development. With simple language formulations *comprehension precedes production* (McNeill, 1966). For example, the child will respond appropriately to sentences like "get the book" and "do you want to eat?" before he can formulate these sentences himself. In complex language, however, the child will use terms like "because," "how," and "why" well before he understands their meaning. Thus, as so often happens in an area as complex as language, we reach a diametrically opposed conclusion—*production does not follow comprehension; rather, production precedes comprehension.*

Upon recognizing this contradiction, one's first reaction might be that the child's use of complex terms is only imitation, not production. Since imitation is known to precede comprehension, the conflict would seem to be resolved with the sequence being imitation, comprehension, and production. The psycholinguists have shown, however, that the spontaneous formulation of particular syntactical structures is unlikely to be imitation. Instead, they are a sign that the child possesses an internalized rule by which to produce an infinite number of sentences of this type. Thus, we cannot simply rid ourselves of the contradiction, for imitation seems to be an unlikely explanation for the production of these complex linguistic formulations.

The contradiction seems, instead, to reflect a real difference between the language of simple association and the language of relatively abstract meaning. With simple associations ("hat," "box," "walk," etc.), the child can glean their meaning easily by acting upon the objects. If he is told to "get the hat" and he selects the wrong object, he can simply try again until one of his choices is finally satisfactory. It only remains for him then to tie the word to the object he selected. Comprehension is possible for the child without his having to attempt any expressive verbal formulations.

No such external referents are available for complex "why," "how," and "what if" formulations. The child can only gain their meaning through producing verbal formulations, and so he is forced to attempt verbal formulations before he can comprehend them. If he fails to do this, he is left in the dark as to the meaning of these words. Such continuing ignorance is intolerable to the well-functioning child who is constantly seeking to clarify the ambiguities in his world.

It is of interest that as the child begins to gain an understanding of these language formulations his actual syntactical productions become distorted. For example, a bright four-year-old upon being asked "Would it matter if your sweater were blue instead of red?" confidently replied "no." When asked "Why wouldn't it matter?" the child literally groped for words and finally produced the formulation "But blue . . . would be . . . still a sweater." This statement, which was far below the child's usual syntactical productions, illustrates the distinction made by Vygotsky between syntactical and psychological organization. Inner speech rarely follows the syntax of external speech. In the young child, who possesses only egocentric speech, no distinction can be drawn between inner and external speech. Instead, as the child begins to use his egocentric speech for more abstract problem solving, we begin to see some of the syntax that is the hallmark of inner speech (i.e., omission of a clear subject, a stress of predication, the predominance of sentence over word, etc.). Thus, words like "why," "what if," and "how" do not automatically provide a concept for the child; they serve, however, as a tremendous and perhaps unique impetus for his conceptual development. *In this view, the child mobilizes a host of problem-solving skills in attempting to solve the complexities of language.*

Once these skills become internalized so that they can be spontaneously and independently applied, the child gains tools of inestimable value. These include the profits to be gleaned from (1) hypothesis formulation, (2) contradictions to expectations, and (3) dialogue with adults. Since these terms seem so much beyond our stereotyped conception of the immature preschooler, it is worthwhile to specify more precisely the role that they might have.

HYPOTHESIS FORMULATION

Some of the most delightful achievements of young children occur when the question form becomes internalized. At this point, the question no longer stands solely as an externally imposed spur requiring an answer (e.g., "Johnny, why don't you want to play with the toy?") but as an internally imposed search for explanation (e.g., a child asking "Why do they put a pit in every cherry? We have to throw the pit away anyway?") (Chukovsky, 1963, p. 21).

The ability to formulate such questions permits the child to search for hypotheses to explain his world. This is not to deny that the hypotheses may be "silly" or "incorrect." The question about putting pits in cherries is a clear sign that the child has overgeneralized the concept of purpose. In his view, nothing comes into existence unless it is put there by somebody; it is as if he sees an assembly line wherein pits are nonsensically being shoved into the fruits as they pass by. Along with the misinterpretation, however, the child is demonstrating important intellectual skills. Through having the concept of "why" available, he has the means by which to question his incorrect assumptions (e.g., if everything has a purpose and this thing does not, what is the reason?). When this occurs, there are almost no areas of experience which can remain free from challenge; everything can be subjected to the test whereby it must justify and explain its presence. Hence the flood of questions that characterize the well-functioning preschool child—such as:

> "If my eyes are so little, how come I can see you
> look so big?"
> "Why does ice melt?"
> "If we have two eyes, why don't we see two things?"
> "Where was I before I was born?"
> "Why can't you see my dreams?"

Once everything can be questioned, the child is no longer restrained by reality; he is only restrained by the limits of his imagination in inventing alternatives to what exists. As a result, he is not bound to what the environment has to offer at any moment, for he can create his own meaningful, exciting, and provocative internal mental world. The child then possesses the "form of effective productivity that makes symbolic representation such a powerful tool for thinking or problem solving: the range it permits for experimental alteration of the environment without having, so to speak, to raise a finger by way of trial and error or to picture anything in the mind's eye by imagery" (Bruner, 1966, p. 37).

When this type of spontaneous questioning is absent, as it so often is in the poorly functioning child (Mattick, 1965), it is a sign that both his intellectual life is seriously hampered and that he lacks the tool for most effective further development. The absence of this behavior in children who come from backgrounds of poverty is not a recent discovery—it was described among the children of the poor in Germany as long ago as the 1920s (Hetzer, 1929). This does not mean that they do not ask questions; it is that few of their questions reveal more than an expression of wanting to satisfy immediate needs (e.g., "When can we have the cookies?"). Questions of intellectual search such as those outlined above are hardly heard.

CONTRADICTIONS TO EXPECTATIONS: IMPETUS FOR CHANGE

Naturally, when the well-functioning child asks these questions.

few of them are of an abstract nature. In line with his developmental level, they are concerned with understanding immediately perceived reality and, as such, are still tightly bound to sensorimotor experience. This is often used as further evidence of the child's immaturity in thinking. But their very concreteness allows these questions to serve an important cognitive role, for such questions can often be confirmed or refuted by direct experience. Because the child himself has raised the questions, their formulation provides him with an internalized source of self-critical evaluation.

To the extent that his ideas correctly represent reality, the child can experience mastery and self-confidence ("Look I was right—you can still drink from the straw even when it is bent"). To the extent that his ideas do not represent reality, he has a major internalized goad for change. For example, when a child explores the insides of a radio because he questions the ability of musicians to "fit into that small place," he has created a situation which will lead to a reformulation of his knowledge. In this way, he is making explicit the discrepancies or disequilibria that are so vital to learning (i.e., the recognition that what is known is insufficient to explain or deal with a situation) (Piaget, 1952; Hunt, 1961; Langer, 1969). The question may not lead to an immediate correct reformulation. Like all of us, he may invent incorrect hypotheses to explain the situation (e.g., "they must have made themselves so small that I can't see them"). Ultimately, his own search for order and logic, however, causes him nagging doubts about the adequacy of his reasoning and he is forced to ponder over these matters until a new equilibrium is reached.

Disequilibria—the feeling, at some level, that one's grasp of a situation is not sufficient—exist at all points in development. If an infant receives a toy different from the toys he has experienced before, he will attempt to accommodate to this new experience by altering his typical responses to whatever degree necessary, and thereby he will increase the range and flexibility of his repertoire. This type of discrepancy between the known and unknown is totally dependent upon environmental opportunities; if the toy is not available, the child cannot adapt to it. Once meaningful, conscious questions are introduced, a qualitatively different factor is added to the equation. These questions reflect explicitly formulated ideas that continually force the child to consider and reevaluate his thinking even when no "real" (external) problem exists (e.g., there is no difficulty in seeing clearly with two eyes; there is only the awareness that the single image is somehow "peculiar" relative to the fact of having two eyes). At this point, the child is thinking simply for thinking's sake about the appropriateness of his ideas in describing, predicting, and evaluating reality. The ensuing self-critical analyses of his ideas become a major prod for cognitive growth.

DIALOGUE WITH ADULTS

The benefits of the child's efforts at thinking are not limited to self-critical analysis. All humans are social beings and any new skill is immediately applied to the interpersonal realm. In the case of attempts at reasoning, this extension is vital since it offers the child a major source of entry into the conversation of the adult world.

Nonverbal communication has been present since the child's birth. When the communication becomes verbal, however, a new dimension is added to the exchange. The child now has the possibility of meaningful dialogue with more knowledgeable persons. Once this occurs, there are marked effects on the child's learning. Much attention has been given to the role of the demanding parent in the high-achieving child. What has been overlooked is the fact that in adopting active (albeit incorrect) attempts at reasoning, the child forces the adult into a directive teaching role. For example, when a child, upon watching her mother nurse a baby, asks "Mommie, do you have coffee there sometimes too?" (Chukovsky, 1963, p. 24) she is creating a situation in which the mother will provide information that could not possibly be gleaned from perceptual observation alone. The learning in this situation need not be automatic or easy, for the child may not be able to accept the information offered. The answer she receives may even cause confusion since it may disturb her conceptual grouping of "things to drink" (e.g., if you can have milk in a cup and coffee in a cup, why can't both of them exist equally well in her mother?).

But confusion need not be a negative force. In many cases communication with knowledgeable persons creates the same disequilibria that are created by self-induced conscious expectations.

The child may perhaps be less affected by adult-induced contradictions than by self-induced ones (see Langer, 1969), since the latter are more likely to be matched to his developmental stage while the former may be so advanced as to be totally beyond the child. Nevertheless, the child's respect for the adult will not permit him simply to disregard the disturbing information. In fact, as his endless question-asking indicates, he willingly places himself into situations where he knows disequilibria may be found. The child's experience tells him that the adult world may not only reject his ideas ("No Johnny, that isn't a dog, it's a cat"), but it may also actually judge them as laughable ("No, don't be silly, cutting down the tree won't make the wind stop"). The child's courage in exposing himself to such possible rejection is an important sign of his emotional strength and security (Erikson, 1950; Frankenstein, 1966). From a cognitive view, however, his statements are clear signs of the effort he is expending to seek the information and advice that is available from the adult world.

If the poorly functioning preschool child is to attain comparable facility, considerable work must be expended to help him formulate and comprehend the prerequisites of problem-solving skills, manifested most particularly in the sphere of "why" and "how" questions. This goal is among the most difficult that education may set for itself. Ultimately, it even reorients the total concept of preschool compensatory programs. Generally, such programs represent an almost literal translation of the term "compensatory"; that is, they attempt to impart directly to the poorly functioning child the same skills possessed by the well-functioning child. Thus, if the well-functioning child has a greater range of concepts, verbal facility, and spatial representation, these would seem to be the same ones that should be taught to the poorly functioning child.

But central to the problem-solving skills cited in this section are their spontaneous nature. This characteristic raises many problems for teaching. It is fairly easy to elicit responses when the behavior is specifically demanded. For example, if a child is shown a broken pencil, there is at least a reasonable probability that he will answer correctly if he is asked "Will this pencil write?" But how can one arouse the will to make meaningful observations and generate pertinent questions on a self-initiated basis (i.e., in the absence of prodding, for the child to say "Oh, this pencil is not good")? It seems a contradiction in terms to think of ways that will compel a person to be spontaneous.

And, in fact, this goal is probably unattainable in a straight-forward fashion. Compensatory programs can directly fill in some of the absent behaviors, but the truly significant gains will occur when these experiences combine in the child to lead him toward independent inquiry. These considerations apply to the Socratic-type tutorial dialogue as well. Nevertheless, because of its structure, it seems to hold the greatest promise for fostering the spontaneous, self-imposed inquiry characteristic of the abstract attitude which the teacher has carefully structured for him in each lesson. In particular, it spotlights cognitive skills for the child by placing them in a context of a sustained, intimate relationship that is precisely geared to his individual needs and level. As a result, the child is stimulated to internalize and ultimately expand the skills he has practiced with the teacher for they have assumed a central place in his daily life.

chapter 3

The Tutorial Interchange

It is clear that the ideas that were emerging could represent a nucleus around which to establish a preschool program. At this stage, however, they offered merely a bare framework of what the structure and content of such a program could be. Thus, it was clear that a tutorial format could be used and that the core of the interchange would be a Socratic type of dialogue. In order to flesh out these ideas, work was begun on the exact types of problems which were to be posed to the children. Rather than attempt to describe these problems in a straightforward commentary, it seems best to illustrate them through an actual dialogue. This was not only our *modus operandi,* but it was also the setting that clearly exposed all the unforeseen problems. (For those readers who are interested in the precise delineation of the techniques, that work will be presented in the second section.)

The following lesson took place after one of the children, Ruth, had been in the program about two months. After entering the room, the child and teacher had a short interchange about the visitor who was recording the session. Ruth spoke with the visitor, examined the tape recorder, and then walked over to sit down with the teacher. The teacher had hoped to start with a review of color concepts that had been taught earlier in the week. To this end, she capitalized on the child's spontaneous comment about her shoes where the child pointed and said: "These are my shoes." The teacher replied,

Teacher	*Ruth*
	1. (Pointing.) These are my new shoes.
2. What color are they?	
	3. Same color as that (pointing to her dress).
4. Right. They are the same color as that. What is that color called?	
	5. (Shrugs) They're the same color.
6. That's right. They're white.	
	7. They're white.
8. Are they (pointing to the shoes) the same color as this (pointing to the socks)?	
	9. No.
10. Right. They're different then, aren't they? What color are your socks?	
	11. I told mommy not to buy me these shoes.
12. Why? What kind of shoes did you want instead?	
	13. (Shrugs.)
14. Did you want sneakers?	
	15. No (emphatically).
16. Did you want shoes without laces? Like the kind you wear to a party?	
	17. Shiny shoes? Oh, I like them.
18. Well, maybe you'll get them next time. In the meantime, let's do something together here. First, please get the play dough.	
	19. All right (She brings over a box of Fit-a-Space puzzles).
20. Oh, I asked for the play dough. But, never mind. We'll use it some other time (turns	

to puzzle). Do you know what these are called?

21. No.

22. They're shapes. Do you know the names of some shapes?

23. They got colors (picks up a circle of red).

24. What color is that?

25. I don't know.

26. It's red.

27. Red.

28. Good. Now, what is this?

29. It's the bumpy side.

30. Good. (Turns over the piece) What side is this?

31. The smooth side (starts searching in the box).

32. Fine. What are you looking for?

33. I'm looking for . . . (voice trails off) (picks on oval).

34. That's an oval. I don't think we ever used that word. An oval looks like an egg. Try and find another like it.

35. I'll get another egg.

36. Oh no, they're not eggs (laughing), they just look like eggs; they're ovals. Now, listen carefully I want you to do something.

37. What?

38. Take this paper (gives child paper) and then find a crayon the same color as this (pointing to blue square).

39. (Looks into box of crayons on the table) I don't know which one.

40. (Picks up yellow) How about this? Is this the same color?

42. And this (a blue crayon)?

41. No.

43. Yes. (Takes it gleefully) I can make a picture (draws a circle).

44. Make a picture? That's a fine idea. What a good circle Ruthie. Now make another.

46. How many did you make?

45. (Does so.)

47. One, two, three, four, five.

48. No, wait a minute, it was two—let's count again.

49. I can make a nose.

50. Oh, okay, you want to make a face. Where do you want to make the nose?

51. Over here (points to place on oval and draws in eyes).

52. You made eyes instead. Where are the eyes—inside or outside the circle?

53. Inside.

54. Good. Very good. And what comes under your eyes?

55. A mouth (and draws a mouth).

56. Yes, it does. And what are these (pointing to child's ears)?

57. Ears.

58. That's right. How about drawing in some.

59. Okay (and draws in some hair).

60. And what's that on the very top of the head?

61. A barret (touching the barret on her hair).

62. Yes, but what did you make in your drawing?

63. I'm making things (starts drawing in the neck area).

64. What is it? What are you making?

65. I don't know.

66. I think you're making a neck because it's underneath the face. (Pause) What shape is this face? What shape did you draw before you put in the eyes and mouth and everything?

67. A circle.

68. Very good.

69. Yeh, I'll draw it—one more thing.

70. Fine and then it will be time to go back to your room.

This interview was one of the kind that prompted us to reevaluate the teaching program. This statement may seem strange since the lesson obviously contained many strengths. The overall tone was one of learning under friendly circumstances. Both the teacher and child liked each other and maintained a pleasant dialogue for the entire time. Although the reader cannot know this, this alone was a sign of progress since Ruth had entered the program as one of the most poorly functioning children in her class. She barely spoke in more than monosyllables—even with her peers—she showed serious weaknesses in eye-hand coordination, and she had great difficulty in concentrating—even though she made obvious efforts to do so. The changes within the first two months were striking both affectively and cognitively. She enjoyed conversation, she volunteered ideas, and she showed pride in her achievements. She obviously thrived on the one-to-one experience, and her teacher in the group remarked on the improvement she displayed.

With all these positive features, why did this kind of interview seem less than satisfactory? After all, the lesson clearly reflected the avowed aim of teaching concepts to the preschool child. But this is precisely where things went awry. The concepts seemed to occur as scattered points, lacking any meaningful connection or framework. At first glance, this may not seem so detrimental since perhaps concepts are learned this way. But a little delving into the interview shows the weaknesses of relying on this technique. In some way, the teaching of the concepts elicited rote responses that were highly idiosyncratic. This is seen most clearly in interchange 29 where the teacher holds up a piece of the puzzle and asks "What is this?" and Ruth replies "It's the bumpy side."

This response might be interpreted as a sign that the child was truly developing finely honed perceptual skills. In part this is true; but, in larger measure, what was occurring was that the teacher was training Ruth in a communication system that was shared by almost nobody else. Thus, rarely in any normal interchange would the spontaneous, initial description of an item be in terms of texture. And it is certainly not the most likely response to the question "What is this?" Yet what Ruth was learning was the appropriate response. It was not incorrect; it was simply a highly peculiar interpretation of the question "What is this" The latter was now a trigger for labeling an abstruse attribute. This would be tantamount to training an adult to say "he's horizontal" as the description for someone who is sleeping.

Even if the response were not idiosyncratic, its rote associational quality would be enough to condemn it (i.e., the concept of "bumpy" was tightly linked to this puzzle; Ruth never used it in any other context). When a response is so tied to a particular context it often fails to generalize to relevant situations if they contain some variation from the original. For example, we have seen children who can count as long as the objects are lined up in a series before them. This is the way they are accustomed to experiencing the demand for number and they respond readily to it. When the same items are placed in an irregular array, the children are often bewildered as to how to proceed; they do not even attempt to count. The concept being taught then does not serve to help the child organize large sectors of his world, but rather is simply another rote detail tied to specific situations.

Even if the individual concepts had been taught so that they were more meaningful, the concepts in combination still possessed a serious weakness—they cast a repetitive, dull shadow on the lesson. It was as if the same refrain were heard again and again, albeit with different labels—first color, then shape, then texture. This was the antithesis of the ever-changing, highly stimulating character of true intellectual inquiry. A problem was not viewed from varied perspectives; there was no search for meaningful relationships; there was no questioning of the unusual or of the unexpected.

This is not to say that such a lesson need automatically be boring. It is possible to compensate for the qualities lacking in the ideas through external devices such as rewards, lively teachers, and attractive material. All of these prove useful and necessary in teaching, but they all fail to deal with the central problem—generating interest in intellectual endeavor for its own sake.

Another disturbing feature underlay the apparently successful learning that Ruth had achieved. In some ways, she still had great difficulty in taking in new information. Thus, every time the teacher asked her for a color name, she responded by shifting the demand to a matching response, adding the verbalization "It's the same color as that." In many ways, this behavior is symptomatic of her newly established mastery—she was no longer helpless when faced with cognitive demands, but rather could offer a relevant, knowledgeable response. Nevertheless, with this response, she failed to meet the specific request made by the teacher. In addition, even after she was offered the information, she failed to retain it (e.g., as occurred with the label for "oval").

These failures are in no way meant to be an indictment of the child; rather, they are important as a sign that the teacher lacked the skills she needed for successfully transmitting much of the information she wished to impart. Frequently, relevant issues were raised (as in interchanges 18, 22, 48, 58), only to be dropped because of the adult's inability to capture the child's attention. It was evident that asking of the questions was not enough; ways had to be developed whereby the question led to a meaningful and responsive interchange.

The first technique that might come to mind toward achieving this goal would be to rely upon the child's lead. Nursery school educators have long known the value of pursuing the child's spontaneous interests as a means of enhancing his learning. The teacher clearly attempted to do this, as in the interchanges on shoes and drawing. This technique seemed particularly appealing in view of the reticence that Ruth had initially displayed early in the program. There were, however, serious limitations to this technique. For example, it permitted the child to maintain a schism between what she was saying and what she was doing. Thus, in interchange 49, when she said she would draw a nose, she proceeded to draw in eyes, with no concern that the answer and action were at odds. At other times, her spontaneous interests merely redirected the dialogue into short interchanges, coming to sudden stops.

This behavior contrasts sharply with that displayed by the well-functioning child in the dialogue setting. His drive for meaning leads him to assume an active role in which he continually seeks to "weigh up what is offered to him, and reject it if it is not up to standard" (Isaacs, 1930, p. 313). For example, Isaacs cites the following incident: "While Mrs. I was sitting near Benjie (4 years, 1 month) helping him to put on his shoe, he said reflectively 'Why do we have to pick up things that we put on the floor?' Mrs. I replied 'Well if we left them on the floor, and were running and trod on them, we might break them, mightn't we?' He said, 'We shouldn't break those big bricks should we?' Mrs. I: 'No, but perhaps we should hurt our feet on them!' This seemed to content him" (p. 312). Because of the child's striving for comprehension the tenet to follow the child's lead is a productive way of determining the sequence and pacing of the teaching.

In the absence of this striving for comprehension, however, the teaching can easily be stymied. The child does not yet have the set to maintain a meaningful interchange, but it must be maintained if thinking is to be fostered. The burden falls clearly on the teacher. To this end, she must modify her tendency to follow the child's tangents and, instead, assume the leadership that only a skilled adult can offer.

With this analysis, we proceeded to redesign the tutorial lessons. The following represents a sample of the type of interchange we were able to achieve.

Teacher	*Julie*
1. Do you remember what we did when you were here yesterday?	
	2. Yes.
3. What did we do?	
	4. I don't know.
5. Let's see if I can help you. Is there anything on this table that we worked with the last time? (A limited variety of materials is presented.)	
	6. (Points to blackboard.)
7. That's just pointing. Tell me what we did.	
	8. We did—we did a square.
9. Right. What did we do with the square?	
	10. (Hesitates.)
11. Think about it for a minute.	
	12. We took it off (child refers to erasing).
13. Good. Now, what did we use to take it off?	
	14. I don't know.
15. (Brings blackboard forward) All right—what would you do if you had a square on here and you wanted to get rid of it? How could you get it off?	
	16. Maybe we could use paper.
17. Why could we use paper? What would it do?	
	18. It could take it off. It could rub it off.
19. Fine. Now, remember what we did? We didn't use paper to take off the square. Do you remember what it was we *did* use?	
	20. A sponge.

21. Very good. Would you get the sponge for me and wet it? Get a paper towel and wet that too. Wet them both.

22. (Goes to sink in room and reaches not for the requested items, but for the soap.)

23. (Follows child over to sink) Do we need the soap?

24. No (takes sponge and piece of paper toweling and starts to return to seat).

25. Do you remember what I asked you to do with the paper and sponge?

26. Uh huh. Wet them.

27. Fine. Then do that.

28. (Wets toweling and sponge) They are full of water.

29. Do you need all that water?

30. (Shakes head to indicate "no.")

31. What could you do to get rid of the water that you don't need?

32. (Squeezes water from both sponge and paper.)

33. What did you do?

34. The water comes out.

35. That's fine, Julie. You really didn't need all that water (they return to the table). Now, I'd like you to draw something for me on the blackboard.

36. What color?

37. What color would you like to use?

38. Green (and selects green crayon).

39. Green is fine. Draw some green lines for me.

41. Okay. We can work with big ones. Oh! Those are very big lines. What will happen if you wipe the sponge on those lines?

40. I'll make some big ones (she proceeds to draw).

43. Think about it, Julie, If you put this sponge over your lines and wipe them, what will happen?

42. I don't know.

45. What's happening to the lines Julie?

44. (Moves sponge over drawing.)

47. (Holds sponge down to prevent child from lifting it) If I lift up the sponge, what color is going to be on the sponge?

46. (With surprise) They're not there anymore!

49. Why white?

48. White.

50. Green.

51. Tell me why you said green. Why do you think it will be green?

52. 'Cause I wipe it off.

53. What did you wipe off?

54. The green color.

55. Let's see if you're right. (Lifts sponge) Green! You're right. Very good.

The discussion went on to consider issues such as the effects on the sponge of erasing different colors, what happens to the chalk after it is erased, how to get chalk out of a sponge, comparison of sponge and paper toweling as erasers, and so forth.

The differences between the two interviews are evident. In

contrast to the scattered "catch as catch can" quality of the first interview, the second was noted by a sustained sequential analysis of a phenomenon. This was not achieved by developing different sorts of questions that would be inherently more successful. Many of the questions in the two lessons were similar (e.g., "What kind of shoe did you want" vs. "What did we do?"–"Go get the play dough" vs. "Go get a paper towel and a sponge").

Nevertheless, there were important differences in the overall pattern of the questions. For example, the second interview was notable for the decline in the teaching of labels. There was nothing comparable to the emphasis that had occurred in the first lesson on size, number, color, and texture. Instead, the concepts already available to the child were used to help her pursue a phenomenon from many different angles. For example, when Julie had difficulty in remembering the "erasing" of the previous lesson, a long interchange was initiated (numbers 9 through 20) in which numerous relevant ideas were raised including memory (e.g., "what did we do with the square"), problem solving (e.g., "if you had a square here, what could you use to take it off"), and rationale for the suggestion (e.g., "why could we use paper"). By contrast, when Ruth failed roughly comparable questions, the teacher either dropped it (e.g., interchange 20, "Never mind, we'll use the play dough some other time") or gave the answer in the form of a single didactic comment (e.g., interchange 48, "no, it was two").

The difference between the two lessons was also achieved by the teacher in the second lesson being willing and able to assume greater control over the interaction. Thus, when she wanted Julie to think about an event, she actually prevented action by holding the child's hand so that the eraser could not be lifted (interchange 47); similarly, when vague answers were given she sustained the questioning so that the child was led to pursue an idea until it was fully described (interchange 7) or explained (interchange 53). Needless to say, this was not done in a harsh, punitive manner, for the latter would have been defeating of both the teacher's and child's interests. Rather, the control was exerted both through having a pleasant supportive tone to the interchange and through providing attractive materials that interested the child (e.g., giving her the opportunity to play with water, to erase the chalk, etc.).

With the mentioning of material, it may appear that the lessons are similar to those taught in more traditional preschool programs. There are naturally many points in common since we have drawn heavily on the techniques that were already available. There does, however, seem to be a key point of difference. More traditional programs emphasize material as a major means for fostering learning. It is generally felt that if the child has the opportunity to play with objects and experience them to the fullest, he will achieve well-integrated, motivated learning. By contrast, in a lesson such as that with Julie, the opportunity to play with desirable objects in an appealing setting is mainly seen as fostering motivation. The introduction of problems within this setting is then accepted by the child because the questions have been integrated into the total play setting.

For example, in the first lesson, Ruth was drawing the neck (interchange 65) but failed to answer the teacher's question as to what she was making. If the teacher wished to pursue this idea so as to ascertain whether or not the child had the concept, she could have stopped the drawing for a moment and asked Ruth to point to that part of the body which was in a comparable position on either herself or on a doll. If this exploration revealed that the child had the information, she could be encouraged immediately to return to her drawing; if it revealed that she did not have the information, the teacher could help her acquire it and then permit her to return to complete the drawing. In either case, the opportunity to draw, which until then had been unconstrained and undirected, is now offered to the child as the relevant and satisfying end point of this particular exchange.

The interruption of activity for dialogue is meaningful, however, only if the teacher is prepared to cope with every type of response that the child may give, including wrong responses that are unrelated, incorrect, or even refusals to respond. In fact, this is *the* most central feature of effective teaching—the ability of the teacher to recognize the child's difficulty and redirect it so as to sustain a meaningful interchange even when the child fails to take up his end of the dialogue. The teachers' competence in this area is the key difference between the two lessons above. Thus, in the first interview, when the child failed to remember that she had been sent to get the play dough (interchange 28), the teacher dropped the question and permitted the child to play with the other item. By contrast, in the second interview, when a similar failure occurred at the sink (interchange 22), the teacher actively followed the child and drew her back to the original request.

The importance of these procedures becomes clear when we compare the teaching that was achieved in the tutorial program with the methods used by more traditionally trained teachers when they are given the opportunity to work on a one-to-one basis. The lesson that follows was given in the same week as Session 2 and it was given to the same child. It was taught by one of the nursery school teachers who had been invited to visit the program. The teacher was told to teach a cognitively oriented lesson that she deemed appropriate for a child of this age.

On this particular day, there were boxes of small plants in the room which the children were to plant outside. As she entered, Julie immediately looked at these flowers. The teacher noticed this and the following dialogue ensued.

Teacher	*Julie*
1. Have you seen the flowers?	
	2. I saw a beautiful flower outside.
3. A beautiful flower? What color was it?	
	4. I don't know. It's a beautiful flower.
5. Did you put it in the ground?	
	6. I picked it up.
7. You picked it up? What kind was it?	
	8. I don't know.
9. Was it little and yellow? Maybe it was a dandelion? Did you plant the flower? Was it a seed and now it's a flower?	
	10. (Nods.)
11. Why don't you draw a picture of the flower and then we can see what color it is?	
	12. I'd like to do any color flower.

13. I'd love to have a drawing of it.

14. I'm gonna make a beautiful flower (child proceeds to draw).

15. Good.

16. What's this (the child is referring to the design from the table which comes through on her drawing)?

17. That's the tablecloth coming up, the pattern.

An interchange about flowers then continued on the assumption that the child, in fact, had something definite she wanted to draw. The teacher did attempt to stimulate the child's recall of the specific flower but for the purpose again used unverifiable questions. After the child had drawn several flowers, the following dialogue was initiated by the teacher.

Teacher	*Julie*
18. Do you know how many flowers you have there now?	
	19. Three. I'm five years old.
20. You're five years old? Maybe you could make flowers for how old you are. Do you know how many more you would need?	
	21. Five.
22. Five *altogether*. And how many do you have here?	23. I'll make one more! What kind of brown is this? It's a tree.
24. Oh, that's pretty, Julie. That's very, very nice.	
	25. I bet it's time to wake up now.
26. What time do you get up?	

28. In the morning? (Incredulously) Do you really wake up at five o'clock in the morning?

27. I get up five o'clock.

30. And what time do you come to school?

29. I do.

32. No.

31. I don't know what time—nighttime?

33. I think so. I got a clock. I'm tired.

It is recognized that the teacher in the third dialogue was at a disadvantage since she was new to the situation and not well known to the child. It is, however, representative of a number of sessions we recorded with cooperative nursery school teachers. Their dialogues typically are in accord with the predominant child-centered, permissive philosophy of nursery school education (see review by Weikart, 1967). That type of program is designed to meet the needs of well-functioning, middle-class children. Because their general intellectual competence can be taken as a "given," language and intellectual development are placed last in a list of desired attributes to be developed. Instead, the guiding principles are focused upon enhancing the child's social and emotional functioning. Thus, the second teacher's lesson cannot be dismissed as chance behavior in the face of novelty. It typifies the branch of education where the pervasive philosophy is to "follow the child's interests."

This philosophy was clearly illustrated by the way in which the teacher limited the scope of the material by focusing on the child's casual comments. Regardless of whether she mistook these remarks for real interest or whether she was guided by a consideration for a child's words, the teacher missed the opportunity to lead Julie toward developing the higher level concepts of which she was capable. On the other hand, when the teacher did initiate material, she posed seemingly simple questions which, in reality, were of enormous complexity (e.g., "was it a seed and now it's a flower?"). Since the teacher did not have the techniques for analyzing where the child's difficulty lay, she assumed that the concepts involved were well beyond the child. Her responses to the child's failure varied; at times, she followed the child's chance associations (e.g., interchange 3), at times she switched topics (e.g., interchange 9), at times she provided brief didactic statements which had little explanatory value (e.g., interchange 22)—but at almost no time did she effectively move the child past the point of difficulty. The teacher's handling of the wrong response appeared to represent a pivotal difference between the last two dialogues. Because this issue is so critical and complex, it deserves much more detailed consideration. It is to this problem that the following chapter is directed.

chapter 4

The Wrong Response

After having raised the issue of the wrong response, we find ourselves in an astonishingly unexplored field in education. There has been almost no consideration given to the treatment of this behavior, even though it is an ubiquitous obstacle to learning. Perhaps its very pervasiveness is a contributing factor to its being neglected—as stumbling in learning to walk and lisping in learning to talk, it seems to be a prerequisite in the development of any skill. Hence, errors are not a source of concern, but merely an expected feature of the normal process of learning which will pass with time.

The behavioral sciences have had a major hand in gaining acceptance for this view (see Kohlberg, 1968). For example, although Piaget has used the wrong response brilliantly for diagnostic purposes, he has ignored any consideration of possible treatment. In fact, attempts at treatment would almost be proscribed since the wrong response is interpreted as graphic proof of the child's immaturity of thinking. In this vew, immaturity will be overcome not by directed intervention, but by the child being allowed to engage in a slow, unconstrained process of interaction with a rich environment. "In a practical sense, the interaction view suggests that limited specific training experiences cannot replace the massive general types of experiences accruing with age" (Kohlberg on Piaget, 1968, p. 1029).

A similar, but more extreme, viewpoint derives from maturational models which conceive of immaturities in thinking as surmountable only through spontaneous internal development and not through externally imposed direction. In general, any approach which emphasizes the self-pedagogy of the child will play down the value of directed intervention in handling incorrect patterns of thinking. These approaches would be reasonable to follow if the outcome that was hoped for was eventually achieved. The poorly functioning child, however, maintains a pattern of failure throughout school. Therefore, his errors cannot be dismissed as symptomatic of "normal developmental immaturity."

Instead, we must recognize that essential differences exist among various types of errors. For example, a child who makes a wrong response while struggling to grasp an idea (e.g., when asked "why do you use chalk to write on the blackboard?" says "It's like a crayon") is quite different from a child who makes an unthinking, irrelevant response (e.g., when asked the same question he says "to make you big and strong"). There is no assurance that the latter behavior will vanish with time. In fact, the opposite is more likely—the error pattern may become entrenched, forming the basis of characteristics commonly termed as "thoughtlessness" and "carelessness." These traits are often dominant in children about whom teachers later despair with comments like "If only he would be able to settle down, I'm sure he could learn." The particular examples used above are not the only types of wrong responses. They are included merely to show the possible variations in this behavior and to indicate the futility of hoping that they will pass.

At this point, it may be premature even to discuss the differential outcomes of various wrong responses, for these behaviors have often not been acknowledged in the preschool setting. The following statement may sound paradoxical since the pervasiveness of errors was just emphasized—if something is omnipresent, how can it be denied? The answer seems to lie in the philosophical underpinnings of current American education. Under the influence of leaders such as Dewey and Piaget, preschool educators were among the first to accept the notion of "learning through doing" and to reject the practice of didactic teaching, for the latter forced the child into a much too passive role. In practice, perhaps the most dramatic consequences for the teacher have been to change her role from one of "telling" to one of "question-asking." The posing of a question is designed to be the trigger to set off the child's independent search for knowledge and understanding.

The emphasis on questions is common in almost all preschool programs which aim to foster cognition, including programs as far apart as those based on Skinnerian behaviorism (Bereiter and Engelmann, 1966), Freudian psychoanalysis (Biber and Franklin, 1967), and Piagetian epistemological psychology (Kamii, 1970). But, in the stress on questions, there has been a peculiar omission—there seems to be the assumption that the asking of the question will surely be followed by the right answer. In fact, this is true in the group teaching situation since someone is bound to come up with the correct answer. When even this does not happen, the teacher adjusts by supplying the answer she originally requested (e.g., "Oh, I'm sure you all remember what we saw yesterday. You know, it was the baby chicks coming out of the eggs"). In effect, when all the children fail to answer, the teacher conducts a conversation with herself. In this way, any single correct response—even an answer from the teacher—comes to serve as the equivalent to the question having been grasped by everyone in the group. These factors have permitted the teacher to avoid any serious consideration of the wrong response.

This avoidance could not be sustained, however, once the tutorial setting was adopted. In the one-to-one situation, the errors stood out graphically and had to be handled. This is where the tutorial setting began to reveal its strengths—it exposed the critical factors which were obscured by the group.

The desire to avoid consideration of errors is understandable. Any teacher must experience discomfort when she finds the child failing to grasp carefully planned material. But the failure need not take on totally pessimistic interpretations. Admittedly, the child is experiencing difficulty, but this difficulty can represent one of the goals that is most sought after in education—it can be the source of the "match" (Hunt, 1961). This term refers to the well-accepted idea that the child will learn from material only if it is appropriate to his developmental level, that is, there must be a match between the child and the material. For example, a farfetched illustration of mismatch would be teaching a three-year-old to do calculus. But when we get to more subtle cases, the problem is really quite difficult. How can a teacher ever be sure that the material she has prepared is appropriate to the child? The curriculum and her knowledge of development offer a gross outline as to what is appropriate, but this can never be specific enough to test out each child's specific knowledge and skills. Diagnostic tests are also of some help, but often they are based on multiple-choice answers which have built-in weaknesses; for example, the child passes many items by chance and therefore his failure remains undiagnosed.

It is for these reasons that errors in the classroom can be so useful. Every type of question that the child fails is an area in which he needs guidance. Once the difficulty is exposed, it becomes possible to help the child move beyond the obstacle. For instance, Ruth failed many questions which required her to attend to or retain simple directions (e.g., get the play dough, draw in some hair, etc.). These errors make evident her need for help in this area. It is apparent that repeated practice alone is not sufficient since repetition of this type of demand will merely lead to additional errors. The actual techniques for treating the failures will be discussed below. The point at issue here is the fact that questions need not be posed for answers alone; rather, they can serve as a barometer of mental performance. In effect, they may function as a wide scanning detection system to expose the areas where the child is not functioning effectively.

This approach stands in contrast to the general view that wrong responses are a deterrent to learning which should be avoided at all costs. Ultimately, the goal of all teaching is the development of productive thinking. This necessitates the elimination of the wrong response. It cannot be eliminated, however, until it is discerned.

On the other hand, a quest for errors should not lead to a distorted perspective whereby we lead the child to repeated failure. No lesson should be such that he fails all, or even most, of the questions. Such failure is a clear sign that the lesson is mismatched at a level well beyond the child. Ruth's failures on the repeated requests for labeling (e.g., color, shape, etc.) are an example of such mismatch. Not only was this aspect of the teaching boring, it was also ineffective. Every lesson, however, should be capable of evoking some error. If it does not, then the lesson is doing little or nothing to facilitate the child's functioning.

One might well question the thesis that wrong responses provide the teacher with valuable clues. It could be argued that errors represent behavior that only interferes with learning and, hence, they should not be encouraged. But errors do not occur because the teacher, or any one else, wills them. They are a "given" of learning—and they cannot be wished away. *The effectiveness of any teaching program critically hinges on the management of the wrong response.*

What then do we have available to help us in this sphere? To my knowledge, only two approaches have given serious consideration to this problem: one is programmed learning and the second is didactic teaching. While both have important roles in the learning process, the handling of this problem is not sufficient for dealing with the difficulties of the poorly functioning child. First, let us briefly examine the usefulness of programmed learning.

A basic principle of this approach is to build up correct responses, while avoiding all opportunities to practice incorrect responses. The material is designed to proceed in such carefully controlled steps that errors in performance will be minimal or nonexistent. This goal is appropriate only if the wrong response represents behavior that can be bypassed with no ill effects. Wrong responses, however, often represent deeply ingrained error patterns which must first be overcome if efficient learning is to take place. For example, a child may have the set to indiscriminately label the most salient characteristic of a situation regardless of whatever question is put forth. Thus, if asked "Why doesn't this cube roll like the ball does?" he might say "because it's white."

It is certainly possible to avoid this error by building in the "correct" response through a carefully programmed sequence of learning (e.g., "Today we are going to learn about cubes. Cubes have sharp corners, count them, etc."). This approach relies on the hope that the wrong response will vanish through lack of reinforcement. Our experience suggests, however, that the more likely result will be that the "correct" response will coexist with, but not displace or even dominate, the "incorrect" response (e.g., "Oh sometimes I can say the color and sometimes I have to talk about the shape"). While this behavior may seem paradoxical, it is consistent with children's well-established tendency to interpret the same event both magically and with rational explanations (Werner, 1957). When this happens, the "correct response" is simply another fact which increases the amount of unsystematized information that the child must retain.

The ineffectiveness of building in the "right" response without eliminating the "wrong" response is evident in the tenuous grasp that results from training young children to achieve concepts such as "conservation" (e.g., the idea that an amount of any substance remains constant despite changes in its appearance, Sigel and Hooper, 1968; Kohlberg, 1968). Even after they have been assiduously trained to achieve the right answer, slight variations in the procedure will cause the children to lose the concept. For example, they may be shown two equal balls of clay and then the shape of one may be changed by pounding it into a flat pancake. During this procedure, they may be given carefully detailed explanations to indicate that the amount of clay has not been altered. They may seem to accept this, since they alter their responses and say that the two pieces of clay are equal—even though they are in different shapes.

But the critical tests come through the presentation of contradictory examples. Thus, out of the child's view a piece of clay may actually be removed from one of the lumps; the two amounts are then put on scales where they naturally are registered as unequal. A child who firmly and independently had the concept of conservation will immediately be skeptical that "something was done to the clay," while a child who was just trained may be unperturbed and conclude that the two equal balls were, after all, not equal. The training seems to vanish with a single, confusing instance. These experiments might be interpreted to support either the Piagetian or maturational viewpoints that training to overcome errors is valueless unless the child has reached the "appropriate developmental stage." This conclusion assumes, however, that all error sets are resistant to modifications as are those on the conservation task.

It may well be an exercise in futility to train children on the

Piaget-type tasks. But significant differences exist between the type of error that occurs on conservation tasks and the type of errors that children make when they select the most salient characteristic in a situation; when they spout ideas which have no logical connection; when they merely imitate what the child next to them has done, and so on. In particular, the latter refers to behavior that is commonly termed as "thoughtless" or "careless." The child is not committed to his error; he did it because it was the easiest thing to do at the moment. By contrast, the former refers to events where the child possesses a strong commitment about his response. His conclusions, though incorrect, represent the best that he was capable of at the time and it clearly reflects his perception of the world at that developmental stage. When the error is of this nature, it is remarkably difficult to alter.[1]

When the errors do not represent this firm misconception of the world, however, they can often be overcome. The child will even be quite amenable to changing his response—provided that he is given sufficient evidence of the need to change it. Such evidence entails the presentation of clear, dramatic examples which demonstrate the inappropriateness of the response. For example, in the cube illustration above, the child can be given a red cube that is the same color as the ball that he just rolled. The problem can then be rephrased, "But look, here's a red cube and it won't roll either. Why won't this cube roll?" If the child repeats his labeling of the color, the irrelevance of this feature can be pointed out by directly comparing the ball and the cube (e.g., "But the ball is red and it rolls. What's the difference between the ball and the cube?" etc.). This type of "confrontation with error" makes the ingenious young child most amenable to recognizing his mistake and accordingly altering his response. (A comparable confrontation in a much more cynical and psychodynamically "defended" adolescent or adult might be a disheartening reaction of "so what?")

This "confrontation with error" contrasts markedly with what is possible in the Piaget-type task. In the latter case, no clear simple

---

[1] Frankenstein (1970) has outlined methods by which disadvantaged adolescents can be led to recognize the inadequacy of these responses, even when they are characterized by firmly held misconceptions. This, however, requires a highly intellectual analysis that is beyond the preschool child.

action or characteristic can be used to show the child that his initial response was incorrect. A flat pancake of clay looks "bigger" (or "smaller" to him, as the case may be) than the ball of clay and little can be done to show, to the child's satisfaction, that his *verbalization* is an inaccurate representation of the *visual impression*. Thus, while all error sets cannot be overcome, it is possible to alter those patterns of error where "proof" can be given to the child to demonstrate the inadequacy of his initial response. This "proof" will, of course, vary with the developmental level of the child, for example, while a young child is bound to concrete sensorimotor reality, the older child can deal with discrepancies on a purely verbal level.

This treatment of errors has much in common with approach outlined by Montessori (1912). She emphasized that an error did not exist until the child perceived its existence. Accordingly, her material was designed to be so highly structured that the child would inevitably be led to recognize a correct from an incorrect response. For example, in a problem involving the concept of size, the various components cannot be fitted together unless the child orders them according to a sequence from large to small. This contrasts with many children's puzzles where the size relationships of the pieces are constructed on a random basis.

But the Montessori material has a major potential weakness. Although it is useful for developing self-guided behavior, the child is not necessarily led to be aware of the concept underlying the objects. Much of the material involves complex perceptual-motor sequences which may be completed through rote trial-and-error behavior. For example, in a problem of size, the child can just keep trying the pieces until he finds that they fit comfortably in their appropriate holes. While the child may reflect on what he has achieved (e.g., thinking something to the effect "Oh, the biggest one has to go here," etc.), such reflection is not essential to completing the problem. Thus, the Montessori material tends to overcome wrong responses—but without the child necessarily confronting the inappropriateness of his wrong response.

The confrontation of error has value which goes beyond helping the child recognize why a particular response is incorrect. The need to examine the "wrong" response not only solidifies the "right" response, but it also leads the child to gradually internalize the "rules" used by the teacher to demonstrate the appropriate response. As a result, even when an adult is not present, the child has techniques by which to evaluate his thinking (e.g., if he has an appropriate idea, he may try it out to see if it works because this is the pattern that has been set by the teacher). Julie, in the second lesson, showed evidence of this internalization in the spontaneous self-correction of her prediction of the color on the eraser (i.e., from "white" to "green"). The internalized rules, of course, cannot be explicit in the preschool child; rather, like language itself (Chomsky, 1957), they exist as an implicit framework for self-critical judgment.

Aside from programmed learning, the second major approach for dealing with the wrong response is didactic teaching. As in the case of programmed instruction, this is a vital aspect of teaching for many types of children and many forms of information. For example, if a child holds up an object and asks the teacher its name, it would be foolish to apply principles of discovery learning to the situation. Nevertheless, didactic teaching is probably a poor method for most preschool children since they are limited in their capacity to be the passive recipients of information.

Didactic teaching is particularly inappropriate, however, for poorly functioning preschool children. Because of their learning difficulties, these children experience discomfort in situations demanding intellectual skills. This leads them to say nothing that might condemn them (hence, the frequency of the "no response") or to something—anything—that will remove the demands on them as quickly as possible (the unthinking "wrong" response). Ruth effectively learned to use the matching response for this purpose. Thus, when she was asked the name of a color, she responded by finding a match and saying "It's like this."

One might suppose that the presentation of information didactically at such a point might lead the children to learn. Since the possibility of failure is greatly reduced when the information has been supplied, the child is theoretically free to devote his energy to the problem being discussed. In reality, however, providing of information can often serve as a deterrent to learning. The child knows that, once the demand for his response is removed, the teacher will not "bother" him again. Hence, he need not continue to attend (see Blank and Frank, 1971). It is for this reason that teaching in the group setting is so ineffective for the poorly functioning child. Regardless of who supplies the answer (whether another child or the teacher herself), the child who failed does not direct his efforts toward incorporating the information.

These considerations make it essential to permit wrong responses to occur. At the same time, however, the teacher must be given techniques with which to cope with them when they do occur. The techniques outlined below represent the work that has thus far been evolved. The basic premise underlying the techniques is that the problem confronting the child must be simplified, but not to the level where he is supplied with the answer. This is done to ensure the child's continued active participation in the problem-solving situation. In almost all cases, the simplification is a first step in leading the child back to the more difficult question that was posed initially.

As the reader begins to examine the list, many of the techniques will have the ring of familiarity. This is particularly true of the initial techniques, which offer almost no degree of simplification. The later ones, however, tend to be those in which a significant amount of aid is given. In part, the range (from simple to complex) depends upon the type of problem failed. Already simple problems can only be further simplified to a minor extent. For example, if a child fails to "pick up the cup" when the only object in front of him is a cup, the range of choices available to the teacher is exceedingly limited, to say the least. By contrast, many aids can be offered to help a child cope with a complex problem such as "Why shouldn't we use Scotch tape instead of shoelaces to tie our shoes?" More detailed specification of the use of the simplification techniques is available elsewhere (see Blank, 1972a).

THE SIMPLIFICATION TECHNIQUES

1. Delay. This technique is geared toward handling failures on relatively simple problems which are not caused by a lack of knowledge, but by impulsivity. It is used only in those cases when the teacher is almost certain that the child is capable of performing the response demanded although he has not done so before because of his impulsivity.

Example:

Teacher—"Pick up the. . . ." Child starts grabbing objects.
Teacher—"Wait a minute. Listen to what I want you to pick up."

2. Focus for Attention.

Frequently, errors occur on relatively simple tasks because (1) the task demand is contrary to a usually performed sequence (e.g., if asked to "try to write with the eraser of the pencil"—the child may be so conditioned to write with the point that he may forget the actual request) or (2) there are strong perceptual components which distract the child (e.g., he is sent to get a cup and he is drawn to a new toy that is present). In these cases, the child can often be brought back to the original request by simply asking him to remember what was demanded of him.

Example:

Teacher—"Go to the sink and get me the pot." Child goes to the sink and reaches for the first thing he sees which is a glass. *Teacher*—"Do you remember what I asked you to bring?"

3. Repeats Demand.

This technique is closely related to "focus for attention," but it makes somewhat fewer demands since it eliminates the need for the child to verbalize the initial request. The demand (whether a question, command, or statement) can either be repeated exactly or in a slightly altered form by changing the emphasis of the command.

Example:

Teacher—"Put your coat on the chair next to the table. No, not on the table; put it on *the chair* that's next to the table."

4. Synonymous Rephrasing.

A child often encounters difficulty with a task because he fails to understand the particular phrase or sentence the teacher used. Many factors exist to cause these difficulties (e.g., the child may lack particular information, he may speak in a different dialect, or he may focus on a main word in a sentence, thereby ignoring key terms such as adverbs, prepositions, etc.), but almost all may be overcome if the teacher has a repertoire of *simple,* synonymous terms to offer the child.

> *Example:*
>
> *Teacher*—"lift the box off the floor." Child—.Teacher—"I mean I want you to pick it up with your hands."

5. Partially Completes Task.   When a child tries to meet a demand, but does not know how or where to begin, it can be useful for the teacher to start the task and leave only a small part unfinished for the child to complete.

> *Example:*
>
> *Teacher*—"What is a pail for?" Child says nothing. Teacher—"It can carry w_____."

THE FALSE USE OF THIS TECHNIQUE

There is a strong tendency to misuse this technique as a disguise for a didactic teaching. As a result, it appears that the child has been left with a problem when, in fact, he was supplied with the total answer.

> *Example:*
>
> *Teacher*—"What do you call this?" Child—. Teacher—"Do you think it's a ball?"

6. Dissects Task Into Smaller Components.   As tasks increase in complexity the child may become bewildered by the number of units with which he must deal. In such a case, the teacher may dissect the task into its various components so that the child can complete the problem in partial steps. The teacher can accomplish this goal in one of two ways:

   a. Isolate individual components by sequentially focusing the child on the various subunits forming the totality

Example:

Teacher presents a group of blocks in a pattern and then says "Now you make the same pattern over here with these blocks."
Child–.
Teacher–"Show me the block at the bottom. Get one like it."

b. Introduce either a perceptual or verbal cue to restructure the situation so as to emphasize its significant characteristics.

Example:

Teacher–"Why do you think we couldn't get this sponge into the (small) cup and we could fit the marble?"
Child–"Because it's a sponge."
Teacher–"Okay, *I'll cut this sponge into two.* Now it's still a sponge. Why does it go into the cup now?"

Both the above techniques share the need for the teacher to decide which parts should be emphasized and the order in which the totality should be dissected. The second technique, however, requires greater ingenuity since the totality is not composed of clearly recognizable units. As a result, skill is required to discern how a seemingly indivisible situation may be dissected and re-structured (e.g., we are not accustomed to seeing sponges that are one inch in size).

7. *Offers Relevant Comparisons.* The essence of this technique rests upon the presentation of clearly incorrect alternatives, alternatives which form a background that propels the correct answer to the foreground. Excessive reliance can easily be placed on this method since it requires only the presentation of a series of con-trasting responses, one of which is obviously correct (or obviously incorrect). Such overuse is harmful since the child will soon realize a bit of waiting will lead to the correct answer being offered in the form of a fairly obvious choice. As a result, he will learn to abandon his problem-solving efforts when difficulty occurs. In order to enhance the usefulness of this technique, it is presented in a variety of versions.

a. Correct from Obviously Incorrect

Example:

Teacher—"What did we open when we came into the room?"
Child—. Teacher—"Well, let's see—did we open the door, the wall, or the ceiling?"

b. Contrast Through Incorrect Alternative

Example:

Teacher—"Where did the ball go" (ball is resting next to the door)?
Child—. Teacher—"Did it go under the table?"

c. Offers Correct for Comparison

Example:

Teacher—"Put these pieces together to form a face."
Child manipulates pieces, does not complete puzzle correctly, but stops, saying he has finished the work. Teacher brings out identical model in completed form and says "Does yours look like this one?"

8. *Didactic Teaching.*

a. Gives Relevant Facts to Child.

While didactic teaching is generally avoided, if used judiciously, it can be helpful. This is particularly true for those forms of information which the child cannot derive for himself (e.g., vocabulary, facts, etc.). Once the information is offered, however, the child should be tested to see if he incorporated it correctly.

Example:

Teacher—"Could you go over there and get me the strainer." Child goes to table and looks bewildered.
Teacher—"Do you know what a strainer is?"
Child shakes head.
Teacher—"Look, this one is a strainer." (The incorporation of this information can then be tested by a demand such as the following. "First, before we use this strainer, go over to the cabinet and see if you can find another one like it.")

b. Provides Model.

Example:

Teacher—"Pour the water out of the glass."
Child does nothing.
Teacher—"Watch, I'll do it first. Now you do it."

9. Makes Child Clarify Response. (Statement or Action). Frequently, in response to request for specific information or behavior, the child makes an appropriate but incomplete response. For example, if a child watches another child pouring water in a bottle and is asked "What is he doing?" his response might well be "water." There is an almost irresistible urge for the adult to accept this answer as complete since the feeling is "He obviously realizes that the water is going into the bottle." While this may be the case, it is also possible that the child only labeled the object most salient for him and did not actually realize what action was occurring. Therefore, it is essential to determine the child's actual grasp of the situation.

Example:

As in the example above, the child said "water" when asked "What's happening?" He might then be told "Yes, there's water, but what's happening to the water?"

10. Repeats Demonstration for Clarification. Frequently, even when a child has witnessed a particular event, he is bewildered when asked questions about it. The repetition of the phenomenon may then be a useful technique to help the child absorb the information. It should be kept in mind that this repetition is not simply a second exposure. Rather, it is a demonstration in which the child's observation may be guided by the question he failed after the first demonstration.

Example:

Teacher—"Where did I put the key to get the door to open?"
Child—. Teacher—"Well, watch again. I'm going to do it over—and
then you can show me."

11. *Relating Unknown to the Known.* A goal of the tutorial program is to help the child realize that even when an answer is not immediately evident, the solution may be derived from information already in his repertoire. This goal is most directly reflected in the simplification technique where the analogy between the known and the unknown is made explicit.

Example:

Teacher—"Now the spaghetti is hard. How do you think it will feel
after it is cooked?"
Child—.
Teacher—"Well, do you remember when we cooked the potatoes? How
did they feel?"

This situation capitalizes on a behavior that is similar to *perseveration* since the message to the child is that the repetition of a previously correct answer is expected. Overuse of this technique is therefore dangerous since it may reinforce perseverative type of behavior in other circumstances.

THE MISUSE OF THIS TECHNIQUE

Relating the unknown to the known can be used when an item in the child's repertoire may be directly applied to a new situation; that is, the child does not have to transform his knowledge in any way (e.g., potatoes become *soft* when cooked so spaghetti will also become *soft;* the package could be *tied with a string,* so the box *could also be tied with a string*). It is precisely because no transformation is required that the technique can capitalize on the child's tendency for perseveration.

We have found, however, that adults often use this technique where analogous reasoning, rather than perseveration, is required.

This seems to occur because of the adult's predisposition to think in superordinate groupings. Such groupings are so comfortable to the adult mind that it eventually leads him to view quite disparate instances as "almost" identical (e.g., if a *spoon* is not available for mixing, a *fork* will serve just as readily because both are *utensils*). Since these groupings are so profitable in his own learning, he tends to feel that they will be of equal benefit to the child. For example, if the child does not grasp the concept of a spoon, the teacher might introduce the concept of a fork as a means of simplifying the task to the already known (e.g., if a child has failed a question such as "Why are spoons good for holding soup" the teacher might attempt to simplify by asking "Well, why are forks good for holding meat").

Even if the child should be completely familiar with forks, (so that it represents the "known"), its introduction at this point is more of a hindrance than a help. From the child's vantage point, spoons are rounded things for eating soup and pudding while forks have sharp points which pick up solids. (One child even refused to mix a drink with a fork when a spoon was not available. He adamantly supported this decision with the statement "Forks aren't used for that.") Thus, the child may be totally confused as to why the adult has paired these dissimilar objects together and, furthermore, asks that he treat them as the same. The second object may be useful once the child has fully understood the first object. Its introduction at that point can then be used to help him realize that both serve "to help us eat." This concept is possible only after both objects have been fully grasped. They cannot be brought in at the initial stages of teaching as a means of facilitating the child's grasp of the "unknown."

12. Directed Action to Recognize Salient Characteristics. Nursery school educators have long emphasized that, if one wishes a child to understand a concept, the child must be given the opportunity to experience and manipulate relevant material exemplifying the concept. Although the teacher in this setting may accompany the child's actions with relevant verbalization, the situation rarely demands that the child attend to the verbal information so supplied. By contrast, the technique cited below structures the situation so that the child's nonverbal behavior must be in accord with the teacher's verbalization. The demands made upon the child, however, are quite simple and generally represent only a simple command which focuses the child on the central features of the concept.

Example:

Teacher—"How is the ice different from the water?"
Child seems unable to answer and so the teacher says "Well let's see. Turn over the cup of water and turn over the tray of ice."
(Commands such as this should be differentiated from the many simple commands that occur in the course of a lesson such as "Get me the play dough now.")

13. Focus on Relevant Features.   When confronted with complex questions, young children often experience great difficulty in knowing even how to approach the problem. There are so many elements and each seems equally important (or perhaps more accurately, equally unimportant). Frequently, progress cannot be made until the child is able to differentiate the relevant from the irrelevant features and, even prerequisite to this, to recognize that some features are relevant and others are not. It is therefore useful to lead the child to focus on what are the relevant properties in the situation—such properties can represent a function, a part, or a characteristic of the material.

Example:

Teacher—"Why did you pull your hand away from the stove?" Child says nothing. *Teacher*—"Well how did the stove feel?"

All these techniques are based on the premise that a wrong response must occur in order for the child's difficulty to be diagnosed. Once exposed, however, nothing is gained by having the child repeat the error. Repetition merely reinforces the particular wrong response and thus fails to move the child beyond the error. Fortunately, diagnosis of the error is not too difficult since the child's response often pinpoints the factors that led him astray. For example, a teacher showed a child two pages in a book, each of which contained drawings of the same set of children but in different positions (e.g., jumping vs. standing). One four-year-old was asked to match the picture of one child with its counterpart on the second page. She completed the task easily for two of the drawings; she was, however, unable to do this for the third drawing. The teacher immediately recognized the source of the difficulty—in one picture, the child was depicted as standing with her back to the "reader"; in the second, she was sitting behind a desk, with her face clearly evident. The marked change in position, accompanied by the absence of facial cues, had led the child to interpret the drawings as being those of two different children.

Unfortunately, diagnosis of the error is a far different cry from its treatment. In this situation, the teacher said "Oh look, it's still the same one. It's just that her back is turned." From the child's response, it was evident that she was still confused. The teacher had stated the obvious (i.e., the child knew that in one case she saw a back and in the other a face). This "obvious" statement failed to establish any equivalence between the two pictures. The "explanation" was an explanation for the teacher, not the child. Nor was the situation ameliorated when the teacher attempted to dispel the child's confusion by saying, "Look, I'll turn around. Now do you see my face?" Child—"no." Teacher—"Now I'll turn around again. Now do you see my face?" Child—"yes." Teacher—"That's the way the girl is in the book." The child was still confused by this accurate but, from her point of view, irrelevant explanation. The teacher, in trying to simplify the situation, required the child to use analogous reasoning ("See what is happening to me is happening to the doll") but the situation was in no way analogous for the child. The teacher was experienced as a single person successively changing positions; the pictures were experienced as dual entities that were static.

The child could be helped over her difficulty only by establishing a situation that, in fact, was comparable to what existed in the book. This involved the presentation of two identical dolls—both of which were seated in identical positions in front of the child (i.e., dissects task to restructure situation). The child, after acknowledging that they were identical, was asked to turn one of the dolls around. She was then asked "Why does this doll now look different from the other one?" The child readily explained that it was because she had turned it around. There were a series of additional questions to solidify this observation (e.g., which doll's face can you see, which one can't you see? are they still wearing the same dresses? on which dress can you see the buttons? etc.). The situation had been transformed so that it was now identical to the situation in the book. At this point, the child was asked "Now, do you see any child on this page" (pointing) "who is the same as the doll on this page" (pointing) "but looks different because she is turned around?" The child was readily able to complete the problem correctly.

This example illustrates the fact that, while diagnosis of the error is essential, such diagnosis does not ensure effective treatment. The latter requires that the situation be analyzed in such a way as to focus on the essential, underlying concepts in the particular problem. Once such concepts are determined, they can obviously not be offered in a simple didactic explanation (e.g., "Don't you see, it's the same girl just turned around"). Instead, the situation must be dissected and structured in such a way that the child is inevitably led to recognize the validity of the "correct" answer. As was illustrated by this example, as the errors become more complex, the task of simplification becomes more detailed, more subtle, and more demanding.

The concept of simplification has some interesting implications for the study of cognitive processes in young children. For example, the fact that one can state that a demand can be simplified implies that the cognitive processes involve a hierarchy of complexity (e.g., focusing the child on the temperature of the stove is a simpler demand than asking him to justify why he pulled his hand away). The existence of such a hierarchy would theoretically make it possible to develop a precise order by which a task may be simplified (e.g., if a child fails a cause-and-effect question, the next logical step might always be a task which focuses the child on a relevant concept). In an overall way, such an ordering does exist and it tends to follow the sequence of the three major areas outlined briefly in Chapter 2 (and expanded in detail in Chapter 9). Thus, problem-solving processes represent the most complex demands that can be placed upon a young child. Accordingly, they require both different and more subtle methods of simplification than do failures in other areas.

Nevertheless, the situation is not yet sufficiently defined to permit the specification of an exact sequence by which the techniques may be applied. A failed response must be considered from angles other than simply which type of cognitive demand was failed. For example, in the cube illustration at the beginning of the chapter, the simplification "But look this cube is red and it also doesn't roll" is possible only if the child has offered an incorrect answer. If the child offered the noncommital answer of "I don't know" the course of simplification would have been different (e.g., the child might be led to focus directly on the corners through a comment such as "Do you see anything over here that will stop the block when we try to roll it").

In addition to the type of failure, proper use of the simplification techniques also requires consideration of the child's personality type (see Blank, 1972b). For example, with passive children who fail to respond, techniques which only reiterate the failed request (e.g., repeats demand, focus for attention, and repeats demonstration) are unlikely to be useful. By contrast, techniques which reduce the demand by partially completing the task for the child (e.g., dissects task, offers comparisons, and provides model) are more likely to succeed. In the case of the hyperactive, overly impulsive child who tends to blurt out responses, it would be self-defeating to use techniques which offer verbal comparisons since this will reinforce his glib verbalization. Instead, it might be better to concentrate on techniques such as delay (to control impulsivity) and directed action (to capitalize on his motor involvement). The complexity of the interplay among these three major factors—the cognitive process failed, the type of "wrong" response, and the personality of the child—makes it impossible to offer a precise sequence of simplification at this time.

Perhaps one of the most surprising features in the simplification techniques is the extent to which they rely upon verbal concepts. For example, a technique such as focusing on relevant features basically requires the child to attend to certain concepts contained in the problem. Since concepts are traditionally deemed to be among the weakest areas of functioning in children with learning difficulties, it may seem unusual to use this means as the route to simplification. The concepts, however, are used in a quite specific way. First, they are largely based on elementary skills of simple labeling and simple actions which are a basic strength of almost all preschool children (e.g., "turn the cup over," "what thing did you see in the picture," etc.). Second, the concepts are raised in an already established context where the child has just failed a problem. Therefore, he knows his information is insufficient. As a result, he is more ready to search for cues that might be helpful. This situation differs from the usual concept training where the conceptual groupings seem like arbitrary, uninteresting exercises ("Put all the red buttons together"). Instead, in the current setting, the concepts are not ends in themselves, but tools for solving more complex problems ("Oh that's *why* the pencil would not write. It didn't have the *black stuff* in it"). Third, for the purposes of simplification, concepts are useful only if they are demonstrable and relevant to the problem at hand.

These restrictions render invalid a large number of seemingly relevant simplification techniques in any setting. For example, during the course of a story about a little boy dressing himself, a question may be asked such as "Why do we need buttonholes?" If the problem is failed, it is possible to ask many questions which appear to be potentially relevant to the course of simplification. For instance:

1. "Do you ever button your clothes yourself?"
2. "Are you wearing buttons?"
3. "Do zippers need buttonholes?"
4. "How do we open and close our clothing?"

All these questions have potential pitfalls. To see this more clearly, it is instructive to consider the limitations of each question in turn.
(1) "Do you ever button your clothes yourself?"—this question attempts to direct the child to already known information in the hope that he will then be focused on the importance of the buttonhole. This question, however, lends itself to a yes or no response. By their very nature, such responses elicit random guessing, especially when the child is already in difficulty. In addition, even if the correct response is obtained, it is difficult to handle. If the child simply says "yes" he may not necessarily be any further along in understanding the purpose of buttonholes. The fact that he buttons his clothes need give him no insight into why he buttons

them. If he answers "no," this line of questioning must be dropped since there is nothing to be gained in pursuing a situation with which the child may be unfamiliar. As a result, the question has simply led to a detour which has detracted the child from focusing on the problem originally posed.

(2) "Are you wearing buttons?"—(in a situation where the child is wearing them)—this question has advantages relative to the first question since it allows greater control over an arbitrary response. Thus, if the child says an unthinking "no," he can be referred to the actual buttons that are on his clothing. If the child's negative answer was not an arbitrary response, but rather a lack of knowledge, then the simplification can serve as a useful starting point for teaching the word to the child. Paradoxically the greatest difficulty with this question occurs if the child answers it correctly. The thinking required for the answer of "yes" may, in no way, have brought the child nearer to a solution to the problem originally posed. The fact that the child has buttons tells him nothing about the purpose of buttonholes.

(3) "Do zippers need buttonholes?"—this question attempts to bring in contrast to focus the child on the central difference. Inevitably, however, it leads to another *why* question. Thus, if the child says "no," the next question will almost certainly be "Why don't they need buttonholes?" Since the child could not answer the first *why* question a second *why* question does not lessen the complexity of the situation. Therefore, the line of questioning leaves the child to cope with two complex questions rather than one.

(4) "How do we open and close our clothing?"—this question has the potential value that it may focus the child on the significant function of buttons relative to buttonholes. The difficulty of this approach, however, is that the concept of open and close has been brought in without adequately preparing the child for it. He was focused on objects (buttonholes); now he is focused on function (open and close). Unfortunately, the child may see no connection between the two. In addition, this question can elicit a number of responses which may lead further away from the question originally posed (e.g., the child can say "I pull them off" or "My mommy does it").

In contrast to these questions, an unambiguous situation results when the child is presented with a bit of clothing that has buttons, but no buttonholes. The child can then be given the simple direction, "Try to button this shirt." This task has several advantages. First, it involves motor movement and so capitalizes on the young child's desire to work through this modality. Second, it involves a simple command which most children would understand. Even should it not be understood, however, it would be a simple one-step process to demonstrate the referents involved (e.g., an intact shirt could be shown and the process of buttoning be illustrated by the teacher). Third, the inability to complete the action leaves the child with a discernible dramatic effect that reveals the relevant properties. Depending upon the child's level, this sequence can be followed by questions demanding expressive language (e.g., "What happened") or those demanding receptive verbalization (e.g., "Could you button it").

One may, of course, question the need for such precision. This doubt arises because of the ease that seems to characterize the well-functioning preschool child's cognitive growth. The parents of such children, regardless of how much guidance they give, do not have to guard every word they say, or do they have to carefully structure every piece of material put before the child. This state of affairs results in the feeling that conversation with a young child is "so natural and easy" that no special safeguards need be taken. This impression, however, is dependent on the almost unrecognized importance of the role of active feedback that the well-functioning preschool child plays in most dialogue situations. Thus, when the teacher asks a question, the child not only answers but often also adds spontaneous comments and questions. This behavior provides a constant flow of information which enables the teacher to regulate her behavior so that it is in line with the child's level.

The significance of the child's role becomes evident when he does not fulfill his expected feedback function. In such a case (e.g., being faced with a child who passively withdraws or, conversely, chatters on his own wavelength) the teacher is frequently left at a total loss as to how to cope (as in the third lesson in Chapter 3). It is for this reason that the questions must be so carefully controlled. The same factors that prevented the child from answering the first question will continue to be present to interfere with subsequent material. Thus, if the poorly functioning child is to learn more effectively, it is necessary to use questions that practically guarantee that he will be helped over his difficulty as expeditiously as possible.

Although the questions outlined above were not suitable for simplification, they would have been suitable if the child's response had been correct. In such a case, they would not represent attempts at simplification, but, rather, attempts at helping the child elaborate the significance of his knowledge. *The interweaving of simplification and elaboration is at the heart of the tutorial dialogue. It reflects the principle that the child's response, more than any other factor, determines each step that the teacher will take.* To illustrate this further, four different sequences of response to a single question are presented below. Each situation follows a chain of two responses from the child.

In this chain, the child is:

1. Correct and then on the subsequent problem correct again
2. Correct and then incorrect
3. Incorrect and then correct
4. Incorrect and then incorrect

Chart 1 lists both the correct and incorrect responses.

CHART 1

The teacher mixed blue and yellow to form green.
The green liquid is then hidden from view and the child is asked,
"What color did the blue and yellow make?"

Sequence of				
Child's Responses	Correct	Correct	Incorrect	Incorrect
		Incorrect	Correct	Incorrect
Child's first response:		"Green."		"Red."
Teacher's response:	"How can we find out if you are right?"		"Well, let's look and see if you are right." "What color is it?"	
Child's second response:	"Give me the jar. I'll show you."	"I don't know."	"It's green."	"Blue."
Teacher's response:	"That's a good idea. Here's that jar. Were you right?"	"Well, where did we see the green water?"	"Right. Do you remember what two colors we used to make green?"	"No, this is green." "Find me something else over there on the table that is green."

106

chapter 5

Cognition in Context

The precision in the sequences just discussed might leave the reader feeling that this kind of teaching requires a degree of skill that can rarely be attained. The difficulty is not to be denied, but it is diminished by a number of resources that can be made available to the teacher. Most of these revolve about a set of principles which govern the interplay between the presentation of questions and the cognitive difficulties of the child. They tend to be grouped into two major categories; the first concerns ways to overcome the confusions and misinterpretations that the child may bring to the teaching setting (the principles of demonstrating the word, duplication of examples, and use of contrast); the second concerns ways to foster more active involvement from the child (the principles of need for relevance, use of action, and indeterminancy in the sequence of questions). The present chapter will be devoted to an elaboration of these principles.

DEMONSTRATING THE WORD

One of the most common error patterns of young children is their failure to independently connect the word to the object.

When this occurs, the dialogue becomes a confused mass lacking any meaningful relation to reality (even when, as in the flower example of Chapter 3, the reality might be immediately before the child).

This potential difficulty can often be overcome if one can demonstrate the relationship between the language and the concrete ("real") world. This constraint does not mean that the child be asked only questions about immediately present events. He can legitimately be asked to evaluate nonpresent material. For example, as in questions of imagery, he can be asked to make predictions about events. Should the child fail to answer correctly, however, the teacher is in difficulty unless she can produce the "real" situation—that is, the situation represented by the question.

For example, imagine a situation where the teacher asks "What color will the cake 'batter' become if I put some red (dye) into it?" and the child replies "chocolate." If the actual materials are not present, the teacher's only recourse is didactic verbal explanation (e.g., "No, not chocolate. It would turn red"). This path is suitable for the older child who can use verbal information even when it is offered apart from concrete referents. It is inappropriate, however, for the young child, especially in a situation where he has already failed a question. Under these circumstances, *verbal explanation isolated from its concrete referents floods the child precisely with the material he is least capable of handling.* The information provided is not a source of help, but a source of added complexity.

PRODUCING THE REFERENT

The situation takes on a new light once the materials are made available to the child. For example, in the illustration above, the child can be asked to execute the action (e.g., "Add some and see what happens"). With this request, the experience of failure is converted into a situation which the child can simultaneously master and recognize the meaning of the verbalization. He now knows that the batter with the red dye turns red, not only because some adult has told him so, but also because he *saw* it himself. "Seeing" under these conditions where it is tied to verbalization is a first step in helping the child achieve "seeing" in its higher level sense of "knowing."

Although the child's preference for perceptual as opposed to verbal evidence can challenge teaching ingenuity, it can also be a powerful aid in the child's learning—it is a tool by which the teacher can make him realize that language must be in accord with perceptual reality. This statement may sound paradoxical, in that the child's strong bond to the perceptual would seem to provide little impetus for him to evaluate seemingly extraneous verbalization. The key lies in turning to advantage the many verbal errors that the child makes.

For example, imagine a situation where a child is shown two toys—a car and a doll—which are then put inside a closed box. Suppose further that, when asked to label the toys that were hidden, the child incorrectly responds "a car and a truck." If the child is then shown the toys and is asked "Were you right?" he almost inevitably will say that he was wrong. The objects he sees do not correspond to the words he used and therefore the words must be incorrect.

In such a conflict, the young child is almost never willing to select his verbal statement; he will almost always side with the visual evidence. Having selected the visual, he must now change his verbalization so that it correctly complements the perception. In this way, the child becomes aware of the fact that verbalization can be wrong. This awareness, in turn, leads him to feel a need to make his verbalization in accord with reality.

THE PERCEPTUAL REPRESENTATION OF CONCEPTS

The keen awareness of language can only be achieved if almost every idea can be subjected to the test of demonstrability. While this may seem to be a reasonable, uncontroversial aim, its realization is difficult. In particular, it renders invalid many of the concepts used in enrichment programs since, from the child's viewpoint, they cannot be adequately demonstrated. For example, concepts such as *evaporation* are sometimes taught by placing pans of water on radiators in order to show that the water evaporates over time. The child, however, experiences no perceptual correlates to the *process* of evaporation. What he experiences is the end product of the changes in which he is expected to fill in the intervening steps (water at the beginning and no water at the end). In effect, he is taught the concept of *present-absent.*

The lack of perceptual correlates for the intervening period may actually reinforce his natural immaturity of thinking rather than encourage logical groupings. For example, it might seem to him that someone poured the water down the drain or somehow it "magically" disappeared since these are ideas with which he is already familiar. Therefore, materials should not simply be demonstrable in some objective sense, but demonstrable in the sense that they are compatible with the grasp that the child has of reality at a given stage. For instance, in the so-called evaporation example, boiling a pot of water on the stove might be the appropriate course. The situation of seeing the formation, rising, and dispersion of steam *may* be a sufficiently demonstrable cue for the child to begin to grasp the concept of evaporation. Thus, the criterion of demonstrability does not mean that certain concepts are teachable and others are unteachable. Rather, it means a careful determination of the potential perceptual correlates that the child may be shown if he is to grasp a concept.

Awareness of developmental stages is vital in this aspect of the teaching. The work of theorists such as Piaget and Werner provides us with the guidelines as to how the child perceives his reality. These guidelines can then be used as criteria against which to assess the validity of the teaching. If there is a discrepancy between the concepts to be taught and what the child perceives as his reality, either the teaching must be redesigned or the concept temporarily put aside.

For example, the teacher may wish to teach the concept *more* by demonstrating that a big cup holds more water than a small cup. For this purpose, it is not sufficient to simply add water to the cups. For example, if the little cup is filled to the brim and the big cup is only filled partially (to show that even a partly filled big cup holds more), then the child's perception is that the little cup holds *more* than the big cup, precisely the opposite of what the teacher intended to teach. On the other hand, if the little cup is filled only a little and the big cup is filled a lot, the child will tie *more* to the level of the water, not to the volume capacity of the cup. Thus, not only has the teacher failed to teach what was intended, but the child also has no correct concept to guide him when he independently confronts other instances of this situation (e.g., such as both cups being filled to the brim).

It is also not sufficient that each cup be filled to an equal level, for in this case the preschool child's subjective reality is that both cups are equally full; he does not think that one cup has *more* than the other.

These difficulties do not mean that this concept is unteachable. The child can be led to abstract some central features of the concept if the situation is carefully *reorganized* through the introduction of two jars of equal size. He may then be asked to pour the water from the small cup into one jar and the water from the big cup into the other jar. The resulting discrepancy between the height of the water in the two jars may help him realize that the water from the big cup yielded "more" water than the small cup. (This example should not be interpreted to mean that the child was taught "conservation" of the concept. If he grasped the lesson, however, he did begin to gain an understanding of the relative concept "more.")

As the child's competence increases so that he is comfortable with verbal communication, it becomes possible to introduce some nonverifiable material. For example, any review of material taught in previous lessons demands that this occur. Such content should be introduced, however, only when the child shows that he is capable of handling it efficiently. Even then, verbalization which is removed from immediately observable reality should not form the core of any lesson.

DUPLICATION OF EXEMPLARS

The poorly functioning child's difficulty in information processing does not mean that only concrete examples must be available; frequently they must be available in duplicate. The need for duplication becomes clear through problems where changes are effected in material. For example, suppose that after making chocolate pudding the child is asked, "Does the" (cooked) "pudding look different now from the way it looked when it was in the box?" If the right answer emerges, no problem exists. But what if the child says "No, it is the same."

This response could be caused by a variety of factors—negativism, a failure to have noted the original material, or a failure to have retained the information even if it had been noted. Regardless of the reason, if none of the original material is available, the teacher's only recourse is didactic verbal correction (e.g., "No it's not the same. Remember it was dry and powdery when we took it out of the box"). While didactic correction can be useful, it can often be defeating with children who have cognitive difficulties. For example, for a child who believes that his incorrect response was correct, the teacher's statement can be interpreted as the arbitrary rejection of his ideas by adult authority. On the other hand, for a child who failed because he did not note the original material, the teacher's correction can be meaningless (e.g., he may not understand what thing is now being described as "powdery" or "dry").

The barrier can be overcome as long as duplicate material is available. With this material, the teacher is able to cope with a wrong response, regardless of its cause (e.g., failure in memory, failure in observation, negativism, etc.). For example, she can simply say, "Look, here is another box that we didn't cook. Is it the same as the cooked pudding?" Once a child is shown the unchanged material, he will generally both abandon his incorrect response and understand why it must be abandoned.

These goals can be achieved only if identical exemplars are available for any material which is altered during the course of teaching. Duplication of exemplars is obviously required for matter that will be altered in state (e.g., ice to water, flour to cake). It is also required for objects (e.g., a whistle, a pencil, a lock) which may have to be taken apart in the course of teaching (e.g., a child may not believe that a pencil will not write if the lead is removed. In this case, the lead may have to be removed. The difference in function can then be most graphically illustrated by comparing the altered pencil to an intact pencil—again calling for duplication of exemplars).

THE USE OF CONTRAST

Although the presence of concrete objects is vital to helping the child grasp ideas, it is not sufficient to enable him to appreciate the full implications of the material. Perceptions by themselves are often devoid of much potential meaning if they are not compared to relevant, previously acquired information. For example, a child could not ask the question "Why does the soap look smaller in the water" (Isaacs, 1930) if he did not have an internalized image that contrasted with the perception of the moment. Therefore, the full appreciation of one's perceptions requires the comparison of new experiences against known (internalized) information.

A major advantage of an abstract attitude resides in its power to impel the child to this spontaneous comparative analysis. The contrast between the known and the newly experienced serves as a major impetus for the question-asking of the well-functioning child. Children who are deficient in the abstract attitude will display few instances of such independently initiated comparative analysis. Teaching programs must somehow compensate for this lack by creating situations which focus the child on the contrast that he fails to perceive.

The usefulness of contrast in learning has long been recognized. For example, Vygotsky (1962), in discussing language development, cites Goethe's saying that "he who knows no foreign language does not truly know his own" (p. 110). This statement epitomizes the failure to appreciate a pervasive skill when it cannot be contrasted with a comparable, but different, skill. It is for this reason that the child fails to appreciate the value and complexity of his first language. In the absence of contrast, the ubiquitous skill is taken for granted. The effort required for second-language learning provides the contrast necessary for a proper perspective on the riches one possesses in the tool of language. Literacy can often have a similar effect since a written language system requires an analysis that is rarely achieved with initial (spoken) language learning.

The principle of contrast, however, is not confined to the appreciation of language. This principle may be the single most important feature in helping the child become aware of any readily available skill. It is evident in the avid manner with which the well-functioning child explores all the most mundane experiences that everyone takes for granted—he is intrigued by the experiences of his eyes (e.g., "Why do we have to blink"), his nose (e.g., "Look, I can hold my nose and breathe through my mouth"), his fingers (e.g., "If I don't use my thumb, I can't pick this up"). He does not simply assert what is—instead he constantly sets up ideas that contrast with the usual order of things—and, through this contrast, he gains a clearer insight into the workings of his world. This is achieved not through enriched abstract subject matter, but through the minute dissection of common, simple perceptual motor experiences.

If the child with learning difficulties is to achieve a comparable degree of awareness he must also be led to attend to his perceptual-motor world—even though it is the world that is least likely to receive his attention. Neglect of sensorimotor experience is not surprising. Although we may be impressed by the seeming chaos in their life, poorly functioning children, like all children, are basically exposed to a world of constancies. Much of their day is taken up with common, familiar activities like eating, walking, running, and playing. In the absence of a well-organized symbolic system which conjures up imagined alternatives to the "givens" of experience, these constancies remain unquestioned and unanalyzed. Just as "the fish will be the last one to discover water," so will the poorly functioning child be the last to discover that his legs are for walking, that his thumb is for apposition, and that his eyes are for seeing.

Yet the sensorimotor world is the only world with which the child is familiar. It would be threatening and perhaps impossible to make him analyze more complex, abstract material. *We thus have the dilemma of being forced to achieve higher level learning through the commonplace sensorimotor world even though this is the world that is the most resistant to analysis by higher level cognition.* Teacher-induced contrast becomes vital at this point, for it provides the means whereby one can create the framework needed to analyze the commonplace, that is, the framework needed to analyze the totally accepted.

The principle of contrast can be applied to many of the questions posed to the child. For example, a typical question such as "Why are boots made of rubber?" can easily be amended, if the child fails, into the form "Why are boots made of rubber instead of paper?" The properties of paper establish a contrasting framework which brings the properties of rubber to the center of attention, thereby leading the child to focus on the relevant characteristics of the material.

Contrast can be achieved in many ways, varying along a perceptual to verbal continuum. For example, a red dot against a field of yellow dots represents a perceptually based contrast in which a single stimulus stands out because it differs from a host of identical stimuli. A totally verbal contrast is created when the child must justify the inappropriateness of a hypothesized act (e.g., "if you want to drink the cocoa, why shouldn't you pour it down the sink"). While both perceptual and verbal contrast is useful, verbal cues have the power of creating striking contrasts in even the most mundane material. For example, the sight of a coat may offer little of interest to the young child. When this item is paired, however, with the ludicrous question "is this coat good to eat?" the contrast motivates a strong response. Not only does the child vehemently deny the proposition, but he is also often impelled to spontaneous verbal elaboration (e.g., "No you put it on, you don't eat it"). Perceptual factors alone rarely contain sufficient contrast to mobilize this degree of involvement.

CONTRAST AND VERIFIABILITY

The principle of contrast in combination with that of demonstrability markedly affects the way in which material is presented and structured. For example, in teaching the concept of *paper*, a teacher might judge its most obvious and useful characteristic to be that "one can write on it." The principle of contrast demands the availability of other items which cannot easily be written upon. This selection may be difficult since the child can write on most items (the walls, the table, books; in fact, as most parents know to their sorrow, this is what the child frequently does). Therefore, if the teacher wishes to avoid an arbitrary edict (e.g., "no, we don't use those things for writing"), contrasting items must be carefully prepared.

In overcoming this difficulty, one might be tempted to rely on logical associations to the item in question, for adults generally find it easier to "make sense" out of objects when they are combined with related instances. For example, the mention of "hot" might easily arouse such terms as "lukewarm," "cool," and "cold." In spite of the adult's comfort with such categorization, this type of clustering can be useless to the child. For example, the adult's associations to paper might be blackboard, pencils, and books.

None of these items, however, offers sufficient contrast to demonstrate the relevant attributes of the concept (e.g., you can write on a blackboard and you can write on paper; therefore, the child may confuse these items rather than see them as distinct). The major road around these obstacles is to analyze the key properties of the concept one wishes to demonstrate. Then items which clearly lack these properties can be selected to provide the appropriate contrast. In the case of paper, such items might be "foam" or "corrugated surfaces" since these items will indicate to the child that paper has unique advantages not shared by all materials.

The contrast to be used depends not only on the concept in question, but also on the child's level of functioning. In general, when a child is unsure of an idea, the contrasts should be gross. The presentation of grossly incorrect alternatives makes the correct answer almost apparent. For example, if a child does not offer the label of a common object such as a shirt, he might be provoked to respond correctly if he is asked "Is it a toy?"

When a child is functioning well, the contrast should be more subtle. Subtle contrasts present the child with complex situations that require careful scrutiny if the correct answer is to be obtained. For example, subtle contrast is a key feature in a question such as "Why do we use sugar instead of salt in making hot chocolate?" The contrasted items are similar in many respects (e.g., color, consistency, association with cooking, etc.), and the child must carefully evaluate their differences if he is to answer the question. Ultimately, this type of analysis is essential in helping the child gain the awareness that is central to a well-functioning cognitive system.

UNCERTAINTY IN THE ORDER OF THE QUESTIONS

While the foregoing rules have been designed to facilitate the child's learning, they were not concerned with directly enabling the child to achieve the abstract attitude. The omission is not due to neglect, but rather to a problem raised in Chapter 1—the spontaneity of the behaviors reflecting the abstract attitude. Characteristically, they are described in the literature in terms such as "voluntarily evoking ideas," "intentionally shifting conceptual categories," and "bringing to mind imagined alternatives"—in brief, it is the careful intellectual analysis that the person elects to conduct in the absence of specific direction (see Goldstein, 1959). Because spontaneity can never be forcibly elicited, it seems necessary to try a more indirect method in fostering its emergence. The only seemingly feasible course of action is to avoid the conditions that will hinder its development.

Among the primary situations to be avoided are those where the child is exposed to the same type of item or task for a particular length of time without any other type of task intervening (e.g., presenting him with a workbook where he must complete a series of twenty items, each requiring him to "cross out" the "different one"). It may be surprising to argue against learning based upon repeated, massed practice since the opportunity for such practice would appear to be an excellent teaching aid for developing learning sets. The term, associated most frequently with Harlow (1959), refers to the fact that when the same type of concept is presented over a series of problems, the problems become increasingly easy to solve. Thus, if a child is given tasks where the first series consist of selecting particular forms (e.g., in the first problem, he must choose a square as opposed to a circle, in the second problem, a triangle as opposed to an ellipse, etc.), he will solve the second set faster than he solved the first; he will solve the second set faster than he solved the first; he will solve the third faster than the second; and so on until he can eventually solve the problems almost without error.

Such rapid and errorless learning would seem to represent precisely the behavior that we would desire. It would be a sign of the total command that the child has over the concept in question. Bereiter and Engelmann (1966) incorporated this technique into their program precisely because of this reasoning. The same line of questioning is repeatedly pursued until the child can answer rapidly and appropriately. For example, a series of questions demanding labels may be asked until the child knows that the correct concept is "to name the thing." Following this, a series of questions may be asked involving adjectives such as color or size. The child practices until he recognizes that he is to label a specific attribute of the object he sees. This technique is of obvious value in any attempt to program in a wide array of correct responses.

But a chief characteristic of the abstract attitude is the flexible shifting across concepts and ideas. The achievement of learning sets need in no way facilitate such performance, for facility in one type of concept may not transfer to other concepts. For example, improvement in solving problems dealing with physical characteristics, such as form, need not facilitate the solution of problems involving other concepts, such as *same-different.*

Lack of positive transfer in itself need not be serious. After all, even if the child does not learn new concepts more easily, he is still better off for having learned the particular concepts he did. But frequently, the absence of positive transfer is not the point of concern; what is troublesome is the presence of negative transfer—that is, learning of the new concept may be even harder than it would have been if the first concept had not been learned (Wolff, 1967).

While this phenomenon may at first seem strange, upon closer examination, it is really quite reasonable. Every time a child must attend to one feature, he must exclude others. For example, if he is required over a series of problems to describe objects in terms of form, then he must learn to ignore other attributes such as color, size, and texture. Having learned to ignore them, the child finds it increasingly hard to notice them again when the situation so demands.

For the poorly functioning child the situation may be even more serious. Once he has achieved rapid learning in a series of problems, he finds the task quite comfortable. Under these conditions, the shift to another type of concept becomes painful in comparison. Unless he has a strong element of curiosity, the child sees little to be gained by switching from a situation where he is coping successfully to a new situation where he has no idea as to how he will fare. Indeed, some failure is inevitable in the switch since learning always involves error. This makes the switch less than desirable from the child's point of view. Thus, resistance to new learning is often the price paid for the information acquired through learning sets.

To the extent that learning sets might be useful in preschool education, they would almost have to be a "metaset"—that is, a learning set of all learning sets. Such a metaset would involve a general predisposition to use all learning sets and to shift flexibly among learning sets as the situation demands. Thus, when the child sees a new problem, his metaset will give him the assurance that information is available to solve the situation; his job is then to determine which of the available information is applicable.

VARIABILITY AND UNCERTAINTY

Metasets can only be achieved if the child is prepared to face any type of reasonable question at any time. He must have no certainty that a particular question will be asked, or will not be asked. This does not mean that he should be discouraged from anticipating the sequence of questions that might logically follow one another. For example, a question such as "Would it matter if the shoes had no laces?" can be answered correctly by the single word "yes." The well-functioning child will often spontaneously extend this response by offering the rationale for his answer (e.g., "Cause they'd fall off," "they'd flop around," etc.), even before the teacher explicitly asks "Why would it matter?" Any effort on the part of the poorly functioning child to extend his thinking in this spontaneous way should be warmly encouraged.

Thus, uncertainty in the order of the questions does not mean that the child should be discouraged from recognizing the logical implications of an idea. It does mean that the order of the questions should not be given in a rigid sequence. For example, if every correct answer to a problem requiring visual scanning of a complex field (e.g., "get me the ball in the closet") were to be followed by a question dealing with the function of the object (e.g., "what do we do with the ball"), the child could easily stop listening. He knows that the next request will simply involve his naming some action associated with the object in question. This development can reinforce the poorly functioning child's tendency to "tune out" information, while giving him the veneer of competence.

The hazards in teaching material so that it has a high degree of certainty become evident when the expected order is changed (e.g., posing a different type of question in place of the expected type of question). In this case, a serious mismatch exists between the question posed and the answer that one is prepared to give—the gulf between the two reveals the inappropriateness of the child's thinking (e.g., because he "expects" a question about function, the child replies "the ball rolls" when in fact he was asked "What else did you see in the closet"). (This type of incongruent behavior can also be seen at the adult level in such rote "unthinking" behaviors as the exchange of traditional greetings. Thus, a person who is set to expect the question of "Hello, how's everything?" may readily say "fine" even though the actual question posed was "What's new?")

The use of a rigid sequence is also contraindicated by the factor of boredom. To the degree that a situation becomes increasingly predictable, it becomes increasingly less interesting. It was this factor that was foremost in the poor quality of the teacher-child interchange documented in the first lesson in Chapter 3. To stimulate interest, it is necessary both to avoid a rigid sequence of questions (e.g., always asking first for the label, then the function, then the negative, etc.) and the pursuit of one line of questioning over a series of items (e.g., displaying a number of different items and repeatedly asking "What is this?" "What is this?" "What is this?" etc.). Even though the items are different, the basic process is an unvarying demand for simple labeling. With the use of such rigid sequences, the teacher loses the motivational aspect of learning that is generated by being faced with the unexpected.

To prevent this, the certainty of rigid sequences must be replaced by uncertainty in the order of the questions. The problems must be continually varied so that the child can rarely anticipate what question will be asked at any moment. This leads the child to develop more discerning responses, for he will be able to handle the problems only by actively attending to the meaning of the language. Variety of demands can occur in two major ways: (1) across questions—in that the type of demand continually shifts and (2) within questions—in that the same demand is presented in many forms.

Variety across questions is nearly self-evident. It refers to the fact that any cognitive demand can legitimately be asked at any point in a lesson, as long as it is relevant to the topic at the moment and appropriate to the child's level of functioning. Variety within questions may be less clear since it has not yet been discussed. It refers to the fact that the same demand can be embedded in different linguistic forms. If this is not done and the same form is consistently used, the child may be led to respond in an unthinking, automatic way to particular questions. For example, if every *where* question requires the naming of a place and every *what* question the naming of an object, then where and what simply become signals for rotely learned responses (much as the commands given to a dog are signals for trained stimulus-response sequences).

Naturally, the variability is limited by realistic linguistic constraints. For example, it is almost impossible to embed a *why* question in a *where* formulation in English. Nevertheless, the variety of possible permutations is quite great. For example, the relatively simple request to locate an object might take on the following forms:

1. "Could you find me the crayons in the closet?" [1]
2. "I think the crayons were left over there. How about looking for them there?" [1]
3. "Please get the crayons from the closet."
4. "Oh, let me see—the crayons are in the closet. Do you think you can find them for me?" [1]

Just as the same question can be embedded in many forms, the same form can contain many different demands. For example, the question word *what* can initiate such different demands as:

1. "What happened to the girl in the story?" (memory)
2. "What made the ball fall?" (cause-effect)
3. "What does this do?" (concept-function)
4. "What made you think the box would be heavy?" (rationale for observation)
5. "What is going on in this picture?" (conversational skills)

THE USE OF ACTION

The principles outlined thus far help to maximize the potential power of a question as a stimulus to cognitive activity; in particular,

---

[1] Although these requests could theoretically be answered by a yes or no response, their conventional (implicit) meaning is otherwise. As in the question "Do you have the time?" one would be dumbfounded if the questionee replied "Yes" and left the scene. Instead, the expectation is that the request will be interpreted as a command and that it will provoke the person to offer the requested object or information without any further discussion of the matter.

they emphasized rules about sequencing of the questions, structuring of the material so that its verbal representation is better grasped, and introducing contrast so that information is seen in a broader framework. The novelty in some of the requests made under these rules may also have some motivational advantages (e.g., children can be tantalized by the unusual juxtapositions entailed in the principle of contrast, such as "If we want to write with the pen, why shouldn't we leave the top on"). The motivational payoff, however, is secondary in that the techniques do not absolutely ensure the desired involvement. As a result, the techniques, no matter how theoretically appealing, will not be sufficient—they may be rendered powerless by the child's lack of interest in the learning situation.

Frequently, the traditional answer to this problem is to design material to be so attractive that the child will become actively involved in exploring and manipulating it. This tack is not sufficient with the poorly functioning child, however, for his cognitive difficulties often do not permit him to grasp the meaning of material, even while he is engaged with it.

But this does not mean that the opportunity for the active manipulation of material is without value. While education has long recognized the importance of "learning through doing" (Dewey, 1900, 1902), action can play another central role in facilitating learning. Young children find it difficult to sustain even brief periods of actionless sequences. If adequate provision is not made for including motor activity into the lesson, the result will be a building up of undirected activity (e.g., tapping, rocking, or gazing) which will prevent attention and learning. The availability of attractive concrete objects, therefore, permits the lesson to incorporate activity that will relieve the child's tension. The opportunity for this activity serves as a major factor in motivating the child's involvement in the learning.

If used properly, this activity can also have a significant cognitive payoff. To this end, the actions must not simply be random behavior to "let off steam"; instead, they must be designed so that the child attends to and follows the verbally directed commands that are initiated by the teacher. With this attention to the words of another, the child has started to become an active participant in the dialogue system. Fortunately, attention to commands requires a type of receptive language that is among the simplest forms of verbal behavior. Even when the child is unwilling to say a word, he is likely to agree to carry out simple actions, such as "Get the ball," "Open the door," and "Push the chair to the table." These verbally directed actions thus provide the child with a verbal task whose demands he can successfully meet and which are in accord with his natural sensorimotor style.

At this stage, the activity need not provide any insight into reality—even if such insight is potentially realizable. Thus, if a well-functioning child is told "Feel the window" he may spontaneously say "Ooh, that's cold" or "Why is it so hard?" The poorly functioning child, on the other hand, may simply touch the window and offer no remarks reflecting further thinking about the situation. He need not realize, however, that his performance is not as full as it might be because he is unaware that he may be missing something of interest in the material. What he does know, however, is that he has complied with the request. Thus, not only has he avoided failure, but he has even experienced a modicum of success. (This is in sharp contrast to demands for expressive language, e.g., "What is this called?" When the child fails a question like this, he is usually vividly aware of his failure.) It has therefore proven useful to interlace each lesson with requests for action, particularly in the initial stages when the children are still functioning at a low level.

Receptive language tasks are also useful in providing an excellent indicator of the child's knowledge. Because they require him to act upon verbal information, they evoke behavior which can be used to assess the child's functioning in any area. For example, if the child brings the wrong shape when he was told to "find the circle" it is likely that he does not understand the referent for circle and that he should be given assistance. The opportunity for activity with concrete objects, therefore, permits the lesson to (1) relieve tension, (2) provide the satisfaction of correctly meeting adult demands, and (3) diagnose points of difficulty in the child's functioning.

THE NEED FOR RELEVANCE

The use of action helps to deal with the initial motivational problems which are concerned with simply getting the child actively involved in the teaching setting. Once this difficulty is conquered, the teacher is left to face the far more tricky motivational problem—the problem of relevance. The child may now recognize that forks do not hold soup, or that pencils without lead do not write—but, in the broader scheme of things, "so what?" If the information does not move beyond this point, the observation is basically not much more than a trick. And, like a trick, it will exist as an isolated bit of information.

Isolated associations are often sufficient for sensorimotor adaptation (e.g., upon seeing a ball, the child may roll it; upon seeing a glass, the child may drink from it, etc.). When this attitude is carried over to more complex material, it can spell disaster for many attempts at enrichment. Even after the child is able to make accurate observations and abstractions, he often fails to see the relevance of such information. The situation is comparable to an adult's being asked to describe everything he sees in an abstract picture. As evidenced by the typical reaction to the amorphous ink blots on the Rorschach test, this can frequently be an anxiety-provoking situation. The person is unsure of what he is to look for; he is not sure if his answers are what might be considered typical, and so on. Even when the anxiety can be allayed, however (e.g., through specific questions which lessen one's doubts such as "Tell me what colors are in it, tell me what shapes you see," etc.), the nagging question remains "What is this all for?" Adults who are long removed from the school setting are rarely faced with these so-called puzzles. When they do confront them (e.g., as in guessing games at parties), the game is of their own choosing and is indulged in for their own satisfaction.

The school-age child has no such choice—he is constantly confronted with problems where he must isolate information, even though he is given no rationale for the task. For the poorly functioning child, this search for information (e.g., concepts of size, direction, color, time, etc.) can be seen as an arbitrary game in which a bunch of nonsense words are applied to a set of stimuli which are of little significance in his life. Why should it matter to him if something is *blue* or if something is *big* or if something is *fast?*

One might legitimately ask why such information matters to the well-functioning child. It matters because the abstract attitude is a hard taskmaster. By its presence, it creates a need in the child to introduce order into the information that he perceives. For example, when a child asks a question such as "What is a knife—the fork's husband?" (Chukovsky, 1963, p. 22), it reflects his endless desire to figure out what wider system of meaning underlies even the most mundane material.

SETTING THE STAGE

Because the poorly functioning child lacks this independent search for meaning, techniques must be developed to make the child feel the need for information. While it is difficult at this time to specify precise methods, the already available materials of nursery school provide a useful starting point since they have been well designed to meet the needs of the young child (e.g., small animals, cars, doll houses, etc.). All of these can serve as attractive goals for which the child will willingly work. In many ways the creation of meaningful situations is similar to setting the stage in a play. It provides the props to make the situation real enough so that the child will be mobilized to participate in the learning situation.

As an illustration of this approach, let us consider the concept of one-to-one correspondence. The idea is complex and many children avoid dealing with it because they do not see its possible relevance. If a situation is designed, however, so that the child needs this information, the concept is seen in a totally different light. One such situation involves the presentation of three dolls and two lollipops. If the child does not comprehend the discrepancy, the teaching of the concept might be initiated by asking "Do you think two will be enough?" Should the child not understand the concept, he might happily take the two lollipops and offer them to the dolls. Then suddenly, to his consternation, he discovers that "they're not enough." At this point, his emotional identification with the dolls propels him to cope with the concept that he had hoped to avoid. In his desire not to leave any doll "out in the cold," he finds himself forced to deal with such complex questions as "Why do you need one more?" and "Why are two lollipops not enough for three dolls?"

The emotional appeal of the material thus serves as a motivational pull for the child. The presence of manageable obstacles related to the material then serves as the cognitive core of the lesson. For example, the teacher may arouse the child's interest by suggesting that they play a game of ball. The ball is present but "unfortunately" not available, for it is locked in a closet. The unlocking of the closet may then serve as the focus of a lesson on keys, locks, and doors. Ultimately, of course, the ball must be obtained if the child is not to lose faith in the teacher. From the child's point of view, the ball serves as the goal of the lesson. If questioned afterwards, he may even say it was a lesson about playing ball. The core of the lesson from a cognitive point of view, however, was the obstacle to obtaining the ball.

THE CONTENT OF THE TEACHING

EMBEDDING THE COGNITIVE TECHNIQUES

The issue of motivational context inevitably raises the question of the content of the lessons. Selection of a particular goal, such as teaching doors and locks, merely illustrates the possible content of one lesson. The teaching will be of use only if a curriculum can be developed which represents a wide range of feasible lessons. This problem is considered at length in Chapter 10. For the present, we will only briefly outline the main factors that guide the lessons.

The goal of the teaching is to foster the child's use of a wide range of cognitive processes. The question of content is thus reduced to the question "What type of materials will allow the cognitive process to be introduced in a meaningful fashion?" For example, one goal might be that the child attain flexibility in thinking (e.g., the ability to see multiple solutions to the same problem). The built-in constraints of certain materials make it difficult to raise this as a legitimate demand in many settings. Suppose that a child is playing with a puzzle that is geared toward form perception (e.g., he must place squares, circles, and triangles in their appropriate positions). It is quite easy to raise memory questions in this context (e.g., which one did you pick up first). Most questions requiring flexibility, however, would be irrelevant in this setting. For example, one could not point to the space for the square and ask "What else could fit in here besides the square?" The question of flexibility, however, could be raised easily in settings which involve appealing action sequences (e.g., "The ladder would help us reach the shelf, but we don't have a ladder. What else do you think we could use").

The bond between particular processes and particular content is not rigid. For example, a lesson with puzzles could be so de-signed to go beyond simple form perception and consider more complex problem-solving questions, e.g., "The puzzle is broken; what could we use to fix it?" and "Why didn't this circle fit into this" (rectangular) "space?" Nevertheless, particular contexts lend themselves more readily to certain cognitive processes than to others. Thus far, five major content areas have been developed. These areas are designed to be broad enough to permit the teacher to meaningfully raise almost every type of cognitive process relevant to the young child's developmental level.

The five areas are as follows:

a. Construction of material—this includes lessons based upon the common and appealing tasks of actually building houses, furniture, boats, and books.
b. Transformation of matter—under this rubric are found lessons dealing with changes in the state of a substance. This is most graphically demonstrated in the area of cooking where innu-merable lessons are possible.
c. Perceptual analysis—lessons in this sphere deal with puzzles, drawing, and sound analysis wherein the child must attend carefully to the analysis of complex sensory experience.
d. Storytelling—and Dramatic representation—in this area, books are used to foster the skills required for understanding sus-tained, complex verbal material.
e. Gross motor skills—lessons here enable the teacher to use cognitive techniques in the comfortable, but rarely analyzed, sphere of large-scale motor activity.

The areas reflect a broad range of experience in the hope that the child will feel that intellectual analysis is not confined to isolated pockets of abstract material, but can be used in every sphere that he encounters. As is apparent, these areas bear great similarity to the material in most preschool programs. The correspondence is intentional, for present preschool materials are generally excellent. Where the material does depart from other approaches is in the organization of the questions. The aim of a lesson is never to teach a predetermined concept (e.g., the concept of size, the concept of direction, or the concept of clothing.). Instead, each lesson is designed to have a broad range of material so that fifteen to twenty basic core questions can be posed. Then, upon the disclosure of the wrong response, the major teaching is initiated. As stated above, Chapter 10 contains a fuller statement of the way the materials are used for these purposes.

chapter 6

Concepts by Principle

The principles of teaching just articulated are perhaps most vividly illuminated in the teaching of concepts. In many ways, they help fill the gaps that exist in the knowledge as to how concepts should be taught to the young child. The lack of specification in this sphere is understandable. From the adult viewpoint, the concepts for the preschool age child are exceedingly simple and we almost cannot conceive of the troubles they may cause the child. "It is curiously difficult to recapture preconceptual innocence. Having learned a new language, it is almost impossible to recall the undifferentiated flow of voiced sounds that one heard before one learned to sort the flow into words and phrases. Having mastered the distinction between odd and even numbers, it is a feat to remember what it was like in a mental world where there was no such distinction. In short, the attainment of a concept has about it something of a quantal character. It is as if the mastery of a conceptual distinction were able to mask the preconceptual memory of the things now distinguished. . . . Concept attainment seems almost an intrinsically unanalyzable process from an experiential point of view" (Bruner, Goodnow, and Austin, 1956, p. 50).

This is not to deny that a substantial body of work exists in the teaching of concepts. For example, De Cecco (1968, pp. 386-87) outlines the following nine stages in teaching the school-age child:

> "Step 1. Describe the performance expected of the student after he has learned the concept.
> Step 2. Reduce the number of attributes to be learned in complex concepts and make important attributes dominant.
> Step 3. Provide the student with useful verbal mediators.
> Step 4. Provide positive and negative examples of the concept.
> Step 5. Present examples in close succession or simultaneously.
> Step 6. Present a new positive example of the concept and ask the student to identify it.
> Step 7. Verify the student's learning of the concept.
> Step 8. Require the student to define the concept.
> Step 9. Provide occasions for student responses and the reinforcement of these responses."

These steps are also relevant in teaching the preschooler. Like the older child, the young child must be able to recognize the positive instance of a concept from the negative instance (e.g., he must know that a rabbit is not a dog); he must be able to recognize which features are central to the concept and which are irrelevant (e.g., color and size are usually not central in defining the concept of a dog), and so on.

The precise application of these principles to the young child is, however, not sufficiently defined. For example, the first step in the sequence requires us to "define the performance expected of the student at the end of the teaching." For the preschooler, a reasonable objective would be that he be able to join the referent and the label, be able to select out all positive instances of the concept, be able to reject noninstances of the concept, and be able to describe the referent in verbal terms. When this is applied to an appropriate concept such as *apple,* this would mean that he be able to say *apple* when he sees the fruit, be able to pick out apples in different sizes and varieties, be able to reject pears, bananas, and such as not belonging to the class of apples, and be able to make such statements as "we eat apples," "some apples are red," and so on. Few would argue with the reasonableness and usefulness of these objectives.

But they contain serious limitations. The difficulties become apparent by replacing the meaningful word and object *apple* with a hypothetical case that involves a novel object and a nonsense word. For example, imagine that one were to teach the class of objects ⋔ which had the name *blip*. Removing the prejudical effects of what is already known forces us to go through the process of developing the concept. As a result, we begin to see the situation almost from the perspective of the still uninformed child.

First, as with the apple, we might join the word and the object (e.g., the teacher holds out the ⋔ and says "this is a blip"). She then adds additional information about the function of the object by telling the child that "we werp with blips." She tests out the child's knowledge by various questions (e.g., "What do we call this?" "What do we do with it"). Having received the appropriate answers, she then presents several types of blips in different sizes, colors, and textures. They are placed among several nonblips so that the child has to carefully examine the situation before making his choice. Even if he selects the object appropriately, the teacher may investigate still further by picking up a nonblip (e.g., ☆) and asking "Is this a blip?" and "Could we werp with this?" She may go further by integrating the concept with already acquired concepts such as "What color is this blip?" "Which blip feels heavier?" "Put all the blips together." Since these have been answered correctly, the teacher feels the child is now prepared to learn *gofs* and *plims* which like *blips* belong to the same family of *werpable* objects. But a curious discomfort is present—it is the feeling that somehow we do not understand what *blips* are.

Having passed the identical criteria as were applied to apple, why do we experience *blip* as so elusive while *apple* is so vitally real? At first, one might assume that familiarity has made the critical difference. This, however, is probably not the reason. *Werp* and *blip* could be joined thousands of times and we would still not grasp their meaning. The difficulty is much more basic than the question of familiarity. In spite of his seemingly adequate performance, the child lacks the essential ideas that should underlie the correct answers. This becomes apparent with the asking of questions that require the child to act upon the information he has received. Thus, if he is requested to "Show me how to werp with blips," it is almost certain that he will not respond correctly. Similarly, if he is given an ambiguous object (e.g., ⊓⊓⊓)

and asked "Is this a *blip?*" a clear decision cannot be made—an answer of yes or no is almost equally likely. Yet, these problems are not trick questions; in fact, they are essential for a full grasp of even this very elementary concept. We expect the child to have this knowledge in all meaningful concepts that we want him to learn. This expectation is revealed by replacing the nonsense words with real words so that the *blip* is really a comb and the ambiguous object a *rake*. In this case, holding up the rake and asking the question "Is this a comb?" is seen as perfectly reasonable.

What has allowed this change? The critical factor seems to lie in intertwining the verbal and nonverbal information in such a way that they enhance each other to form a coherent, organized unit. For example, the child could only profit from adding the concept of *werp* to *blip* if he knows the referent for *werp*. We have long recognized the need for showing a clear instance of the object (e.g., showing an apple, a truck, a house, etc.); we have placed much less emphasis on the need to show a clear example of the verbalized action (e.g., the meaning of *eating, driving, living in*, etc.). It is somehow assumed that the presentation of the object is enough. It is, however, insufficient. Both the object (blip) and the action (werp) must have clear, concrete referents that are combined on an intimately intertwined verbal-perceptual basis. Without this, the child may encounter serious difficulty. In the absence of this intertwining, the language questions can be answered without reference to the object (e.g., a child could easily answer "What is this?" and "What does a blip do?" even when the object is meaningless to him) and the questions about the object can be answered without reference to the language concepts (e.g., "get me another one like this" can be done without any need to examine the words *blip* and *werp).*

This lengthy examination of the *blip* concept may be misleading. The concept is so simple that it may give the impression that our concern is largely with elementary labeling. This is not the case. The child is unlikely to be at a loss with most concrete objects since he experiences them frequently in his daily life; that is, an eighteen-month-old may use a comb correctly and spontaneously bring it into play situations, even though he is unaware of its name. Therefore, he is unlikely to be thrown by having a word attached to this already familiar object. The above discussion therefore was not designed to show the importance of correctly teaching simple objects. Rather, it aimed to demonstrate the possible failure of teaching that can occur even in the seemingly simplest situation. If it can occur here, it is overwhelming to consider what might happen in far more complicated situations.

These potential confusions do not mean that the general principles of concept teaching are not applicable to the young child. They suggest, however, that the principles must be modified to ensure greater precision. Since we cannot "recapture our preconceptual innocence," any modifications can only be based on educated guesses at what might be most useful to the child. The sequence presented below is therefore not definitive. It does, however, offer a promising framework in this effort.

The sequence is delineated into six stages, with each stage following one or more of the teaching principles outlined in the previous chapter. The principle overriding all six stages is the principle concerned with the use of action. For example, the first step is to show an instance of the concept and then have the child use this instance in some simple action (e.g., "touch the *top* of the bookcase the way I just did"). The next step is to present an almost identical instance among new, dissimilar instances and have the child select the correct object; the selection inevitably entails a motor action for the child must grasp or point to the item. At each step, the child is given a minute bit of information and the situation is immediately structured so that he must act on this information. The need to act both relieves any restlessness the child may have and leads him to consider the information he has just been offered. In addition, the activity offers the teacher an indicator of whether the information was accurately incorporated (e.g., if the child selects the wrong item, the teacher knows he has not grasped the information). In order to gain an overview of the sequence, the steps are outlined briefly in Table 1.

In detail, the steps are as follows.

1. A Clear Instance. This step is similar to most current procedures for teaching concepts in that the child is focused upon a well-defined example of the category. In the case of nouns, it might be saying "this is an *apple*," in the case of verbs, "this is a boy *walking*," in the case of adjectives, "this is a *large* box,"

TABLE 1
Sequence for Teaching Concepts

Step	Example	Principle Underlying the Demand
1. A clear instance of the concept.	"This milk is liquid. Here you feel it."	Demonstrability, action.
2. A clear definition of the function or attribute.	"If it's liquid you can pour it. You try pouring it. And after you pour it, it drips. Look. You do that."	Demonstrability, action.
3. Extension of concept to similar instances.	Shows play dough, water, and cotton wool. "Which one of these is a liquid?"	Demonstrability, action. Contrast.
4. Extension of concept to less obvious, positive instances.	Shows some paint in a jar, some cars, and a plate. "Which of these is liquid?"	Demonstrability (if needed), action, contrast.
5. Consideration of subtle negative instance.	Shows salt. "Is this a liquid?" (While it meets the criterion of *pouring* it does not meet that of *dripping* and therefore the child can be led to reject it.)	Demonstrability, contrast.
6. Extension of category	"What kinds of liquid can you drink? Tell me one you can't drink."	Relevance.

and so on. Since this step is so familiar, it need not be discussed in detail. The major aim is to offer the child a clear example of the concept in question so that the word gains a demonstrable reality for the child.

Since only the barest amount of information has been given at this point, any request for action to test the child's comprehension must be elementary. Generally, it consists of a simple command which focuses his attention on the item under discussion. Frequently the request can be for imitation of what the teacher has just done (e.g., a request such as "touch the square that I just touched").

2. A Clear Definition of the Function or Attribute of the Instance. It is at this point that the teaching begins to diverge from the usual methods of instruction in concept formation. Just as the understanding of *werp* was vital to understanding the concept of *blip,* so too is the young child aided if he has a clear grasp of the function or attribute of any concept. This statement may at first seem peculiar since concepts connoted by adjectives (e.g., "small," "pretty," etc.) and adverbs (e.g., "fast," "awkwardly," etc.) are already attributes. Therefore, how is one to give an attribute of an attribute?

The situation is not as difficult as it first appears. Many attributes can be discussed and represented through concepts that are already available to the child (e.g., "up" is "as far as you can go on anything," "soft" is "when you can squeeze something," etc.). The aim is not to offer a precise definition of the concept; instead, it is to focus the child on some of the chief characteristics that cause an instance to be grouped into a particular category.

For example, in discussing *corner,* the teacher might say "Look at this wall, now look at this other wall, see where they meet, you have to turn here because you can't keep going straight. The child need not understand every word of the explanation; rather he must (1) recognize the key words and their physical referent and (2) grasp their relevance in this situation (e.g., corner—turning at the place where the lines meet). In effect, this technique capitalizes on the child's well-established predisposition to spontaneously define concepts through function—"a hole is to dig, a hat is to wear, a puddle is to kick in." The teaching extends this tendency by showing the child how it may apply to a broader range of concepts, including those that he finds most confusing.

Without this explicit definition, concept attainment becomes a guessing game with enormous potential for frustration. For example, in a traditional method of teaching concepts such as emotions, the child may be presented with several pictures of happy faces and several of nonhappy faces. As each picture is shown, he is offered the appropriate label (e.g., "this person is happy," "this one is sad," etc.). In effect, the child is placed in a problem-solving situation where he must independently abstract the features that determine the placement of an instance into a particular category (e.g., from a rather *adultomorphized* point of view, his thinking is supposed to go as follows: "both the happy and sad people have hair, so hair cannot be a relevant feature; all the happy faces are smiling, maybe that's important," etc.).

This procedure is excellent for studying self-directed concept attainment in the young child (e.g., how does a child begin to exclude irrelevant characteristics? how fast is his learning? etc.) (Wittrock, Keislar, and Stern, 1964; Stern, 1965; Huttenlocher, 1962). It may not, however, be the most fruitful means of fostering concept development in an actual teaching situation. A heavy burden is placed upon the child who must test a long series of hypotheses before he can accurately determine the referent for the label. This type of self-directed learning is often intolerable for the child who is weak in cognitive functioning. In effect, it places him in a situation similar to the *blip* example for, from his point of view, he is being given a nonsense syllable with the expectation that it should give meaning to the concept. As the concepts get more abstract, the situation becomes even more difficult. *Blip* at least referred to a clear, circumscribed object which the child easily perceives. But what of concepts, such as relational properties, where no such clear referent is present (e.g., *smaller, straighter, faster,* etc.)? The presentation of endless instances of such concepts in no way guarantees that they will be comprehended, for the child does not know to which of the many attributes the word refers. It is for this reason that a clear definition of the function or attribute is so helpful. It gives the child a mediating rule by which to identify members of the concept.

This emphasis on creating functional attributes in the teaching of concepts might at first glance be seen as reinforcing a Piaget-type view that early concepts are simply "interiorized actions." Further analysis, however, suggests that this interpretation is insufficient. When the actions are used, without any accompanying verbal explanation, they become nonsensical movements. For example, if the child were to be taught the concept of *second* without any verbal explanation, he might be shown to hold back from picking every first thing in a sequence. This type of unexplained delay would result in confusion and frustration, and not the awareness of the concept of *second.*

The child's consternation becomes apparent when one observes the difficulties of teaching so-called abstract concepts to young deaf children. One teacher, for example, reported no difficulty at all in teaching verbal labels such as *ball.* As soon as she showed one or two balls and gave the label, the children could select any ball, regardless of variation in size, color, or texture. The graphic quality of the roundness was sufficient to unify an abundant number of stimuli in this category. When she attempted to teach a word like *top*, however, almost insuperable difficulties were found. The children looked at her in total bewilderment as she attempted to use the word *top* to unify such disparate objects as the "top of one's head," "top of one's desk," and "top of one's shoe." Any attempt to teach this concept through actions which are not accompanied by verbal explanation only add other aimless cues to an already confusing setting. For instance, in the effort to emphasize the height to which she referred, the teacher might run her hand across the top of the desk or point to the tops of both shoes. This action might lead the child to think that the relevant concept was not *top*, but concepts such as *two things* or *flat surfaces.*

Therefore should a child not know a particular concept, teaching efforts which are confined to nonverbal representation are almost certainly doomed to failure. Admittedly, words alone are not sufficient to enable the young child to grasp the concept. For example, with a concept like *second* if only verbal terminology were used, it would have to be so complex as to be beyond the child's grasp (e.g., a statement such as "one thing must always precede the one you choose," would be necessary, and it would be totally incomprehensible). Actions must be included to help the young child grasp the verbal referent. Thus, a relevant verbal-motor rule for the concept of second might be "don't pick that one; go on to the next, pick that; that's the second one." With this rather peculiarly formulated, but nevertheless appropriate, rule, the child can begin to use his action sequences to abstract the concept of second.

For this orientation to prove useful, it is necessary to be aware of the fact that one cannot use just any action simply because it happens to be capable of being performed on the object. For example, in teaching *crayons*, it would be misleading to use an action such as, "Look, the crayons can be put in the box." Admittedly, they can—but this action reveals nothing distinctive about the crayons. The mediator must represent a distinctive feature of the concept which the child can readily perceive and abstract. For example, a distinctive feature of a *circle* is the absence of corners. Once the child grasps this information, it can serve as a rule by which he can test whether new instances are or are not members of the category (e.g., "a circle has no corners, this thing" [a square] "has corners; therefore, it cannot be a circle").

In general, in the case of things (nouns), the key mediators are functions of the thing ("food is to eat," "clothing is to wear," "tools are to fix things," etc.). Help in this area need be minimal, however, since the child finds the labeling of *things* to be relatively easy (John and Goldstein, 1964). His greatest confusion arises not from concepts dealing with objects (nouns) but from those dealing with *actions* (verbs) and *attributes* (adjectives and adverbs). This area includes the common preschool concepts of size, direction, shape, speed, and sequence. A reference point for the teaching of these concepts must be found which is comparable to the usefulness of function in teaching objects. This reference point seems available in the use of clear perceptual or motor referents. For example, the referent for *hard* can be *the inability to bend the material;* the referent for *sharp* is that *it hurts when you put it on your finger;* the referent for *smiling* is *an upturned mouth;* the referent for *top* is that you *go up as high as you can on something until you cannot go any further.*

Again, as in step 1, the test of how well the child has incorporated the information is generally a simple direction (e.g., "Oh, this is hard, I can't bend it. Here you try it—does it bend?"). The attribute which he is testing is, of course, not a full definition of the term. In fact, it would probably be inadequate for distinguishing more subtle instances of the concept. For example, an initial formulation for *liquid* may be that *it pours.* This is a useful and valid definition for a vast number of instances of things that fall under the category *liquid.* But what of *sand*—it pours, but it certainly is not a liquid. The rule is therefore not absolute nor complete. Rather, it is an initial formulation which focuses the child on a *demonstrable* central feature of the concept. (Interestingly, the lack of unique derivative characteristics for instances within the categories of color [red, blue, green], brightness [dark, light], and laterality [left, right] may be a major reason for the poorly functioning child's difficulty in grasping these concepts.

Nothing he can do to these qualities will reveal any distinctive characteristics by which one instance can be differentiated from another.)

Selection of a clear, verbalized attribute can be extremely difficult. For example, in teaching set theory to young children, it is common to explain a set as "things that go together." While this is reasonable and seemingly appropriate, it rapidly proves its weaknesses once it comes upon the set of *one*. For a young child, "one thing that goes together" just does not go together—it is illogical. If presentation of the set of *one* could be delayed until the child had fully grasped the idea of a set and was now beyond this verbal rule, the situation might be salvageable. But the set of one is too basic and too common to be held off until its appearance is more fortuitous. Therefore, a much more adequate mediator must be found or the child is left to cope with a bewildering and major exception.[1]

In our experience with the tutorial program, this potential distortion is not the most common one. Perhaps it is because the children are younger and therefore expectations in the verbal sphere are fewer. In any event, the most common teaching error is not the establishment of inappropriate verbal mediators but rather the tendency to treat perceptual encounters as sufficient mediators. For example, in teaching the concept of *wet,* one teacher had the child place his hand in water while she explained that it was *wet.* She then had him place his hand in sugar as an instance of a clear, nonwet exemplar. Although the teacher was certain that the combination of the tactual experiences and the label was unambiguous, the child looked at her in a confused way.

Analysis of the situation indicates that the child's puzzlement was predictable and comprehensible. From his point of view, he had not been shown the feature that clearly differentiated the substances, but rather the feature that united them—they both could be felt and manipulated! His confusion disappeared only after he was shown the differential effects of the two substances.

---

[1] This criticism ignores the other bewildering experience the child undergoes in this situation—namely, to say that "this one is a set of one" is something so blatant as to be puzzling. It is as if you were told "this building is a building." The usual reaction being "Yes I see that. So why are you belaboring the obvious?"

When he removed his hand from the sugar, it was pointed out to him that almost nothing remained on his hand. By contrast, after he took his hand out of the water, the *wet* substance remained on his hand and slowly dripped down. In this way, the child was given a critical recognizable attribute by which to initiate a meaningful differentiation of wet versus nonwet substances.

3. Extension to Similar Instances from Among Grossly Dissimilar Instances. The example contrasting water and sugar brings us to the next step in the sequence where the child must select other instances of the concept which vary slightly from the original example (e.g., "find me another corner of the room, find me another square"). Like step 1, this step is quite similar to methods currently in use, in that the negative instance makes an important appearance. Its presentation is critical in determining whether the child has begun to grasp the concept. Negative examples also serve to create a background which gives the concept being taught greater salience by forcing it to the foreground.

At this point the negative instances should be so grossly different that the child will have no confusion about rejecting them as not being instances of the concept. The criterion for confusion is quite straightforward. An exemplar is deemed to be confusing if it is possible to apply the verbalized mediator to it. For example, if the mediator for a *chair* is the statement "you can sit on it," then a table would be a potentially confusing noninstance of the concept; by contrast a wall would be a clear noninstance of the concept. In effect, the child is presented with a presence-absence condition. All members of the concept have the specified attribute while all nonmembers lack it. If the problem is posed as a multiple choice, the teacher must select the particular noninstances of the concept, for example, she brings out an ellipse, a circle, and square, and asks "which one of these is a square?" If the problem is open-ended (e.g., "find me another corner"), then the teacher must be sure to remove potentially confusing noninstances of the concept.

In general, all items that might possibly share the same function should be avoided at this point. This means that items from the same superordinate grouping should *not* be introduced together, for example, pencil and crayon should not be compared, while objects from totally different superordinate groupings can be combined, for example, a pencil can be contrasted to an ashtray. This suggestion is contrary to the almost ubiquitous effort to teach concepts in accordance with their superordinate grouping. The adult emphasizes such groupings largely because he finds them useful in his own thinking, and not because of evidence that the child finds them useful. If anything, the work of investigators such as Piaget and Vygotsky indicates that superordinate groupings are beyond the ken of the preschool child (e.g., he cannot see that an object can simultaneously be a member of a class such as fruit and a subclass such as apple). In addition, superordinates have a high likelihood of sharing the same function or attribute, for example, apples are eaten, and so are pears; therefore, by being grouped together, the categories may become fused rather than be seen as distinct and separate. Or put in terms of the language of Chapter 5, the principle of demonstrability cannot be met—it is extremely difficult to demonstrate that negative instances from the same superordinate grouping are different from the concept being studied.

For the same reason, it is also helpful to avoid contrasting objects that are closely associated in time or space with the concept being taught, even if these objects have totally different characteristics, for example, in demonstrating *pen,* a clear noninstance might be *paper.* Such a choice would be inappropriate, however, since *paper* is too closely associated with *pen* and the entire writing situation. Other comparable confusions to avoid might be plate and spoon, toothbrush and glass, and bat and ball.

Two different principles of contrast govern the selection of negative instances; one relates to the teaching of whole objects, the other to part of objects. In the teaching of whole objects or attributes of whole objects (e.g., size and shape), contrast is created by the presence of other whole objects which clearly lack the function or characteristic being taught. In addition, the objects should be of comparable size and position (e.g., a door should not be compared to a pencil, but it can be compared to a bookcase). In the teaching of part objects (e.g., the *handle* of a valise, the *point* of a pencil, or the *button* on a dress) the background is formed by the object itself. Hence, the function or characteristic of the part is best demonstrated not by comparing it to other objects, but by removing the part under discussion (e.g., comparing a pencil with a point to a pencil without a point; comparing a valise with a handle to a valise without a handle, etc.). The function of the part can then be made immediately evident by having the child attempt to perform the usual action on the object containing the missing part (e.g., "try writing with the pencil without the point").

Stages 2 and 3 in teaching the concept clearly follow the principles of demonstrability and contrast. Nevertheless, the relevant objects can be selected without too much premeditation. As long as the concept can be clearly shown, the other characteristics of the item need not be carefully controlled. For example, if one is demonstrating the concept of hard, it is possible to use such different objects as a wooden chair, a brick, a spoon, or a metal box.

There is one class of concepts, however, that demands more careful control of the material—this is the area of relational concepts (e.g., big-little, near-far, high-low, etc.). Any instance of a relative concept requires a minimum of two objects, for such concepts are not embodied in a single entity; they exist only insofar as they define a relationship between two items or events. Frequently, adults may appear to use relative terms as if they were absolutes ("Oh yes, that place is near"); in fact, however, they rarely use them in this way—it is simply that the relevant continuum is implicit, rather than explicit (e.g., the moon is "far away" when the implied continuum is distance to the earth, but it is "near" when the implied continuum is the distance to the sun). On the other hand, because of their limitations in thinking, young children actually do treat the relative as absolute. This predisposition is precisely what must be overcome if they are to develop a true concept of the relative.

In setting up the necessary instances for the child, one might be led to pair any items (e.g., a cup and a ball) since the attributes of the objects are irrelevant to the concept (e.g., it is not its "roundness" that causes the ball to be farther away than the cup). Because of the child's concrete level of functioning, however, pairing of dissimilar items might cause difficulty. It might lead him to focus on the differences between the objects themselves (since these are so obvious), rather than on the relationship between them. By contrast, if identical (or near identical) objects are used at this point, the child is helped to recognize that the items themselves are not in question. He may not yet recognize what idea is in question—but at least he is no longer fixed on the qualities of the items themselves (e.g., he recognizes that the teacher is talking about some new and unique feature; yet, the items are identical—therefore, the feature must be something over and above the items themselves).

Once the child has been able to identify the concept correctly in three or four problems involving identical pairs of objects, he must be led to move beyond identical pairs and use the concept with nonidentical objects (e.g., "Now which is farther—the chalk or the box"). At this point, the use of nonidentical pairs is as essential as the use of identical pairs was earlier in the teaching sequence. Just as the use of pairs of different objects in the beginning of the teaching might have led the child to think that relative concepts refer to something about the differences between the objects, so too may the continued use of pairs with identical instances lead the child to think that relative concepts apply only to identical pairs of items.

Although the need for control of material in step 3 places complex demands on the teacher, from the child's viewpoint, the stage is simple. It presents him with clear, nonthreatening situations in which he is made aware of the fact that the instances of the concept must be differentiated from the noninstances of the concept. This awareness is prerequisite to the true development of a concept where the child cannot only select clear examples of the concept, but can also confidently evaluate potentially confusing exemplars (e.g., a pencil is not a pen, even though both can write; the glass in a window and the glass in a bowl are the same material, even though they look quite different). In other words, confusion refers to instances where thought must be exercised to determine whether the exemplar is or is not a member of the class. It is to this goal that the next two stages are directed.

4. Extension to Less Obvious Positive Instances. After the child has been able to select similar instances of the concept, he should be asked to select potentially confusing instances. The confusion should lie in the fact that the new instance looks quite different from the original exemplar, while still belonging to the category under discussion. It is at this point that the verbalized demonstrable function or attribute from step 2 again is vital, for regardless of how different the instances look, the same verbalized mediator should be applicable to both (e.g., the child may be asked to choose the *corner* of a desk after having learned the *corner* of a room, the *inside* of a pocketbook after learning the *inside* of a large cupboard, etc.). If the child is confused, he should be led to use the mediator to handle the problem (e.g., the child seems bewildered when asked to "find the corner of the desk" because he expects *corner* to be a part of the room. The teacher can repeat the verbalized mediator by saying "remember, look for the place where you have to turn," etc.). The child should be led to handle three or four potentially confusing instances of the concept.

5. Consideration of Subtle Negative Instances.   When a child has been able to extend a concept to a variety of differing instances, he must be led to recognize the limits of this extension. This can be achieved by having him judge potentially confusing negative instances of the concept. In the potentially confusing positive instances, the examples were grossly different physically, but clearly shared the essential function or attribute. The situation is reversed for the negative instances—the dominant physical characteristics should be similar to the concept demonstrated, but the essential function or attribute is (upon examination) clearly lacking. Thus, if *pencil* is being taught, a subtle negative instance might be a long, thin stick; if *square* is being taught, a subtle negative instance might be a triangle; if *top* is being taught, a subtle negative instance might be a position almost but not quite reaching the top. The recognition process in this type of problem is thus totally different from discrimination required to reject a grossly negative instance. In the latter, the inappropriateness of the choice is almost immediately obvious (e.g., showing a ball and asking if it is a pencil); in the former, the inappropriateness of the choice is barely apparent (e.g., showing some salt and asking if it is sugar).

It is of interest that the subtle *negative instance provides one of the rare situations where recognition can be more difficult than recall.* This seeming paradox is caused by the fact that recognition in this situation requires the careful evaluation of the negative instances. As a result, there is a high probability of interference from the similar but irrelevant characteristics, for example, the whiteness and texture of the salt makes it seem so similar to sugar. By contrast, a demand for recall does not require the child to grapple with subtle negative cues. Instead, he can concentrate his full effort on producing a single positive instance of the concept, for example, if told to think of something sweet, sugar would likely crop up and salt would probably never enter his mind.

In presenting the subtle negative instances, it is helpful if the child can be led to verbalize the reason for his acceptance or rejection of the item ("Why is" or "Why isn't this a pencil"). If, after such explication, the negative is still accepted as a positive instance of the concept, the child should be led to realize that the relevant function or attribute is missing (e.g., if a child says a long stick is a pencil and it will write, he can be given the simple request—"Okay, let's take some paper and see if it writes"). This is not meant to be said in a challenging fashion, but rather to show the child the importance that you attach to his words and to show him the need to consider information carefully. In addition, with the execution of the act the child experiences the inappropriateness of his words with a vividness that a teacher's explanation could never arouse.

6. Extension of Category. Once the previous levels have been obtained, the concept can be extended so that the child sees its relevance in the scheme of things. In the case of attributes, the child can be led to appreciate the significance of the characteristic in situations in real life. This can be achieved by creating problems where the information he has gleaned becomes vital to some adaptive behavior (e.g., "Okay, let's see if this *small* cup can hold all this water"; "Can we walk through the doorway when the door is *closed*"). In the case of objects, the child can be led to a beginning grasp of superordination. This extension can be achieved by combining the verbalized mediator with the concept of *not* (e.g., "Now, let's find something that *writes* that is *not* a pencil"; "Now, let's find something to *drink* from that is *not* a cup," etc.).

In this aspect of the teaching, only one new label should be presented at any time. Thus, after testing the child's knowledge, if it becomes clear that he did not know the labels for either *pencil* or *pen,* these items should not be taught simultaneously. This injunction applies as well to the teaching of opposites (big-little, tall-short, and up-down)—if the child is unfamiliar with both polar terms, they should not be taught together. The pairing of such terms (e.g., this is the top and this is the bottom) leads the child to combine them in an indistinct, undefined category. Even adults commonly show confusion with strongly paired words such as lay-lie, teach-learn, borrow-lend, or imply-infer. And similarly it is remarkably common not to know which member of the team is Laurel and which is Hardy, and exactly who wrote the libretto and who the score in the Gilbert and Sullivan team.

The potential for confusion is rampant when new terms are paired. The words tend to be retained as a unit in which the presentation of one label elicits the recall label of the other (rather than the recall of the appropriate referent). For example, many young children can correctly complete sentences such as "My house is not big, it is _____" even when they have no grasp of the concept of size. Similarly, when asked to state the color of an object, they chant off a sequence such as "red?" "blue?" "green?" "brown?" until the teacher finally accepts one as correct. The children need have no understanding of the referents for the labels; rather the word *color* triggers off a host of verbal associations.

The prohibition against simultaneous presentation of multiple instances applies only to the teaching of new *labels.* The simultaneous presentation of concrete negative and positive *exemplars* of the concept should always occur. For example, if the child does not know any of the labels for a group of objects (e.g., pencil, stick, or ruler), then only one label should be taught (e.g., pencil) and the other objects either referred to as "not X" (e.g., "not a pencil") or simply brought into focus without being named (e.g., in comparing the stick to a pencil, the child can be asked "Is this a pencil?" There is no need to ask the child to label the stick).

The reader will have noticed that the sequence of teaching concepts follows a rather rigid plan. Since much of the teaching is designed to have the flavor of spontaneity, one may wonder why the concept teaching conflicts with the general pattern. Upon reflection, however, it is evident that the demands represent a hierarchy of complexity. The complex stages embodied in steps 4, 5, and 6 would fall on deaf ears if introduced before the earlier steps. Therefore, the teaching should more carefully follow a sequence. Nevertheless, the sequence is not rigid and the teacher, need not feel that a departure violates some written script. For example, step 2 and 3 can readily be interchanged. In addition, excursions can be made (1) to follow up relevant comments by the child (e.g., "yes we did use a crayon to draw the picture last week; do you remember what we drew with the crayon"); (2) to initiate greater involvement from the child (e.g., with a withdrawn child, more movement can be introduced to encourage greater manipulation of the material; (3) to review known concepts while teaching unknown concepts (e.g., "yes, you found another *valise;* is that as *big* as this valise"). Chart 2 that follows outlines the sequence of development of a number of different, but fairly typical, concepts for the preschool child.

The sequence of concept teaching contains several basic assumptions. First, the material must be carefully structured by the teacher so that the child will have no difficulty in comprehending the information which he is given. For example, the initial mediator (step 2) for a concept such as *farther* may be "You have to go a longer way for it. Look, this one you can pick up from here—but this one, you have to *walk to,* that one is farther." Once given this mediator, the child should be able to use it in all situations until the point where the concept is securely grasped. Thus, as subtler instances of *farther* are used, the distances between the objects will be reduced. Nevertheless, in case the child experiences confusion, it is essential that the mediator still apply—and it will apply as long as the child has to take even one step to reach the "farther one."

Because the child may not appreciate something as small as the "one step," the teacher must be capable of magnifying the smallest of movements so that they take on a significance they would not normally have. For example, a small step can take a seeming eternity in time, if the teacher says "Don't move—can you reach it? No—okay, move a teeny bit, can you reach it? No—a

CHART 2

Illustration of the Teaching of Concepts Relevant to the Preschool Child

Type of Concept	1* Clear Example with Simple Direction	2 Verbalized Attribute	Extension to			
			3 Similar from Grossly Dissimilar Negative Instances	4 Less Obvious Positive Instance	5 Subtle Negative Instance	6 Relevance of the Category
Concrete Object	"This is a pencil. Pick up the pencil."	"Look, the pencil has a point and we can write with it."	"Find me another pencil" (from among cup, box, and zipper).	"Find me another pencil" (the other pencil in this case is different in size, color, width, etc.).	"Is this a pencil" (a long stick)?	"Do you see anything else that writes but that is not a pencil?"
Location	"This is the top of the box. Put your car on the top of the box."	"Top means you go up as far as you go until you can't go anymore" (takes child's finger and moves it along); this is the top."	"Which of these toys is on the top of the box" (one is next to the box, one is on top of the box)?	"Show me the top of the door"; "Show me the top of the basket"; "Show me the top of your shoe."	"Is this the top" (referring to a point near but not at the top of an object)?	"Why did we put the cover on top of the jar and not under the jar?"
Emotion	"The boy in this picture looks unhappy. Touch	"Look, he has tears in his eyes. Point to the tears" (in the picture). "Look his mouth is	"Which one of these boys in the picture is unhappy" (a smiling child vs. a	Pictures of adults and other children are shown and the child is to select	A picture of a child with a neutral expression is shown and the child is	"What do you think made him unhappy?"

152

Mass Noun	"the boy who looks unhappy." "This is sugar. You taste it."	"down like this. You put your mouth down like that." "How did it taste" (where possible use child's words such as good or nice")? If the child says nothing say, "it tastes sweet. Feel it. See, it feels rough and sticky."	sad looking child)? "Which of these is sugar" (offer a choice between sugar, cocoa, and nonsweet dry cereal)?	"the people who look unhappy." "Look inside these paper bags and find me some more sugar" or "There is some sugar over there that does not look like this, it is in little squares—go over and find it and see if it tastes like sugar."	asked "Is this girl sad?" "Is this sugar" (referring to salt, flour)?	"Can you think of anything else that tastes sweet like sugar?"
Size	"This doll is bigger than this one. Show me the big doll."	"Move your finger along the doll." (Takes child's finger and moves it along from the bottom to the top.) "See with this other doll (the smaller one) you can't go any further, but with the big doll, you can keep moving your finger up and up."	"Which of these is bigger" (compare similar material such as blocks but of grossly dissimilar size)?	"Which of these is bigger" (referring to two very different objects such as a chair and a bookcase)?	(Give two identical blocks) "Is this one bigger than this one?"	"Look at the doll house. Will this doll (referring to doll too big for the opening) be able to go through the door?"

[1] This teaching is based on the assumption that it follows after the child's behavior (e.g., wrong response) has indicated that he does not know the concept in question.

153

teeny bit more—still not—now, just a little bit more—did you get it? Good, okay then which one was farther away?"

Second, each demand placed upon the child should be carefully scrutinized to determine whether it actually tests the child's knowledge. For example, in teaching color, the teacher may draw a yellow line, retain the yellow crayon, offer the remaining crayons to the child saying "Draw a line that's a *different* color." Since the yellow crayon is no longer present, any crayon that the child selects is technically correct even though he may have no notion of the concept of different. This same demand represents an appropriate test if the teacher reinserts the yellow crayon among the others before offering them to the child. In this same vein, the child should not be given problems which merely reinforce preferred responses (i.e., responses that the child would make even in the absence of overt demands). Thus, if a child prefers red, but does not know its label, it is no test to give him a set of blocks and say "Give me the red one," for he would make the same response if he were told "Give me any one." It is appropriate, however, to say "Give me one that is *not* red" or else to teach a different color that does not reflect a preferred choice.

Third, if the child is experiencing difficulty with the concept, the teacher must avoid the strong attraction to switch to another concept within the same family. For example, if the child has failed *big*, it is confusing to switch to *small*, for this leaves the child to face two unknown labels, rather than one. (Only the teacher knows that *big* and *small* are related—not the child.) It is even more essential to avoid the analogous use of terms when the child is experiencing difficulty. For instance, a child may not understand that a handbag *opens*. In an effort to explain the idea, the teacher says "See, it's just like the drawer. That *opens* too." Shifting the frame of reference in this way when the child is already confused is likely to aggravate his difficulty.

Fourth, the most important implicit assumption in the entire sequence is that the teacher have no predetermined notion about teaching certain concepts in any lesson (e.g., she never says "today, children, we are going to learn about big things and little things"). If the child already knows the concepts, such teaching may serve as a useful review—but it will not extend the child's repertoire. Instead, *the teaching of concepts is initiated only when the child's behavior indicates that he does not have the particular concept. This can only be determined by the presence of the wrong response;* that is the signal that the child lacks the concept. The wrong response can appear in a variety of forms. For example, if asked to place the ball (that he is holding) *under* the desk, the child may look at the teacher with confusion (no response); he may place it on top of the desk (the incorrect response); he may ask "where's under?" (a request for help). All these varied behaviors share the feature that the request has not been met. It is not yet certain that there is genuine lack of knowledge on the child's part. Upon further examination, it may become evident that it was simply a failure in hearing, a brief lapse in attention, or even whimsical playfulness. But whatever the cause, the wrong response must be explored. If it is determined that the cause was a lack of knowledge, it is then appropriate to initiate the concept teaching sequence. In this way, the wrong response is pivotal, for it becomes the focus around which instruction is centered.

chapter 7

The Permutations of a Lesson

It is apparent by now that the most central element of one-to-one teaching is the opportunity it offers to tailor each lesson to suit the child's strengths and weaknesses. There can be no predetermined sequence of questions since the child's response at each point determines how the lesson will proceed. In order to obtain a more graphic illustration of this process, the following material examines the seemingly same lesson that was given to two five-year-old children. One is with a well-functioning boy who had no need of the tutorial program. Because this was the only lesson he received, it took place in a context of total novelty—the adult was strange, the room was different, and the tutorial relationship was new. Despite these seeming disadvantages, he (like most well-functioning children) maintained a lively cheerful competence throughout. The second child, a girl, had been in the tutorial program for about three months. She showed considerable progress at this time, including a rise in IQ from 81 to 95. Nevertheless, she continued to show many deficits, chief of which was a smiling withdrawal when confronted with cognitively demanding situations. If she was urged to answer, she would offer inappropriate, unthinking guesses.

Both dialogues concern a charming and popular children's book entitled *Are You My Mother?* by P. D. Eastman. It is a story of a baby bird who is hatched while the mother bird is away from the nest, searching for food. Upon emerging into the world, the baby bird longs for its mother and begins a trek to find her. On the way, he naturally encounters many things, both animate and inanimate, each of which he hopefully asks "Are you my mother?" As with all good children's tales, the story ends happily with the baby and mother reunited in the nest. While the story contains imaginary material, the lesson is geared to reality-based cognitive skills necessary for an appreciation of fantasy.

The first interview is with the well-functioning five-year-old boy. There had been a preliminary dialogue about what we would find when he entered this new room and some exploration of the recorder used to tape the session. Following this, the teacher and child sat down at the table.

Dialogue	*Interpretation*
Teacher—Now I'm going to read a story.	
Child—That story is like a story from the library in the school.	The child spontaneously and relevantly elaborates on the material.
Teacher—This school has this book?	
Child—Not the same thing. It's like the same picture.	This response shows how carefully he can delineate his ideas and communicate them to others.
Teacher—Oh, I think I know what you mean. There is a whole series of books that look like this. The man who wrote this wrote a lot of books. Do you know what we call a man that writes books?	
Child—(Shakes head.)	

Dialogue	Interpretation
Teacher—Do you think it might be a pilot or an author?	Because the child cannot derive this information himself, the teacher directs him to the correct information by offering a verbal choice.
Child—Author.	
Teacher—Yes. Why wouldn't it be a pilot?	Since child was sure of his knowledge, the teacher extended the discussion to the complex process of making him give the "rational for the incorrect."
Child—Cause pilots fly planes.	Objections can be raised to this questioning on the grounds that a man can both be a pilot and an author. The young child, however, has difficulty in simultaneously considering two attributes of the same phenomenon. Therefore, the aim here is limited to securely establishing the connection between a job and the person who performs it.
Teacher—That's right. The name of this book is *Are You My Mother?* That sounds strange, doesn't it? Let's find out what it is about. It starts "A mother bird sat on her egg." Do you know that this is a mother bird?	The dialogue is presented within a framework of comments which are often quite complex (e.g., "that sounds strange"). Such comments enhance the variability of the dialogue. However, no demands are placed upon the child to understand all the complex, varied statements.
Child—(Nods assent.)	
Teacher—How could you tell?	Child is made to justify his response to the teacher.

Dialogue	Interpretation
Child—(Points to bird's head which is sporting a kerchief.) Cause she has this.	
Teacher—What is that?	Teacher pursues the question. Even though the child's initial response was correct, he did not indicate whether he possessed the relevant label.
Child—I don't know.	
Teacher—I didn't know if you knew the word. It's kerchief—and usually only ladies wear those things. "The mother bird sat on her egg"—where is she sitting, anyway?	The teacher gives the correct information but does not pursue it further at this time. If every single failure were pursued, the lesson would become monotonous. The question "Where is she sitting?" shifts the child's focus from the occupants of the nest (i.e., the bird and the egg) to the nest itself. This quick shifting is useful in helping the child develop flexibility in viewing material.
Child—In the nest.	
Teacher—Right, she's in the nest. The egg jumped. What do you think is happening?	This presents the child with an open-ended question (many options are possible) that demands expressive verbalization.
Child—The baby's coming out.	
Teacher—You're right! " 'Oh oh!' said the mother bird. My baby'll be here—he will want to eat." What do baby birds eat?	Because the child has given complete, correct responses, the teacher is free to offer any number of questions here. For example, instead of asking "What do baby birds eat?" she could have asked "Who has to get the food for babies?" or "Why can't babies get the food for themselves?"

Dialogue	*Interpretation*

Child—Worms.

Teacher—That's right. She looks kind of worried. Right?
Child—(Nods.)

Teacher—How do you know that she looks worried?

Child—Cause the look on her face.

Teacher—Yeah. What part of her face looks worried?

Child—Her eyes.

Teacher—Her eyes. And those things above her eyes. Do you know what those are?

Child—Eyebrows.

Teacher—Good. And she says " 'I must get something for my baby bird to eat'.... So away she went." How did she go?

The pattern of the tutorial method of storytelling is being revealed. A bit of content is read and is then used as a point from which to take off and pose a series of relevant cognitive questions.

Child—With her wings.

Teacher—Does she need anybody to fly her?

This question may seem redundant, but it is necessary to set the framework against which to contrast the flight of a plane and the flight of a bird.

Child—No, she can go by moving her wings.

Teacher—Can you think of anything else that has wings that can also fly?

Dialogue	*Interpretation*

Child—No.

Teacher—It doesn't have to be a bird. Can you think of anything with wings that can fly?	The teacher poses the same question in a more limited form. The hope is that, by having discarded the categories of birds, the child may be led to a correct answer.

Child—No.

Teacher—If you wanted to take a very long trip and you didn't want to go by train or by car, how could you go?	Since restatement did not work, the teacher is led to focus on the relevant object by comparing it with members of its traditional superordinate grouping.

Child—By plane.

Teacher—Yes—so what has wings?	This question is to refocus the child back to the original question.

Child—A plane.

Teacher—That's right (laughing). Is it a bird? *Child*—No (laughing in response). *Teacher*—Can a plane fly by itself?	(At this point, because the teacher is pursuing the correction of an error, she has less freedom in selecting questions. She must select only those questions that will lead the child to correct his misinterpretation.)

Child—Yes.

Teacher—What kind of plane flies by itself?

Child—All planes.

Teacher—Do you think so? All planes? What did you tell me was	This dialogue could have been pursued easily even if the concept

Dialogue	*Interpretation*
the name of the man who doesn't write books? What kind of man was the one we talked about at the very beginning. I gave you a choice. I said he was an author or a. . . .	of pilot had not been raised earlier. By reverting to this concept, however, the teacher capitalizes on the opportunity to show the child how previous information can be useful later in the discussion.
Child—A pilot.	
Teacher—So how can the plane go by itself if you said it had a man to fly it?	
Child—Oh, yeah!	This exclamation shows that he has gained insight into a problem which was not available to him before. In addition, he has begun to develop a more differentiated concept of "flying."
Teacher—That's right. It has a pilot. Now "The egg jumped . . . and out came the baby bird." How did he get out?	
Child—By breaking the egg.	
Teacher—That's right—by breaking it. What part of him, do you suppose, broke this egg?	This sequence illustrates the delving that is possible with even the most seemingly simple observations.
Child—His *beak*.	
Teacher—Oh, his beak. Why does his beak do it? Why doesn't his head do it?	
Child—Because his head isn't strong enough.	

Dialogue	Interpretation
Teacher—That's right. How do *you* break an egg?	This question is designed to help the young child realize that the eggs in stories about birds bear a relationship to the eggs they experience in their real life. (Frequently, eggs in books are seen as *totally* different entities from eggs in life.)
Child—With our hands.	
Teacher—Just with your hands? Do you just squeeze it? What do you do?	
Child—You bang on it.	
Teacher—That's right—and that's pretty much what he does with his beak (goes back to the book). Do you know the very first thing he says when he comes out of the egg?	This is an open-ended question which the child may well fail. However, the child is well functioning so that it is useful to lead him to deal with the increasing amount of implicit information that is present in more complex dialogue.
Child—(Shakes head.)	
Teacher—What might he say if he broke out of his egg and he looked around and he was the only one there?	In the context of a story about a baby the phrase "was the only one there" is a sufficient cue to focus the child on the concept of mother.
Child—" 'Where is my mother?' "	The identity between the child's statement and the title of the book is not coincidental. It reflects the child's ability to bring in relevant material that he has previously experienced, when the situation demands.
Teacher—That's exactly what he said, 'Where is my mother?' And	

Dialogue	*Interpretation*
he looked for her. Where did he look, Bobby (pointing to picture depicting the bird's search)?	
Child—Up in the sky.	
Teacher—And where else?	These questions are included to present simple questions which the child will almost certainly solve. This is necessary to prevent the child from being flooded solely with demands for higher level problem solving.
Child—Down.	
Teacher—How can you tell he's looking up?	The child's accurate response reflects his competence in perceptual analysis; this question is designed to make him reflect upon the way this competence is achieved.
Child—Cause I see the picture over there.	
Teacher—What part of him is looking up?	
Child—His head.	
Teacher—Right, his head. But look at which part of his head. Look at this (pointing to the picture of the bird's beak) pointing straight up (raises her head so that her nose is pointing upward).	The teacher again reverts to a concrete demonstration because the child is unclear as to what is demanded. (This demonstration is particularly important for poorly functioning children because it shows them that the content of a book represents aspects of the real world around them.)

Dialogue   *Interpretation*

Child—(Imitates teacher's gesture)
His beak.

Teacher—Put your head straight   This question is designed to use
up. Is your beak pointing straight   humor rather than didactic teach-
up?   ing to help the child recognize the
                                     limits of a concept.

Child—(Laughs) I don't have any
beak.

Teacher—(Laughs) Oh, we don't
have any beaks; that's right. I
forgot you weren't a bird! So, "he
looked down"—and "he did not
see her!" Where was she, anyway?

Child—Looking for food.

Teacher—Right. In the market?
(Child and teacher laugh) Where
was she?

Child—I don't know.

Teacher—Where might she find a   Because child had difficulty with
worm? Where do worms live?   the open-ended question (i.e.,
                                     "Where was she?") the teacher
                                     focused him on the concept of
                                     worms to help him recognize the
Child—In holes in the dirt.   answer.

Teacher—Then where do you
think she's looking?

Child—In dirt.   This example demonstrates how
                                     the child's perseverative response
                                     can be channeled for simplifying
                                     a complex problem.

| *Dialogue* | *Interpretation* |

Teacher—Absolutely! " 'I will go and look for her' he said"—he's going out to take a walk and find her. What's going to happen to this bird (showing the picture of a bird walking out of the nest)?

This question is designed to make the child recognize the implications of the new content that he has just been offered.

Child—He's going to fall!

Teacher—Why is he going to fall?

Child—Cause he can't walk on air (laughs)!

Teacher—But—why can't he just fly and find her?

The teacher makes the child extend his excellent observation by posing a question which requires him to define further the limitations of the baby bird.

Child—Cause he's not strong enough.

Teacher—I think you're right. Babies are really not strong enough "Down, out of the tree he went." . . . "It was a long way down" and "the baby bird could not fly. He could not fly but he could walk. 'Now, I will go and find my mother' he said." But "he didn't know what his mother looked like." Why was that?

Child—Cause he never saw his mother.

Teacher—That's right. But over here he doesn't even stop when

Dialogue	*Interpretation*

he passes her by (shows picture where the baby bird is separated from his mother by a rock). Why does he go right by her?

Child—Cause the rock is in the way.

Teacher—It certainly is hard to see through a rock!

Child—Cause its blocking your way.

Another sign of spontaneous elaboration in the well-functioning young child.

Teacher—What would this have to be made of in order to see through it?

The question is designed to focus him on the property of a rock that "blocks" vision.

Child—Glass.

Teacher—Right—I never saw a rock made out of glass! (Both laugh) Who does he come to here (show pictures)?

Child—A cat.

Teacher—Do you know what this silly bird says to this cat? You won't believe it! He said "Are you my mother?"

The statement ("you won't believe it") is most relevant with a well-functioning child. A poorly functioning child may not understand what about the material is supposed to be unbelievable.

Child—(Laughs.)

Teacher—Could a cat be his mother?

Dialogue	*Interpretation*
Child—(Laughs) No.	
Teacher—Why not? What kind of babies does a cat have?	This question is difficult for most young children. Therefore, even before the child made an error, the teacher simplified the question form "why not" to "what kind of babies."
Child—Kittens.	
Teacher—Right. So the cat just looked at him—and didn't say a thing—not a thing. The cat was not his mother so he went on until he came. . . .	
Child—To a chicken.	
Teacher—That's right. What does this chicken have that the bird has?	This line of questioning not only serves to review previous concepts (e.g., beak) but it also requires the child to see similarities in the face of differences.
Child—Feet.	
Teacher—What else?	
Child—A beak.	
Teacher—Yep. " 'Are you my mother?' he said to the hen." Why might he mix up this chicken with his mother?	This question is vital in showing the child the usefulness of having observed the apparently meaningless similarities between the bird and the hen.
Child—Cause she has wings and a lot of things like her.	
Teacher—What things?	

Dialogue	*Interpretation*
Child—His wings, his feet, and his beak.	The use of *his* is a lovely illustration of the weaknesses in the child's grasp of the sexual role, even though (1) he has, for years, been using gender correctly in his grammatical formulations and (2) he can unequivocally differentiate between male and female humans.
Teacher—Yes (returns to reading). "The cat * was not his mother," and "the hen was not his mother." Now he came to a dog and asked the same silly question. What do you think he asked the dog?	
Child—(Peering intently at pages) Are you my mother?	
Teacher—"I am not your mother. I am a dog, said the dog." Then he came to a. . . .	A simple demand for labeling to keep balance between simplicity and difficulty.
Child—Cow.	
Teacher—Right. Is he going to ask the same thing?	
Child—Yes.	
Teacher—He doesn't learn very much. "'Are you my mother?' he said to the cow. 'How could I be your mother?'" she answered. "'I	

---

* The word in the text was "kitten." However, since the child introduced the word "cat" and it was appropriate to the context, it was decided to use it in the dialogue.

Dialogue	*Interpretation*
am a cow.' " What are baby cows called?	This questioning is designed to raise common concepts (e.g., names of baby animals) within a context that is meaningful for the child.
Child—I don't know.	
Teacher—Are they lambs or calves?	
Child—Calves.	
Teacher—That's right. And "the hen was not his mother" and "the cow was not his mother" and the dog was not his mother. " 'I did have a mother' said the baby bird . . . 'I have to find her.' " And he began to run. I think he's getting a little bit anxious. What does anxious mean?	
Child—I don't. . . . Excited?	An example of the way a well-functioning child can use context to grasp the meaning of a quite abstract term.
Teacher—That's right; excited and a little bit worried.	Teacher acknowledges his idea but extends the meaning somewhat. It would be possible to teach this concept much more extensively. Because the lesson is nearing its end such a departure at this point might frustrate the child.
Teacher—"Then he saw a car. Could that old thing be his mother?"	No *why* question is asked here both (1) to avoid establishing a set sequence in the questioning

Dialogue	*Interpretation*
	and (2) to move more quickly to the end of the story.
Child—No (laughs).	
Teacher—It could not. "The baby bird . . . ran on and on" and "he looked way, way down. He saw a boat. 'There she is,' said the baby bird. He called to the boat but the boat did not stop. The boat went on." Why didn't the boat answer him?	This *why* is quite different from the *why* in "why couldn't *X* be his mother?"
Child—Because she couldn't talk.	The child had no difficulty in making the shift that this question required.
Teacher—Right. He looked up until he saw a big plane. " 'Here I am mother,' he called out! But the plane did not stop." It went on.	
Teacher—"Just then, the baby bird saw a big thing." What is this big thing?	
Child—I don't know. I forgot the name.	
Teacher—What does it do?	Before giving the label, the teacher tries to determine the extent of the child's knowledge by asking for the function of the object.
Child—It picks up dirt.	

Dialogue   *Interpretation*

Teacher—Right. It's called a steam shovel. This must be his mother. " 'There she is,' he said, 'there's my mother.' He ran right up to it. 'Mother, mother. Here I am mother,' he said to the big thing! But the big thing just said 'Snort.' 'Oh, you're not my mother,' said the baby bird. 'You are a Snort! I have to get out of here.' But the baby bird could not get away. The 'Snort' went up. It went way, way up. . . . And up went the baby bird" with it. "Oh, oh" where was the snort going? " 'What is this Snort going to do to me? Get me out of here!' " Do you think he's happy?

Child—No.

Teacher—He's getting a little worried. What is the word I used before for worried?

The teacher is reintroducing the concept of anxious. She did not teach it fully before and therefore the child had not been required to remember it. Nevertheless, this well-functioning child did learn something just from exposure. (Even with his level of brightness, however, exposure alone was not sufficient. If the word were to have been taught, the tasks outlined in Chapter 6 should have been used. It would be unwise to do this, however, at this late point in the lesson.)

Child—(Hesitating) Scan?

Dialogue   *Interpretation*

Teacher—Anxious. You say that.

Child—Anxious.

Teacher—"Just then the snort came to a stop. 'Where am I?' " (teacher using whining voice), "said the baby bird. 'I want to go home! I want my mother.' Then something happened." What happened, Bobby?

Child—The baby bird fell in the nest.

Teacher—Isn't that funny. Way up there to his home. Right back in the tree, the baby bird was home!

Child—Yeah (very softly).

Teacher—Just then the mother bird came back to the tree. " 'Do you know who I am' she said to her baby." She had to introduce herself to her child!

Child—Hm (very softly).

Teacher—" 'Yes I know who you are,' said the baby bird. You are not a "—cat. Whom else did he meet? "You are not a"—

This simple labeling is both easy for the child and serves to review the story.

Child—Dog.

Teacher—Right. What else?

Dialogue	Interpretation
Child—Or a steam shovel.	The child has remembered the word offered by the teacher, even though it was not actually taught.
Teacher—A steam shovel.	
Child—Or a cow.	
Teacher—Right! Or a—what was it? Remember when he looked way, way down. What was that?	
Child—The boat.	
Teacher—The boat. You're not any of these things." 'You're a bird and you are my mother' " I think they look pretty happy now! Do they look anxious?	Teacher now reviews the concept of anxious by demanding only its receptive rather than its expressive use.
Child—No.	
Teacher—How do you know they don't look anxious?	
Child—Because they did a smile on their face.	Child's response shows that he has grasped a major part of the concept.
Teacher—That's right. That's the way you look when you're happy. Right! It was very nice.	

The second interview with the same story is conducted with a poorly functioning five-year-old girl, who was in the same class as Bobby. Many of the same questions are intentionally used in both sessions in an effort to achieve greater comparability between the dialogues. The child had been a regular student of the tutorial program and therefore was quite familiar with the room and its materials. The lesson began by allowing the child to explore the tape recorder. The teacher then introduced the book.

Dialogue	*Interpretation*
Teacher—Did you ever see this book?	The teacher and child had read this book together about a month previously.
Child—One time.	
Teacher—That's right. We read this together a long time ago. Sometimes I like to go over things we did a long time ago. We call this book *Are You My Mother?* Do you remember the name of the person who writes a book?	
Child—Uh, uh (shakes head).	
Teacher—Do you think he's called a doctor?	Only a single clearly incorrect alternative is offered. Multiple alternatives are avoided (is it a doctor or an author?) because the teacher knows of this child's tendency to unthinkingly select any options when several are offered. In addition, doctor is used rather than pilot since all the children in the school were well acquainted with doctors through their medical checkups. The teacher could not be sure that the child had a comparable knowledge of pilots.

Dialogue	Interpretation
Child—No, he checks people?	This spontaneous elaboration is a marked sign of progress in this child. Nevertheless, even when she was correct she was so unsure of herself that she phrased many statements as questions.
Teacher—That's right. You know who writes books—an author. You say "An author writes books."	The prodding of a clearly incorrect alternative was not enough to help the child's recall. Since the information is a label, it is given to the child didactically. This simple imitation will not ensure memory, but it helps to focus her attention and to augment her generally poor expressive verbalization.
Child—An author.	
Teacher—Say the whole thing—an author *writes books.*	Carol can obviously speak in full sentences. Therefore, this request for sentence imitation may seem strange. It is made to help the child both solidify the discussion and consciously attend to a skill that she has long used with little awareness.
Child—An author writes books.	If the child had not been capable of imitating the sequence, it would have been reduced further to two phrases. *An author—writes books.*
Teacher—Perfect. Now, what is happening on this very first page of the book?	

Dialogue	*Interpretation*
Child—The baby inside.	The response indicates that she recalls the story, but as sporadic, unelaborated details.
Teacher—Inside of what?	This question is designed to help the child clarify and elaborate her thinking.
Child—Inside the egg.	
Teacher—I think you're right. You remembered what we read before!	A question such as "How can you tell there is a bird inside?" is specifically avoided because it is not only complex, but unverifiable (i.e., the reason for her statement is just memory). Thus, if the child fails this "How can you tell" question, the teacher can do little to help her over the difficulty.
Teacher—Let's see what it says. "A mother bird—sat on her egg." How do you know this is a mother bird?	
Child—Uuhm. Because it's big?	The child's questioning, although correct, response indicates a growth in her thinking but a continued lack of assurance about her skills.
Teacher—That's right. Very good. But the daddy bird is big too. How do you know that this is *not* a daddy bird?	Although this is a difficult question, it is worthwhile to attempt it since the child is answering well. In addition, the teacher aids the child by assuring her that her response was correct, and by specifically stating the reason that

Dialogue	*Interpretation*
	makes the first response incomplete.
Child—Uhmm. Because the fathers go to work and the mommies stay home.	This seems like a high level response. Nevertheless, it is likely that the child is just offering one of her verbal associations to father and mother. In this case, she will not have determined the clues that led her to recognize the figure as the mother.
Teacher—That's right, mommies usually stay home. But there's another reason we could tell this is a mother bird. She is wearing something that ladies wear. Do you see it?	This question is designed to help the child realize how pictorial evidence is used in thinking. This is particularly important for this child who shows strong verbal associations, but poor verbal perceptual analysis.
Child—(Shakes head) No.	
Teacher—(Points) What is this bird wearing that makes us think its a lady?	
Child—Uh—a kerchief?	An interesting illustration of how verbal labeling is often not seriously deficient in these children. In fact, on this item, the child answered an item which the first child failed.
Teacher—Perfect! A kerchief. Daddies don't wear kerchiefs on their head! What do you think's happening here?	A question demanding a yes-no answer (e.g., do daddies wear kerchiefs?) is avoided with this child since it lends itself to her unthinkingly saying yes as readily as no.

Dialogue	*Interpretation*
Child—Uuhm—the baby, the baby is probably trying to get out?	The use of the word such as "probably" shows that the child is beginning to incorporate more complex lexicon.
Teacher—You're *probably* correct. The baby bird is *probably* trying to get out. You know what? I *like* the word "probably." That's a most grown-up word. Look at the mother bird's face (points to picture) over here.	
Child—He's mad.	The most significant aspect of this response is not the confusion in gender, but its spontaneity since it occurred without a direct request from the teacher. This was a marked sign of progress in this child's functioning for it indicates anticipation of content.
Teacher—I think you're right. Something is wrong. How come you don't think she's happy?	The look is supposed to be one of worry, not anger. This is a subtle distinction which would be difficult to teach because of the absence of clear perceptual illustrations. Instead, the question is worded in the negative ("not happy") to make the child recognize what in the picture led her to recognize a *negative* mood (as opposed to a specifically angry mood).
Child—Because she got a sad face.	This response suggests that sad, mad, and so on, exist, in this child's mind, as a composite con-

Dialogue	*Interpretation*
	cept to indicate negative emotions.
Teacher—What about her face looks sad? What part of it? *Child*—The eyes.	This question requires the child to focus on part, rather than the whole face.
Teacher—Good. But there's something on top of the eyes that are all squeezed together.	This continued probing is designed to help the child carefully analyze and evaluate perceptual information.
Child—The eyebrows?	Her statement is in a hesitant question form. It reflects not only her lack of confidence, but also her inability to judge the adequacy of information. She still views answers as arbitrary bits of information.
Teacher—Yes. Look at my face (teacher puckers her lips and knits eyebrows together). Do I look happy or worried?	Because the child has relatively good command of this area, the teacher takes the chance of formulating a question with alternatives. This is done to save time since the alternatives focus the child directly on the desired information. The alternative is to lead the child through a complex set of questions which will eventually lead to the desired concept.
Child—Worried.	
Teacher—What part of my face looks worried?	This question is designed to reinforce the concept raised in con-

Dialogue	*Interpretation*
	nection with the picture.
Child—Eyebrows?	
Teacher—Fine. And when you put your eyebrows together like that you just plain don't look happy! If she were very happy, how would she look? Make a happy face for me.	The use of commands which require only receptive verbalization (e.g., "Make a happy face") is an excellent way to involve the child actively in the lesson.
Child—(Smiles.)	
Teacher—That's good. Now I'll make a happy face. What am I doing?	The smiling is brought in to create a more extreme contrast between smiling and the concept of worry.
Child—Smiled.	The syntax is incorrect but the response shows a grasp of the concept.
Teacher—Good. Now is the bird smiling?	
Child—No.	
Teacher—So we know she's not happy because she's not _____.	It would be preferable to get the child to make the concluding statement. However, the sequence has been long and the child has not yet used the extensive expressive verbalization needed for this type of summary. Rather than confront the child with failure at the end of a sequence, the teacher completes most of the task, and only requires the child to fill in at essential points.
Child—Smiling.	

Dialogue	*Interpretation*
Teacher—Right—and her . . . (pointing to the eyebrows).	
Child—(Pause) Eyebrows.	
Teacher—Are all squeezed together (teacher returns to book). " 'Oh, oh,' said the mother bird," in a kind of worried voice, " 'my baby will be here! He'll want to eat' " (pause—looking at child). What is he going to want to eat?	
Child—Grass?	This response is good since it shows that the child has recognized the items surrounding the bird.
Teacher—That's a very good idea. There's a lot of grass around the tree where the baby bird lives. But you know what? The thing he likes best lives down in the dirt underneath the grass. Do you know what that is?	
Child—(Shrugs shoulders.)	
Teacher—They're worms. He likes worms?	
Child—Yea (emphatically and spontaneously)!	
Teacher—Yea! Fooey! So do you know what his mother has to do?	
Child—Dig to find worms.	This response shows that the child is beginning to develop expressive

Dialogue	*Interpretation*
	verbalization in cognitively demanding situations.
Yegh (with facial expression of distaste)!	
Teacher—Yegh. I'm *glad* I'm not a baby bird or a grown-up bird.	
Child—Me either.	
Teacher—What is the mother doing now (showing picture)?	
Child—She's going to fly.	
Teacher—And—	
Child—And she's going to get— she's going to dig and then she going to get some worms again and she's going to feed the baby bird.	This extensive verbalization illustrates the importance of motivation in helping the child mobilize her cognitive skills. In this case the motivation may stem from the child's identification with the baby bird.
Teacher—Yes-siree. Let's see. "So away she went." Did she take a car?	Preposterous questions are used because their humor is highly motivating. In addition, they often lead the child to elaborate the correct answer spontaneously.
Child—(Sitting on edge of seat in order to see better) No.	The lack of any smile indicates that she does not yet appreciate the humor in this idea.
Teacher—Did she take a bus?	
Child—(Hesitating) No!	

Dialogue	*Interpretation*
Teacher—What did she do?	
Child—She's flying by herself.	
Teacher—That's right.	
Child—(Looking at book) There goes the baby!	The child is now spontaneously selecting out information in the story.
Teacher—How do you know that?	Because the child is doing well the teacher chances a complex "how do you know" question.
Child—Cause he came out.	
Teacher—Yes, he's coming out. But look at the egg on this page and the egg on this page (pointing). What's the difference between them?	This question is designed to help the child focus on the cues she used to arrive at her conclusion.
Child—It's trying to break the egg.	
Teacher—Carol, you're really great. The egg is breaking and then what happened?	
Child—The baby came out of the egg.	
Teacher—That's right! Look at these pieces of egg over here (pointing to page).	
Child—They're little.	An additional sign of spontaneous comparative behavior.
Teacher—The pieces are little now	The teacher uses the child's words

Dialogue	*Interpretation*

Dialogue

because they're broken. But how did he break them?

Child—Ah—(hesitating).

Teacher—How do you break open an egg?

Child—You got to crack it on something.

Teacher—You're right! What do you think he used to crack it?

Child—The nest?

Teacher—The nest isn't hard and we need something hard if we want to crack open an egg. Look at his face—do you see anything that might be hard?

Child—I don't know.

Teacher—Do you think his eyes are sharp?

Interpretation

while at the same time redirecting the child's attention.

The child is guessing, but the guessing is not as wild as it was when the tutoring began. She is selecting out appropriate objects that are associated with the objects in question.

If real objects (e.g., a nest, an egg, etc.) had been present, the questioning would have taken a totally different turn (i.e., they would have been directed toward showing the child the inappropriateness of her verbalization). In the absence of these objects, the teacher could only bring in limiting (verbally imposed) conditions ("the nest isn't hard") and then quickly shift the questioning to focus on the right response.

Dialogue	*Interpretation*
Child—(Looks at picture) No.	
Teacher—How about his mouth? Do you think that—	
Child—(Interrupting) Yeah.	
Teacher—Yes, that is sharp. A bird's mouth has a special word. Do you know what it's called?	
Child—I don't know.	
Teacher—You might not know that. It's beak. Say "beak."	
Child—Beak.	
Teacher—Show me his beak.	
Child—(Points correctly.)	
Teacher—Now he looks around and he sees that he is all by himself and he doesn't want to be alone. Who do you think he might look for?	
Child—A friend.	The child's difficulty in handling this type of open-ended question shows that she is not ready to deal with material that relies upon implicit meaning (i.e., the discussion has only been on the bird and the mother, yet the child is unaware that the idea of mother might be relevant here).
Teacher—But he doesn't have any	The teacher attempts to handle

Dialogue	*Interpretation*
friends yet. He doesn't know anybody yet cause he was just born. But who was in the nest just before he was born?	the difficulty by showing the child why her response ("friend") is not feasible.
Child—His mother?	
Teacher—Yes, I think he wants his mother and I think he's going to look for her (turns page). So, what did he do?	
Child—He's going to fly?	
Teacher—I think he's going to try to. But first what does he do? What's he doing in the picture?	The teacher directs the child to analyze the pictorial information further.
Child—(Looks at picture) Looking up.	
Teacher—Perfect. Now you look up.	
Child—(Does it.)	
Teacher—Now look down.	Contrast is used to help the child analyze the central differences between situations. If the child had not understood the concept of up, the polar term down would not have been introduced.
Child—(Looks down.)	
Teacher—Does it feel the same way?	This type of questioning is to help the child grasp the pictorial evidence, as well as to focus more discerningly on her own bodily sensations.

Dialogue	Interpretation

Child—No.

Teacher—Which way does your neck feel stiff and funny—when you look up or when you look down?

Child—Up.

Teacher—Right. Now the bird looked up.

Child—And he looked down.

The child spontaneously completes the teacher's phrase "looked up" with the phrase "looked down." This is a sign of the strong verbal-to-verbal associations that are present even in poorly functioning children.

Teacher—And he didn't see her at all (turns page). Well, he's going to look for her.

Child—Look at that!

Teacher—What 's going to happen?

Child—He's going to fall?

Teacher—Oh (mock terror). Why is he going to fall?

Child—Cause one foot is off the egg.

This is one of the first signs that she can now identify the reasons for her interpretations.

Teacher—Right, his foot is off. But

The questioning is elaborated to

Dialogue	*Interpretation*

why can't he just walk off the egg onto the ground? Where is this nest?

help the child extend her reasoning.

Child—On a tree.

This sounds correct but the child has still not shown that she has grasped the concept of height.

Teacher—And where is the nest in the tree?

Child—(No response.)

Teacher—Near the ground?

Child—High up in the tree?

The posing of an incorrect alternative led in this case to the correct elaboration of the response.

Teacher—That's right! And if he just walks out high up in the tree what will happen to him?

Child—He'll fall out.

Teacher—That's right. I guess he thinks he can fly. But why can't he fly? His mother can fly!

Child—He and the bird can fly.

The pictorial information told her that the bird would fall; her verbal associations to birds are that they fly. This is an illustration of how the child comfortably holds two opposing views without any awareness of their conflict.

Teacher—You think he can fly? Let's see (turns the page).

Child—He fell.

Dialogue	*Interpretation*
Teacher—Why did he fall? Why didn't he just fly?	
Child—Cause, cause he took one foot off of the nest!	A good use of memory, but still an incomplete answer to the question "why didn't he fly?"
Teacher—Yeah. But his mother took one foot off of the nest and what did she do?	This question is to help the child realize that her initial response is obviously not correct.
Child—She didn't fall out.	
Teacher—Why not?	
Child—(Shrugs shoulders.)	
Teacher—Who's bigger and stronger? The mommy bird or the baby bird?	While this question poses an alternative which may cause difficulty, the child's strong verbal associations make this a reasonable option to chance.
Child—The mommy.	
Teacher—And who can fly?	
Child—The mommy.	
Teacher—That's right. But the baby bird cannot fly yet because he is not strong. His wings are not strong enough to help him fly. What could happen?	The teacher concludes the sequence since it would probably be too difficult for the child to do it, especially at the end of a lesson. Nevertheless, a question is left for the child to answer in order to make her use some of the information she has been given.
Child—He'll fall out.	

Dialogue	*Interpretation*
Teacher—That's right. He fell "Down, down down! It was a very long way down. And the bird could not—"	
Child—Fly down.	
Teacher—Why?	The teacher uses this opportunity to review what had been taught.
Child—Because his wings need to get more bigger.	This appropriate answer to a why question is one of the surest signs that the child is incorporating information that she is offered.
Teacher—That's right! "He could not fly yet, but he could walk!" So when he got to the ground, he began to walk and he said " 'Now I will go find my mother.' " But you know what, we've been reading such a long time that it's time for you to go back to your class. But tomorrow when you come in, we'll finish the story. (Teacher picks up a book mark) Do you know what I am going to do with this?	The bookmark involves a review of a concept that had been taught several weeks earlier.
Child—Put it in the page?	This correct response is another sign that she is retaining information.
Teacher—Why? Why should I do that?	Because the response was correct, the teacher goes on to pose a question of rationale.
Child—Because—ah—	

Dialogue	Interpretation

Teacher—Well, which page were we at when we stopped reading?

Child—This one (pointing).

Teacher—Yes, and that's the page we want to go back to next time so I'm putting the marker here.	Because it is the end of the lesson, the teacher does not wish to introduce the sequence necessary for the child to fully learn the idea. But she does not totally drop the discussion without explanation; instead, she offers a relevant comment to at least convey to the child the idea that there is a rationale to the action.

The commentary accompanying the dialogues dealt with most of the central points of the lessons. It seems useful to add only a few additional comments. Perhaps the most marked feature of the lessons is the predominance of correct responses, despite the children's different levels of functioning. (Approximately 80 percent of Bobby's answers were correct, while Carol had approximately 70 percent correct.[1]) A high percentage of correct responses is sought intentionally. If the child were exposed to frequent failure, he would quickly abandon his efforts at learning.

The high level of success is achieved by lowering the demands to fit the child's level of functioning. It was for this reason that Carol was not asked questions such as:

---

[1] This estimation is imprecise since there are inevitably difficulties in categorizing responses. For example, many questions demand information that the child could not be expected to know (e.g., "When the bird came out of the egg, what did he say?"). In this case, an incorrect response is inevitable and it therefore seems unfair to count it as incorrect. These difficulties arise in part because questions in the tutorial program are often used as attention-getting techniques rather than as genuine requests for information. Nevertheless, it is possible to categorize most responses with little difficulty. Therefore, while any categorization of a particular response may be questioned, the overall proportion of correct to incorrect responses is fairly reliable.

"Is your beak pointing up?"
"What would the rock have to be made of to be able to see through it?"
"Why couldn't the cat be his" (the baby bird's) "mother?"
"Why might he" (the baby bird) "mix up a chicken with his mother?"
"What does anxious mean?"

It would have been possible to chance *any one* of these questions with Carol. Even if the single question were failed, one additional wrong response would be of little concern. In fact, the teacher did chance one such question. For example, "Did she" (the mother bird) "go by car?" shares the preposterous quality of the question "Is your beak pointing up?" Carol's failure to recognize the absurdity of the question indicated that she was not ready for such material. While one such question need not detract from the lesson, the child might become seriously bewildered if many such questions were asked. As a result, the number of complex questions (i.e., complex for the particular child) must be carefully controlled.

Carol's lesson was marked by a reduction in content as well as a reduction in complexity. This is evident in the fact that the story could not be completed within her lesson. The reduction in content results from the numerous simplifications that the poorly functioning child requires. For example, when asked "How could you tell this is a mother bird?" Bobby immediately pointed to the kerchief (even though he did not know the label).

Even when Carol's answers were correct, they were often incomplete. For example, when asked "What is happening on the first page?" she replied "The baby inside." In order to be assured that the child understood what was occurring, the teacher had to ask a second question "Inside of what?" Because of the incomplete quality of her answers, almost every question required two or three questions before the idea was fully defined. This, of necessity, implies a reduction in content.

Teachers frequently view these additional questions as unfortunate obstacles that should be bypassed, if possible. This interpretation stems largely from the content-oriented emphasis in education which views teaching as the transmission of a set amount of material. The teacher has a predetermined set of information to teach and anything that keeps her from this goal is considered detrimental. For example, in the dialogues above, content-oriented education would view the goal of the lesson as "the telling of the story." The failure to complete the story then represents the serious transgression of "not having covered the material."

Content is vital to learning and it would be a serious mistake to underplay its significance. For example, in teaching reading, the teacher could not decide that teaching fifteen letters well is just as good as doing all twenty-six. But content is of little value if the child does not possess the means for incorporating it properly. Because of this, content assumes different roles at various stages in the teaching. With the young child, content is the vehicle for developing the system that will make learning meaningful. No specific amount has to be taught; the amount is determined by the child's ability to comprehend the material. As the child develops secure skills of reasoning and reflection, the focus can then shift increasingly to the content itself. This shift must be delayed until the child is capable of grasping consensually validated information (i.e., when he can understand the meaning of verbally communicated information, without having to undergo the experience itself). When this point is achieved, the child can begin to profit from the verbal transmission of knowledge available in the culture—including that available from didactic teaching (see Ausubel, 1968).

Both lessons are also marked by the absence of concrete rewards. Verbal rewards were used, particularly with Carol whose confidence needed bolstering. It is paradoxical that the amount of praise often fails to correlate with the quality of the performance. Children who perform well do not require much praise since their interest in learning is often sufficient motivation for them. As a result, in spite of their good performance, they receive relatively few plaudits. Poorly functioning children, however, are highly dependent upon external support. Therefore, in spite of their less adequate functioning, they elicit a great deal of praise. The praise, although liberal, is offered only for correct responses. Incorrect thinking is not criticized, but it is also not praised.

The most notable characteristic of the tutorial sessions is the precisely detailed framing of the questions. One may easily be skeptical of the need for this specificity. We are accustomed to viewing children's learning as a spontaneous process that occurs with little outside intervention. As a result, the questioning may seem to be an unnecessary examination of minutiae. The great skill that underlay Bobby's functioning, however, was precisely in this area of so-called minutiae. Like Bobby, well-functioning preschool children enter enthusiastically into this type of dialogue, even when they have had no experience in the tutorial program. They elaborate spontaneously, they shift attention easily, they delve into concepts, they can rationalize their thinking, and they are secure enough about all these skills so as to enjoy intellectual absurdity.

The basic assumption of the tutorial approach is that this spontaneous, accessible system represents the central cognitive difference between the well-functioning and poorly functioning child. Only further research can determine the validity of this assumption. If it is correct, however, then precise questioning is essential. It represents the major tool by which the teacher can lead the child to develop skills necessary for intellectual achievement.

chapter 8

An Anatomy of the
Teacher-Child Interchange

The detail that has been hypothesized as essential to effective teaching fortunately contains more than simply increased demands for teaching skill. Within this seemingly overly minute dissection are contained the rudimentary tools for the precise analysis and quantification of the teaching-learning process.

Such an analysis is vital if we are to understand the changes that are effected through any educational effort. Most assessments of teaching programs are global; that is, they involve undifferentiated measures such as intelligence test scores, achievement test results, and teacher evaluation of child behavior. These measures are both legitimate and helpful, and, like other investigators, I have used them in assessing the results of the tutorial program. These results have been published and are available to the reader (Blank and Solomon, 1968, 1969; Blank, 1969; Blank, Koltuv and Wood, 1972). Because they yield limited insight as to what has occurred in the learning situation, they will be sketched here only in brief outline. After this, we will proceed to an alternative analysis that can be developed for a finer dissection of the effects of educational intervention.

The tutorial program has thus far been used in a series of three studies, all of which involved children ranging in age from three to six years old. Since relatively few tests are available to assess functioning at this age, the well-known Stanford-Binet in-telligence test and the Wechsler Intelligence Scale for Children were selected as the measures of performance.

Although the program had the single guiding idea of one-to-one structured teaching, within this framework many relevant issues were open for testing. These included the amount of time the program had to be maintained, the type of training necessary for the teachers, and the effectiveness relative to other methods of instruction. The most central factor, however, was obviously the one-to-one interchange itself. From almost any perspective, whether it be that of psychoanalytic theory (Freud, 1938; Erikson, 1950), stimulus deprivation (Spitz, 1945; Hebb, 1966), or imitative modeling (Bandura and Walters, 1963), an opportunity to have a close, sustained, and concentrated relationship with a single adult is likely to affect behavior. Because of the potentially overriding importance of individual attention, all studies controlled for this factor.

Because funds were limited, it was necessary to be selective about the other issues which were most central to the development of the program. For example, rather than maintain a small group of children for a relatively long period of time, it was decided to teach more children for shorter periods. This allowed us both to replicate the results and study a wide range of individual needs and differences. Thus, in the three studies, any child was seen for a maximum of six months.

A total of 150 children took part in the research, with approxi-mately one-third seen in the tutorial program, one-third in one-to-one instruction along more traditional lines, and one-third who received no additional attention other than their regular classroom experience. In all three studies, children in the tutorial method showed significantly higher gains on the IQ test than did either of the other two groups. The average improvement was approxi-mately fourteen points, but some children showed gains as high as thirty-two points. In no study did children who received one-to-one traditional instruction show rises that were significantly greater than those of the classroom controls. This strongly indicated that the improvement could not be attributed to the role of individual attention alone. The results also suggested that the gains correlated with the amount of instruction per week in that children seen five times a week showed more improvement than those seen three times a week.[1]

These gains were most promising. But as stated at the beginning of the chapter, they were far too vague to indicate the exact ways in which the change was effected. It is here that the precise analysis of the teaching began to prove its worth. It led to the development of an instrument through which there could be constant monitoring of the tutorial sessions.

Initially, it had been planned to assess the child's patterns of response. The analysis soon developed a twofold purpose, however, for not only was it applicable to the child, but it also showed itself applicable to the teacher. Thus, rather than having to assess the teacher's performance with such traditional global comments such as "That lesson was too high level" or "You didn't establish a good relationship with the child," it became possible to delineate the precise area of difficulty with comments like "The child's verbal expressions are limited almost solely to labels. Therefore, he can't answer any 'why' and 'how' questions since they demand far more verbalization than he can muster in the teaching setting. It would be preferable if requests were reworded so that they demanded receptive rather than expressive language."

In order for the reader to have more than this limited glimpse into the methods that were devised, a fuller description of the analysis seems called for. The basic model involved the development of a method whereby each interchange between the teacher and child could be coded and quantified. With the rising interest in the educational process, a number of systems of this nature

---

[1] Within the three studies, a total of ten teachers were trained. Although the program was obviously complex, I had not anticipated just how complex it would be to transmit. There was no predetermined curriculum; it had to be improvised according to the child's every response. This demanded rapid assessment of what the child's response meant and then immediate readjustment of demands to meet the child's particular level at that point. Both phrasing and rephrasing of the problems required sensitivity to personality factors, as well as to cognitive ones. To achieve this, we found that an intensive daily training period of approximately four months seemed to be required. Throughout this time, each teacher worked directly with children under close supervision. In some ways the training of the teacher paralleled that of the children; it was highly individualized, it was intimately tied to the reality presented by the child's behavior (as opposed to general theoretical principles of teaching), and it involved the practice of new techniques until they became so much a part of the person's style that they seemed to be second nature.

have been devised (see Simon and Boyer, 1968). While these systems have been designed to assess teacher-child interaction, none was directly applicable to the tutorial situation.

First, most have been devised with a view toward analyzing the classroom group setting. Therefore, they would have to be considerably modified for application to the one-to-one situation. For example, any one child's refusal to respond will not interfere with the progress of a group lesson. The teacher will always find someone who will answer. In the one-to-one setting, the silence cannot be escaped. Her method of handling the silence is a critial measure of her success as a teacher.

Second, many of the systems have been influenced by the idea that the teacher has self-fulfilling prophesies about the child (Holt, 1964; Rosenthal and Jacobson, 1968). These prophesies come to life through the climate for learning that the teacher creates (e.g., the level of stimulation she provides; the amount of support she offers, etc.). Measurement systems that are guided by this philosophy are naturally most interested in assessing parameters that are viewed as representative of "good teaching"—for example, (1) the amount and quality of the praise used by the teacher; (2) the amount of attention she gives to the child; and (3) the type of intellectual demands she makes in the class.

In general, these systems focus to such an extent on the teacher's behavior that they do not give sufficient attention to the way the child's behavior must modify what the teacher will do. As a result, they undervalue the interactional nature of the teacher-pupil relationship. When ratings are confined to the group setting, many of these differences in treatment need not be considered. There are usually a sufficient number of well-functioning children in any class to permit the teacher to maintain all the recommended teaching principles. For example, if the teacher asks a question in the group and receives a wrong answer, it is relatively easy for her to withhold criticism, turn to another child, eventually get the right answer, and then offer the appropriate praise. In the one-to-one situation, however, there is no other child to whom to turn. In this situation (as in the group situation), it is appropriate to withhold condemnation, but it is equally appropriate to withhold praise from the child.

This example illustrates how the sustained one-to-one interchange forces attention on vital factors that may easily be diffused in the group setting. It also illustrates the reasons why the available scoring systems could not be used in the present circumstances. Instead, a system had to be developed which would capture the feedback nature of the one-to-one setting; that is, any bit of behavior could not be assessed by itself, rather it had to be assessed according to its relevance as to what the other member has just done. Relevance can be judged along both affective and cognitive levels. For example, on the affective level, if a child answered a problem correctly, praise may logically follow; such praise might be inappropriate, however, if the child made no effort to handle the problem. Similarly, on the cognitive level, a question demanding primitive cause-and-effect reasoning might be appropriate if the child with reasonable expressive verbalization had just answered a question correctly. Such a question might be inappropriate, however, if the child with limited expressive verbalization had just answered a question incorrectly.

Assessment of this feedback situation is further complicated by the fact that each member of the pair functions according to quite different rules. We would readily question the skill of a teacher who decided to teach astrophysics to six-year-olds, or of a teacher who screamed at her children that they "would never learn." We could do this with a guilt-free conscience because the teacher is clearly not fulfilling her expected role. If, however, the child chooses to ignore the teacher's requests, or chooses to jump around the room, or chooses to change the topic, our conceptualization of childhood does not permit us to condemn him. At most, the teacher is expected to modify the child's style of responding (even the desirability of such modification is often questioned at the preschool age since it may be deemed an unnecessary constriction of the child's spontaneous drives). These examples point up the special nature of the teacher-child situation. The teacher has a definite role to perform entailing clear demands and restraints; the child has no such obligation—yet he is just as active a member in the interaction. This state of affairs has two important implications. First, the measures for assessing the teacher's behavior will be different from those for assessing the child's behavior. Second, judgmental processes (e.g., was the behavior appropriate?) will be applicable to the teacher's behavior, but not to the child's.

This distinction has been present throughout the techniques described in the book. The teacher was given a wide set of rules by which to function with regard to the types of questions she could ask, the way in which she had to structure material, and so on. But how might these varied categories be summarized into manageable, quantifiable groupings? The overall cognitive orientation of the tutorial program is of major use here since it provides the framework by which the teacher's behavior can be assessed. For example, within this orientation a major factor is obviously the type of cognitive demand she places upon the child. These demands were described in broad outline in Chapter 2 (in the discussion on cognitively directed perception, concepts, and problem solving). They are much more fully elaborated in Part II, with the result that they make it possible to code every type of demand that is put forth (e.g., is the demand one of a request for imagery, exclusion, directed dialogue, etc.). A second major category for describing the teacher's behavior is available through the simplification techniques for coping with the wrong response which were given in Chapter 4 (e.g., when the child has incorrectly answered a problem, does the teacher "dissect the task," "provide a hint," "repeat the demand," etc.). At this point, we have two major areas in which to assess teacher's performance: (1) the cognitive demand imposed and (2) the simplification technique used.

Although these two groupings encompass a significant part of the teacher's handling of the cognitive sphere, they omit a major aspect of her behavior, namely—its appropriateness in the immediate context. It is here that we begin to see more clearly the constant emphasis on the need for the teacher to evaluate the child's behavior at every point. Thus, it is not possible to judge, in the abstract, whether the teacher should, or should not, pose any set of particular questions to a child. A relevant judgment can only be made by taking into account the child's behavior at the particular time. To give a rather extreme example, if a child has been speaking in monosyllables, it would be inappropriate to pose a *why* question since the latter is bound to require fairly extensive, free-flowing verbalization. Thus, any judgment about the appropriateness of the teaching can only be assessed by taking into account what the child has just done. Therefore, the third major grouping for coding teacher behavior is organized with reference to the child's functioning. For example, the first category represents the teacher's behavior when the child has responded correctly, the second category represents her behavior when he responded incorrectly, and so on.

The behaviors are further grouped into A and B categories. In general, the methods listed under A tend to be what would be deemed positive or appropriate responses, and those under B tend to be what would be considered negative or inappropriate responses. The full scale is presented in Part II. At this point, only one subscale is completely outlined.

TEACHER'S RESPONSE TO CHILD'S RESPONSE

I. *When Child Is Correct*

A	B
1. Praises.	1. Fails to praise a novel or well-formulated idea or question.
2. Acknowledges child's response (either explicitly or implicitly) by continuing to make appropriate demands relative to subject being discussed.	2. Ignores child's response (or a central part of his response).
3. Uses word or phrase introduced by child in continuing appropriate demands.	3. Accepts and/or praises an incomplete response.
4. Elaborates a statement made by child.	4. Makes child explain, elaborate, or justify nonexplainable fact ("Tell me how you know it's a line").
5. Gives rationale related	5. Simplifies question before

| to idea or material being discussed. | giving child a chance to respond. |

6. Uses humor.

The remaining subscales delineate the teacher's behavior.

II . *When Child Is Incorrect*
III. *When Child Fails to Respond*
IV. When Child's Response Is *Irrelevant, Ambiguous, or Not Totally Suitable*
V . *When Child Requests Help*
VI.When Child Is Confronted with New *Information or New Situation*

This scale permits a rating of appropriateness for every interchange in which the teacher takes part. Her overall sensitivity cannot be assessed, however, through any single response. For example, although the teaching is designed to help the child overcome his errors, the teacher in a particular instance may elect not to treat a wrong response (e.g., it may have occurred late in the lesson when the child's attention is lagging). But these mitigating factors cannot be taken into account at each point. If they were, the ratings would become meaningless as they were bent to the influence of each observer's personal interpretation. Therefore, even when the teacher has an excellent reason for her behavior, it would still be scored under category B. The occasional seemingly inappropriate response does not detract from the teacher's skill. The appropriateness of her behavior is not judged by single instances, but by the general pattern that emerges across the range of her responses. The single A or B response is not significant; it is the overall balance between A and B responses that is critical.

This analysis provided sufficient measures for assessing the teacher's behavior. It did not give consideration, however, to the other vital partner in the lesson—the child. A scale of his behavior was essential if we were to begin to assess his learning. Accordingly, a scale for this purpose was developed. However, unlike the three measures used for the teacher, the child was assessed in only a single sphere—his reactions to the cognitive demands posed by the teacher. At first glance, the most obvious categories for these purposes would seem to be the ratings correct-incorrect (i.e., did the child correctly meet the problem posed or not). This dichotomy is, however, far from sufficient. An incorrect response can range across an array of behaviors, some of which are indicative of reflection while others are lacking any attempt at thinking. For example, one three-year-old who had just been taught the label bulletin board, was asked if she knew the name of the things (tacks) on the board; to this, she answered "bullets?" This is an example of a wrong response which is of a different nature from an answer such as "I don't know," for it is original, it displays analogous reasoning, and it merits high praise from the teacher—even though it will have to be corrected. In order to represent these various responses, the child's behavior was coded according to seven major groupings. These are:

1. Correct
2. Incorrect
3. Irrelevant
4. No response
5. Asks for guidance
6. Questionable
7. Behavior when no request has been made

Each of these categories, in turn, contains subgroupings that define the child's response more precisely. For example, under the category of correct responses, the child's answers could be coded as:

1. Correct.
   a. Verbal—correct
   b. Nonverbal—correct
   c. Partially completes task—not fully adequately
   d. Spontaneous observation of significant properties
   e. Asks a question indicative of thought or requesting information
   f. Anticipates questions of dialogue that are forthcoming

The full scale is presented in Part II.

With these scales, it becomes possible to code each bit of behavior that occurs between the teacher and child. In order to obtain a clearer picture of how this is done, in Chart 3, a sample from one of the dialogues (in Chapter 3) is presented along with the ratings that would be accorded each response.

This coding permits us to define the precise differences between the dialogues of the teacher trained in the tutorial program and of the teacher trained in a more traditional program (the last two dialogues of Chapter 3). For example, from the complete coding of the lessons (available in Part II), it is clear that the teacher in the second dialogue used a wider variety of cognitive processes (e.g., imagery, directed dialogue, memory, etc.) than did the teacher in the third dialogue (thirteen versus five) and a wider variety of simplification techniques (six versus two). In addition, the second teacher almost always failed to offer a simplification when it was needed. Most significantly, the teacher in session 2 used responses from the A grouping forty times and from the B grouping only two times; while the teacher in session 3 used responses from the A grouping seven times and from the B grouping nineteen times.

Although the results are quantified, they are still liable to the charge of subjectivity (e.g., it is possible to dispute the validity of any particular A or B rating). Nevertheless, it would be difficult to dispute the accuracy with which the ratings depict the teacher's overall pattern. For example, the teacher in session 3 clearly resorted to unverifiable questions when the child failed problems. All such unverifiable demands unequivocally receive B ratings.

Unverifiable questions, by themselves, need not pose any difficulty—if the child is functioning well in the lesson. In such circumstances, the teacher may attempt to move the child past the immediately experienced events. This, in fact, would be a major goal of any cognitive program. When the child is functioning poorly, however, such demands often add to his difficulties. They are particularly inappropriate when used as attempts to simplify a failed request. Yet the second teacher consistently used them in this way. For example, when Julie failed to answer questions about the flower, the teacher plied her with unverifiable demands such as "Did you put it in the ground?" "Was it little and yellow?"

CHART 3

	Dialogue	Coding of Child's Response	Cognitive Tech-nique Demanded	Coding of Teacher's Behavior		
				Simplification Used	Response to Child's Response	
Teacher:	Do you remember what we did when you were here yesterday?		Memory-recall (over previous session)		(Not applicable to first question.)	
Julie:	Yes.	6a (Questionable)				
Teacher:	What did we do?		Memory-recall	Makes child clarify statement.	(When child's answer was unclear—teacher continues to make appropriate demands relative to subject being discussed.) IV A 2	
Julie:	I don't know.	3c (No response)				
Teacher:	Let's see if I can help you. Is there anything on this table that we worked with the last time? (A limited variety of materials is present.)		Memory-Recognition	Offers contrast.	(When child failed to respond—teacher gives rationale for task.) III A 3 (Teacher perseveres on task.) III A 1	
Julie:	(Points to blackboard.) Gesture is correct.	1c (Correct)				
Teacher:	That's just pointing. Tell me what we did.		Directed Dialogue		(When child was correct—teacher gives rationale for statement.) I A 5 (Teacher perseveres on task.) I A 2	

*The words in parentheses represent the definition of the numerical code.

"What kind was it?" The difficulty evoked in the child by this line of questioning is evident in the performance she displayed. Thus, if we examine the types of responses that the same child gave in the two lessons, we see:

TABLE 2

Child's Response

	Correct	Incorrect	Irrelevant	No Response	Other (requests for help, spontaneous comments, etc.)
Session 2	21	1	2	4	2
Session 3	1	1	9	5	6

It is clear that the session within the tutorial program led to predominantly correct performance, while the other session led to predominantly incorrect performance. In effect, that lesson was mainly an opportunity for the child to reinforce her patterns of error. Further analysis of Julie's failures in the first session reveals why nonverifiable questions were so disastrous in the third dialogue. Of her seven noncorrect responses (incorrect, lack of response, etc.) in the structured tutorial lesson, five were caused by questions dealing with nonpresently available information (i.e., memory and imagery questions). This difficulty clearly contraindicates the use of nonverifiable material for the child. In other words, if the teaching in the last dialogue were to be effective, the teacher had precisely to avoid the type of questions that dominated her lesson. One might be tempted to dismiss this proscription as facile *post-facto* advice (e.g., "That's easy to say after the lesson. But how was the teacher to know this difficulty when she had never before laid eyes upon the child"). This criticism overlooks the fact that the child's behavior in the lesson itself offered sufficient cues for the teacher to retreat from the path of unverifiability—if the teacher had been attuned to the difficulties that can mark the thinking of the young child.

It is necessary to be cautious in extrapolating the findings beyond the sessions thus far analyzed. Much more extensive analyses of other teachers and other children will have to be done in order to demonstrate the usefulness of this system. Nevertheless, the analysis does appear to offer a useful beginning for answering key questions about both teacher and child performance. For example, with regard to children's behavior, the following type of questions can be dealt with:

1. What are the specific cognitive processes on which the child succeeds; which does he fail?
2. When a failure occurs, to what level of simplification must the problem be reduced before the child can arrive at the answer?
3. What is the pattern of the child's errors?

With regard to the teacher's behavior, the following questions might be answered:

1. What is the range of cognitive processes covered by the teacher?
2. What is the pattern of the teacher's behavior when the child is not correct?
3. What are some of the specific differences in teaching style among different teachers?
4. What types of failure by the child can the teacher cope with successfully and what types of failures does she have difficulty in correcting?

A tool of this sort can obviously be used for negative as well as positive purposes. For example, it has been an all too common experience to rivet on the teacher as a major cause of children's failure. She becomes the source upon which to lay blame. The analysis above could easily be put into service of this sort (e.g., "the teacher never followed the child's interests, remarks," etc.). It was not intended for this purpose. The teaching of children is a remarkably difficult skill and often we have not provided a clear enough definition of the elements which are essential to its success. Therefore, rather than educators considering this analysis as a challenge, I hope that they will look upon it as a potential aid in their work. It is obviously far too intricate to be used on any kind of daily basis. It can, however, be used in many key situations where there is a need to delineate the major elements in operation, such as when one wishes to analyze the reasons why a particular child seems unreachable, what are the precise characteristics of a teacher who seems unusually effective, and what curriculum seems most profitable. For those readers who wish to pursue this aspect of the work, further explication of the techniques and methodology of the tutorial program is presented in Part II.

part II

Delineation of the Tutorial Techniques

The remainder of the book contains a more detailed exposition of the tutorial program. It is designed primarily for those readers who are specifically interested in applying the ideas that have been raised earlier in this text. After the presentation of this material, there is a short summary statement which is applicable to the entire volume and which may prove useful to all readers. It attempts to present an overview of the general ideas that underlie the tutorial program.

chapter 9

Posing of the Problem

It is evident from the discussion above that the success of the tutorial dialogue critically hinges on the type of problem that is asked. This aspect of teaching is familiar to everyone, since children are commonly faced with questions such as "What is the weather outside today?" "What shapes are the cookies?" and "What did we see when we visited the post office?" Questions of this nature seem right from an intuitive standpoint. If, however, we are to use them to enhance cognitive skills, it is necessary to have a much more precise understanding than is afforded by intuition alone.

From this perspective, the framework of dialogue provided in Chapter 2 will be used to analyze the demands that are placed upon the child and the possible intellectual yield of each demand. In accordance with that outline, the first set of skills will deal with the techniques which help the child to tie language to his familiar perceptual world.

LANGUAGE FOR OBSERVATION AND COMMUNICATION

The tasks in this area are designed to lead the child:

1. To refine and extend his visual skills, along the dimensions of past, present, and future
2. To attend to and retain the more transitory sensory experiences, particularly those in the auditory and tactual sphere.

The major techniques in this area are given below.

SELECTIVE VISUAL ATTENTION

This category refers to problems where the child must carefully scan a complex array with the purpose of selecting a particular object (e.g., a teacher might show a page with many different pictures and ask the child to find a particular object such as "the white cat"). This type of request can foster such varied functions as labeling, categorization, and perceptual discrimination. The multiple gains from such a simple question show the potential available in the most elementary linguistic demands.

But, given the power of language to guide perception, the yield may even be greater. When not bound by the restraints of language, perception is often dominated by physical saliency. One is inevitably drawn to objects with potent perceptual qualities (e.g., the blast of a horn, a whirling disc, etc.) since they are obvious, exciting, and least demanding of concentration. Regardless of how attractive the color or design of an object may be, however, *attention can easily be shifted to other characteristics* (e.g., size, weight, texture, or function) *if one is given specific verbal instructions to do so.* Thus, if language begins to control behavior, attention can gradually shift from exclusive domination by the obvious to awareness of the more subtle.

Poorly functioning children's difficulty with language may be responsible for some of their seeming perceptual deficits. Although the children easily recognize common objects, their behavior frequently becomes disorganized when these same objects are grouped together in a complex array. Because they lack the controls gained through language, they become overwhelmed by the multiplicity of objects. If the children are hyperactive, the complexity leads to impulsivity and wild grabbing; if the children are withdrawn, it leads to a narrow focusing of attention on a few limited objects.

The problem of perceptual complexity has long been recognized. Frequently, the proposed solution is to simplify the perceptual field so that the child will focus more discerningly on the objects remaining (Deutsch, 1966). For a variety of reasons, this approach may be insufficient. Mental order is not a reflection of externally imposed organization, but rather represents a careful, internal process of search and analysis. Therefore, external order may have little to do with helping the child achieve internal (mental) order. In addition, artifically constrained environmental arrangements may encourage the child to develop patterns which can never be used in other than the simplified school setting. While this may lead to certain adaptive patterns in school (e.g., knowing where to hang his coat, knowing where to get his chair, etc.), the child may still be in difficulty when he must handle situations with increased stimulus complexity.

It is here that the seemingly simple request for selective visual attention can be so helpful. When used in the appropriate context, it introduces language as a tool by which the child can compare a number of objects or characteristics in a considered, deliberate manner.

When This Technique Might Be Applicable.   When the perceptual field contains a multiplicity of objects, the child can be led to focus on one of the many objects through verbal instructions. The instructions can vary considerably in the type of verbal knowledge demanded.

Example

Teacher shows child a page in a book with many drawings and says—

1. Verbal label

   "Show me the picture of the pencil."

2. Verbal by function or attribute

   "Show me the picture of the thing we write with."

3. Perceptual match

   Holds up a pencil and says,

"Find me one like this."

4. Perceptual memory

Holds up a pencil, then withdraws it, saying,

"Find me a picture of the thing I showed you."

This list of examples is by no means exhaustive. Even if it were, however, it would not be sufficient. Unless carefully controlled, the techniques may raise more difficulties than they solve. For example, one teacher related a story where she attempted to foster prescientific concepts by demonstrating that celery put in red water gains a red tint. The following day, a child was quite perturbed because he had gone home, put some celery in milk, and found that "it didn't turn red." The error, which was caused by an insufficient number of exemplars, was of little importance in this case because the child's independence and curiosity brought it to the surface. Many other children, however, would never question the experience, even though they had emerged with the same mistaken impression. As a result, they would maintain the error—an error that would never have developed if they had not been exposed to the so-called enriching experience.

In order to deal with this problem, it is necessary to be aware of the potential misuse of the techniques. To this end, suggestions are given not solely for the appropriate uses, but also ways of inappropriate application. Because exact rules cannot as yet be specified, a wide variety of examples is given. Each instance of inappropriate use is concerned either with (1) the context (setting), or (2) the child's level that might contraindicate the use of the technique.

When Selective Visual Attention Might Not Be Applicable.

SETTING

If the objects are in disarray (e.g., a heap), this request should not be made since the field lacks the organization necessary to help the child direct his search.

Example

Teacher refers to a pile of toys in a box and says, "Would you go over to the toy box and see if you can find the doll."

LEVEL OF CHILD

When the child is timid, it is threatening to ask him to search through a large variety of objects, particularly if the search requires him to move far from the teacher.

Example

Child seems frightened and barely speaks; teacher says,
"Look at this picture of a doll. We have a doll in the closet.
You go over to the closet and get the doll."

ATTENTION TO NONVISUAL STIMULI

Although, complex visual analysis should be fostered, the child does not evidence his most serious handicaps in this sphere. Like other primates, humans are so oriented to this sensory modality that they can gain an incredible amount of information from visual stimuli—even in the absence of verbal elaboration. The reliance on vision frequently means that nonvisual cues become redundant information that can easily be ignored. For example, a child who feels pieces of material (e.g., sponge and felt) may be unaware of their different tactual impressions; their clear differentiation is achieved through visual representation alone.

Skills in the nonvisual areas (e.g., hearing) must be developed, for the child to function adequately in many academic tasks (e.g., reading) (Deutsch, 1966; Blank, 1968a; Wepman, 1960). The well-functioning child easily achieves this mastery; possibly through his interest in language, for the latter focuses acute attention on the auditory modality. The child's spontaneous efforts at rhyming and other forms of word play are an example of this process (Weir, 1962). In order to help the poorly functioning child achieve comparable facility in the nonvisual areas, emphasis can be placed on language-based techniques which require the child to identify objects and their attributes on the basis of their non-visual characteristics.

When Applicable. If an object possesses clear nonvisual cues (auditory, tactual, or gustatory) a problem can be created whereby these nonvisual cues become the focus of attention. Because the child will rely on visual information if it is available, competing visual cues must be eliminated.

Example

Teacher moves a zipper up and down, while it is out of the child's sight. She then exposes three objects—a ball, a hammer, and the zipper—and asks "Which one of these made the noise?"

When Not Applicable.

SETTING

The various modalities have differential capacities for discrimination. For example, much finer size discriminations can be made in the visual modality than in the tactual modality. Thus, even when identical objects are involved, it may not be possible to make the same request in one modality as in the other modality.

Example

The teacher, knowing that the child can make a particular visual discrimination, presents the same problem tactually and says, "Close your eyes, I'm going to give you two sticks" (six inches vs. seven inches). "You feel them and tell me which one is longer." (This request would be appropriate if the child was presented with the larger contrast necessary for an adequate tactual discrimination.)

LEVEL OF THE CHILD

If the child has difficulty with expressive verbalization, it is inappropriate to demand a verbal identification. He can, however, be given simple nonvisual tasks requiring receptive verbal skills.

Example

Child barely says more than a single word or two. Because he knows a circle and a square, however, the teacher says, "Now feel this block.

Tell me what shape it is." (It would be preferable to present the child with both blocks, saying "Give me the circle.")

DEVELOPMENT OF MEMORY

In a well-developing cognitive system, the child does not simply analyze the material that is in front of him at the time. He also spontaneously stores the information in memory so that it can be retrieved in relevant situations. When a child has difficulty in this area, it can easily be underestimated because of our present methods of assessment. Thus, most attempts to measure memory present the child with explicit demands for this behavior. Children will often have less difficulty in retaining information when the situation is structured so that this is clearly demanded of them (e.g., "look at these toys; when I take them away, tell me which things you saw"). By contrast, they will frequently fail to retain this information when external requirements are not imposed (Gotkin et al., 1968). In other words, spontaneous retention is often more deficient than the performance to specific demands would indicate. In developing this area, it is useful to question a child about material after it has been withdrawn, without giving any hint that such demands will occur. In this way, the child can begin to realize that he should have stored certain information, even if he had not been forewarned.

When Applicable. When the child has experienced a particular situation, the cues can be (temporarily) removed and questions asked to determine how much information was retained. Because they involve different modalities of input and the different types of information, a distinction is made between actually perceived material (e.g., visual, tactual impressions) and verbally related material.

Example

1. Actually perceived

   Teacher had mixed blue and yellow water to form green. She hides the green liquid from view and asks "What color did the blue and yellow water form when they were mixed?"

2. Verbally communicated

> Teacher is telling a story to the child. After saying "Then the boy's hat fell in the water" she stops and asks "What fell into the water?"

When Not Applicable.

SETTING

Memory questions are inappropriate if the teacher has failed to keep the relevant items available, for she is then unable to guide the child when he answers incorrectly.

Example

> Teacher made chocolate pudding with the child, but neglected to keep any of the original powder mix available. She then asks "How did the pudding look before we put the milk in it?" (Should the child reply "I don't know," the teacher has no material available by which to demonstrate the original appearance.)

LEVEL OF THE CHILD

Hyperactive children tend to blurt out answers without bothering to reflect upon their meaning. Therefore, memory demands, especially demands for other than immediate memory, often have the unfortunate consequence of reinforcing their irrelevant verbalization.

Example

> Child is chattering away in a stream of consciousness about a trip to the supermarket with his mother. The teacher then says, "Tell me what you bought in the store." (It would be useful to capitalize on the child's interest in the trip. This can be done more productively by structuring relevant concrete material [e.g., toys representing food] which will be able to guide the child's language so that it is more geared to reality.)

DIRECTED DIALOGUE

When confronted with cognitive requests demanding extended expressive verbalization, poorly functioning children frequently use gestures or give single word responses (Bereiter and Engelmann, 1966; Hertzig et al., 1969). For example when asked "Why is she buying milk and bread?" the child might reply "eat" since that is the most salient feature in the setting. Because of the adult's empathic response, these gestures and monosyllabic responses are often interpreted to mean that "the child surely has the appropriate thought, but is merely not giving verbal expression to it."

This explanation is *not* accepted when the same behavior occurs as part of the normal development earlier in life. For example, the child in learning to speak commonly uses a single word like "daddy" in a global, undifferentiated manner to refer not only to his father, but also to any situation with men in general (Lewis, 1936). At this stage, the response is not taken as an indication of high-level thinking, but rather as a "vocable . . ." "in which agent, action, and object are intimately fused" (Werner and Kaplan, 1963, p. 116).

When the same monosyllabic response occurs in the older child, our empathy is such as to deny its primitive quality with the reaction "he must mean. . . ." Nevertheless this reaction is not based upon the child's real performance, but upon what we know is the potential available to the well-functioning child. This very human response is ultimately defeating for the poorly functioning child, for it allows the teacher to accept lower level performance as indicative of adequate functioning. A first step in helping the child overcome these difficulties is to have him construct verbal formulations which are relevant descriptions of reality.

When Applicable.

DESCRIPTION OF EVENTS

When the child has a reasonably well-developed set of verbal associations to a particular situation, the teacher may ask a question that requires the child to select among the various associations in accordance with particular demands.

Example

Child is playing with a ball and teacher says, "Now tell me what you're going to do next with the ball."

LANGUAGE TO DIRECT ACTIONS IN OTHERS

Even when a child is capable of accurate verbal descriptions, he is often unaware of his ability in this area. The child can be helped to be made conscious of his skills in this area by switching his role in the teaching situation. Instead of responding to the suggestions of others, he must define a course of action for some-one else to perform. This technique, commonly used in many educational programs, has the obvious motivational advantages of allowing the child to assume the power role.

Example

When the child has executed a series of tasks correctly, the teacher might say, "This time you tell me what to do with the blocks."

IMITATION OF SENTENCES

Occasionally some children are so withdrawn that they are ill at ease with almost any need for verbal expression. Since the above techniques may then be too demanding, it would be useful first to develop expressive verbalization on the level of sheer imitation.

Example

Teacher—"Look what happened to the water. It spilled on the floor. You say that."

When Not Applicable.

SETTING

Demands for directed dialogue should not be made in situa-tions involving sequences of change since an accurate description of a sequence would require an interrelated host of sentences.

Example

Teacher and child have just made a cake and teacher says, "Now tell me all the things we did to make the cake." (This demand is reasonable if it is asked not in the expectation that it will be answered, but rather as an introductory statement to review the sequence of cake preparation.)

LEVEL OF THE CHILD

When the child is extremely withdrawn, he finds it threatening to have to answer any problem requiring verbal elaboration.

Example

Child has been giving muted, monosyllabic responses throughout the lesson; the teacher says, "Now tell me what the doll is doing with the toy dog."

SELF-MONITORING OF VERBAL RESPONSES

Much adult conversation with the young child is a stereotyped exchange that lends itself to pat, seemingly appropriate responses (e.g., "How old are you," "What do you like to do," "Do you like ice cream"). As a result we frequently fail to notice the irrelevancy that marks so much of a child's language. Yet the child's "mastery of the irrelevant comment" can deal a fatal blow to attempts to develop relevant verbal descriptions of the world. For example, when asked "Why do you use chalk on the blackboard?" one poorly functioning four-year-old said "To make you big and strong." (The why in this case was probably associated with questions such as "Why should you drink milk," and "Why should you go to bed early," and it therefore triggered the clichéd response bound to these questions.)

All children are prone to this behavior. The well-functioning child, however, increasingly begins to monitor the verbal responses of both himself and others. Isaacs, in a section called "corrections and self-corrections," cites instances such as a child watching an aquarium and asking, "Why is the snail sinking at the top?" A second child replies, "It couldn't sink at the top. If it sinks, it goes to the bottom." He then goes on to explain that if it stays at the top, "it's floating, not sinking" (p. 154). The child is displaying a precise attention to meaning that shows him to be an astute judge of relevant as opposed to irrelevant verbalization.

Because the poorly functioning child fails to achieve this distinction, he is exposed to a world of confusion. He is aware that the adult world views certain answers as acceptable, while others are somehow unacceptable. However, he lacks the criteria for this verdict. Hence, he is led to feel that arbitrary, incomprehensible judgments are constantly being used to assess his responses. For example, when asked a question such as "Which is more—2 or 3?" a child with a poor grasp of numbers knows that an answer is expected and he will guess. If his guess is wrong, he faces confusion, humiliation, and fear. Inevitably withdrawal from these contacts results, until the classic picture of the withdrawn, disinterested nonlearner emerges.

This problem has been recognized by nursery school educators, for they have long emphasized the importance of not associating shame or humiliation with a wrong response. But given the generally permissive nursery school philosophy, this approach has often meant that a wrong response is met with the same degree of acceptance as a right response (e.g., if the child were asked to select a yellow crayon and he chose green, the teacher might well say, "Oh, I see you want to play with green today—that's fine"). This tactic not only fails to give the child tools by which to cope with his wrong response, but it also stands in danger of encouraging the child to think that any response is as meaningful as any other response. If the child is ultimately to be able to function effectively, he must therefore be given the means by which to test out the appropriateness of a response so that he can discard what is inappropriate.

When Applicable.   This technique can be applied whenever the child has answered a question whose truth or falsity can be demonstrated. *Correct responses must be questioned as readily as incorrect responses, for otherwise the child will interpret the question solely as a signal that he is wrong.*

Example

Teacher—"How many fingers do you have on one hand?"
Child—"Four."

Teacher—"Okay, let's count and see if you're right."
Child—(He counts) "Five."
Teacher—"So were you right before when you said four?"

When Not Applicable.

SETTING

This technique should not be used if the problem presented to the child does not permit direct validation of his verbalization, (e.g., labeling—thus, one animal is called a *cat,* another a *dog;* the labels themselves have no logical relation to the object). Although the teacher may give correct didactic information in these cases, it is not possible to show the child the reason why his response is incorrect.

Example

Teacher—"What is this called" (pointing to ink)?
Child—"Paint."
Teacher—"No, it's ink. So were you right when you said paint?"

LEVEL OF CHILD

When the child is just beginning to gain confidence, it can be threatening to question his wrong responses. He can easily interpret such questioning as a rejection of his effort. It is, however, useful to question his correct responses so as to reinforce the fact that he was correct.

Example

Child is timid and teacher asks "What will cut the paper?" Child says "Pencil." Teacher shows him it will not work and then says, "So were you right when you said the pencil could cut the paper?"
(It is preferable for the teacher to simply state, "No, the pencil didn't work, can you think of anything else that we could use?")

The techniques outlined thus far require the child to use relevant language to describe, analyze, and retain information in the physical reality surrounding him. This development, though essential, is not sufficient. If the child is to have full command of the skills available through verbal labeling, he must grasp the rules underlying this linguistic coding. The following techniques are designed for this purpose.

THE CODING PROCESS

VERBAL CONCEPTS

When the idea of linguistic coding is applied to the preschool age, the issue of concept formation is immediately raised since the latter is so crucially involved in the coding process. A great deal of work has already been developed to define the range of verbal concepts that are appropriate to the preschool child (see Bereiter and Engelmann, 1966), and all teachers use these concepts in their interaction with children. In fact, this area is so familiar and so much in the forefront, that the major difficulty is knowing where to expend one's effort. The list of potential concepts is so long that it seems well nigh impossible to cover all the entries. At the same time there are few criteria by which to assess whether one concept should be taught rather than another.

As a beginning effort in handling this problem, it seems useful to group the concepts into a few major categories, according to the demands they place upon the child. For example, the labeling of simple objects can be considered as a single category, even though the list of instances within the category seems endless. Thus, if the child can label objects like "car," "chair," and "doll," he is likely to be able to master terms for other common objects such as "spoon," "pencil," and "table." He may, however, have difficulty in abstracting the attributes of objects (e.g., "dark," "heavy," or "sharp") since the demands are far more complex. Accordingly, labeling of attributes is considered as a separate category from the labeling of objects. With these ideas in mind, the concepts have been grouped into eight basic categories as follows:

1. Simple labeling of objects or actions (e.g., cup, spoon, etc.)
2. Selection of object through function or attribute (e.g., "get me a thing we write with")

3. Abstractions of physical properties (color, size, form, texture, weight, etc.)
4. Simultaneous consideration of multiple properties (e.g., big and red, round and flat, etc.)
5. Abstraction of nontangible properties (e.g., direction, sequence, number, order, etc.)
6. Establishment of relations (e.g., "show me the part of the candle that has the flame")
7. Conceptual auditory skills (e.g., "a word that rhymes with man")
8. Vocabulary (e.g., "what is a car?")

The demands on a child, however, may vary not only across the different categories of concepts, but also within each concept as well. For example, in discussing a concept such as "handle," the child might be asked a problem demanding receptive language (e.g., "show me the handle") or a question demanding expressive language (e.g., "what is this called"). These different demands must be considered in evaluating the type of situation that causes difficulty for the young child.

These different demands and the various conceptual categories are outlined in Table 3.

When Applicable. The techniques related to concept formation are applied when an idea comes up in the context of a lesson and the child's behavior indicates that he does not possess the concept.

Example

In the course of telling a story, the teacher feels the child is confused by the concept "next to." She says, "The boy stood next to the tree. Show me where he would be if he stood next to the chair?" (If the child fails the question the concept teaching sequence may be initiated.)

When Not Applicable.

SETTING

When there is no cue (whether a perceptual attribute or a function) which can identify the key features of the concept.

TABLE 3
Instances of Conceptual Demands

	Single Object*		Alternative Objects*	
	Positive	*Negative*	*Expressive*	*Receptive*
1.	"Is this a cup?" (Referring to a cup.)	"Is this a cup?" (Referring to a spoon.)	"Is this a cup or a bottle?"	Shows cup and bottle, "Which one is the cup?"
2.	"Is this the thing we use to hold juice?" (Referring to a glass.)	"Is this the thing we use to hold juice?" (Referring to fork.)	"Do we use a fork or a glass to hold juice?"	"Do we use this (fork) or this (glass) to hold juice?"
3.	Is this the block at the bottom?" (Block is at the bottom.)	"Is this block (Pointing to one on top) at the bottom?"	"Is the block at the bottom or is it next to the chair?"	"Is this the block at the bottom (pointing to it) or this (pointing to one on top)?"
4.	"Is this a red, long line?" (It is a red, long line.)	"Is this a long, red line?" (It is a short, blue line.)	"Is this line long and red or is it short and blue?"	"Is this the long, red line or is this the long, red line?"
5.	"Did you touch the red block first?" (He did.)	"Did you touch the red block first?" (He did not.)	"Did you touch the red block first or the blue block first?"	"Did you touch this one first or this one first?"
6.	"Is this (pointing to the wick) the part that will have the flame?"	"Is this (middle) the part that will have the flame?"	"Will the wick or the bottom have the flame?"	"Will this part (wick) or this part (bottom) have the flame?"
7.	"Does 'pan' rhyme with 'man'?"	"Does 'bread' rhyme with 'man'?"	"Which rhymes with man—'bread' or 'pan'?"	
8.	_____			

* Differentiation should be made between the gross contrasts (e.g., "Is this (a cup) a pen?") and the subtle contrasts (e.g., "Is this (a knife) a scissors?"). Gross contrasts are used when a child is poorly functioning and requires a clear differentiation of the correct from the incorrect item. Subtle contrasts, on the other hand, present the child with a complex setting where he must carefully judge the relevance of particular attributes for specific tasks.

Example

Teacher says, "Yes, the lamp operates on electricity. Is there anything else in the room that is electric?" (If the child is wrong, the concept cannot be demonstrated. Instead, the only recourse is appeal to authority, such as the teacher didactically explaining, "Electric means that there are wires inside the wall that carry current.")

LEVEL OF CHILD

The more complex concepts should not be attempted unless the child has shown that he has mastered the simpler levels.

Example

Before ascertaining that child can even cope with abstraction of spatial dimensions (e.g., size, direction, etc.) teacher demands abstractions of temporal dimensions by saying, "Tell me which sound came first—the bell or the whistle?"

It is evident that the list of conceptual demands outlined above has not exhausted the potential conceptual categories. But, more importantly, it has omitted subsidiary skills that can greatly enhance the development of the coding process. Such skills are evident in the well-functioning child's delight in word play. For example, a kindergartener excitedly announced to his teacher his discovery that "You know what, a W is a double U." When a child has this conscious awareness of words, he is beginning to gain mastery of the coding process.

Such mastery is not to be assumed to arise automatically with the acquisition of words. In fact, words can create misapprehensions for the child. For example, the young child's magical thinking frequently leads him to view the word as part of the object. This difficulty is exemplified in the classic anecdotes of children's refusal to accept the fact that things could just as easily be called by different names. Thus the suggestion that a "cat" could be labeled "dog" is sufficient to arouse most children to vehement denial. The label is not perceived as a useful device for talking about things, but as something inextricably linked to the object it represents.

This process is not confined to single words; it also occurs with longer language phrases. For example, young children bind verbal commands (e.g., "go to the door") to the actual execution of the act. Even when they respond appropriately, they have no conscious awareness that the word "go" in "go to the door" is the same word that occurs in the phrase "go shopping." The total phrase is so linked to the behavioral act that the individual words have no meaning independent of the phrase in which they occur.

This phenomenon is not without its advantages. For example it is essential in allowing us to achieve the degree of comfort with language that is necessary for free and easy communication. If we were constantly to separate the word from its referent, verbal interchange would be well nigh impossible. It is probably for this reason that this phenomenon is never fully overcome. For example the same tendencies are evident in the adult—they are simply displayed somewhat less readily. Generally, an unusual situation is required for these misinterpretations to surface. This occurs, for example, when people are traveling overseas and hear a child speaking a "foreign language." Regardless of what their intellect tells them, their feelings reverberate with the message that this must reflect some unusual talent because "our way of speaking" is the "only natural one." Thus, as with so many phenomena in an area as complex as language, opposing skills must be fostered— on the one hand, the word must be bound to its percept; on the other, it must be somewhat independent of its percept.

The demands of school clearly indicate that we expect the child to have achieved some proficiency in this latter sphere by five or six years of age. For instance, the teaching of written symbols (i.e., reading) assumes that the child can establish a connection between the word and its referent, even when the word appears in an unusual guise. Thus, for the child, the written word "CAT" conveys little of the meaning that seems almost to be inherent in the identical word when it is spoken. Yet, it is expected that he will treat the spoken and written words as equivalent. Before the written level is attempted, therefore, the child must achieve the skills that permit him to recognize that spoken words also exist independently of the referents they denote. The techniques described below are designed to achieve this goal.

THE WORD AND ITS REFERENT

When there is total identification of the word with its referent, the word can actually distort the perception of the object. The distortion can work in conflicting directions, depending upon whether single or multiple labeling is involved. Examples are given below.

i Similar items with different labels lose their similarity, for example, a house and a garage are almost never seen as alike once their differentiating labels are acquired. This predisposition creates particular difficulties for the disadvantaged bilingual child who has different labels even for identical items. For example, "dog" at school is called one word, and at home, another word. If the child does not comprehend the idea of coding, he is liable to think that the same object changes its identity according to the context in which it appears. (These difficulties are not caused by multiple labels per se, for bilingualism does not create difficulties in the well-functioning child [Peal and Lambert, 1962]. Language development may even be enhanced when the child can appreciate the fact that different symbols can express the same ideas.)

ii Subtly different items with the same label lose their distinctiveness, for example, so many different kinds of animals are called "dogs" that the child overgeneralizes this label to almost any four-legged furry animal.[1] This overgeneralization is not solely a function of the physical resemblance between the objects, for we know that, depending upon the label, objects that are seen as nearly identical in one culture are seen as quite distinct in

---

[1] By contrast, the child generally fails to see any similarity among grossly different items with the same label. For example, a bright four-year-old child who had been shown how to make the symbol "2" turned to her teacher and said, "How much is two and two?" The teacher held up two fingers on each hand and indicated that the child should count them. The child looked at her in confusion saying, "I don't mean that 'two' (two fingers), I mean this 'two' (the written symbol '2')." Although the child had seen endless examples of two, all the prior instances had, in fact, contained two separate units (two eggs, two pins, two apples). In this new situation, the child was required to recognize that a single unit (the symbol "2") was equivalent to these dual units. Her understandable difficulty indicated that she had not abstracted the meaning of the word "two," so that it could be applied to these very different perceptual experiences. Thus the child appears to have two rules for the use of the "same word." If the same word is applied to fairly similar objects, he overgeneralizes its meaning. On the other hand, if the same word is applied to apparently dissimilar objects, he fails to even attempt to generalize its meaning; he seems to treat the words as though they were homonyms.

another. Thus, Eskimos have nine labels for different types of snow, while in our culture we group (and perceive) all kinds of snow as a single entity (or perhaps as two entities, as typified in the rather imprecise terms of "wet snow" and "dry snow") (see Brown, 1968). It is, of course, not necessary to perceive all the varied types of either snow or any other substance that we may encounter. Nevertheless, this does not negate the fact that the unifying word can serve to blur rather than highlight our perceptions of what are in reality quite varied substances.

The rigid tie which the child establishes between the word and the thing is not simply a sign of unthinking behavior. For example, the child is correct when he treats items with different labels as different. In most cases, differently labeled items are different and therefore this is an economical rule for the child to employ. When it is overgeneralized, however, this rule becomes self-defeating. In order to maximize the gains of coding, the child must develop a set of rules which establish more subtle distinctions between the word and its referent. The child will be helped in this effort if he is led to focus on the fact that objects have characteristics which go beyond the label itself. In this way, the object takes on a set of explicitly formulated distinctions which are richer than those contained in the single label.

ANALYSIS OF REFERENT APART FROM ITS LABEL

When Applicable.   It is useful to require the child to define the essential similarities and differences of various exemplars of a concept with which he is already familiar (e.g., as indicated by the fact that he can easily label the different exemplars).

Example

a. The child has verbally identified a house and a garage. Teacher—"Good, can you think of anything that's the same about a house and a garage?"

b. Child has verbally identified chalk and pen as "things to write with."

Teacher—"Yes, we can write with both of them. Is there anything we can do with the chalk that we cannot do with the pen?"

When Not Applicable.

SETTING

When the differences between the objects being discussed cannot be clearly demonstrated to the child.

Example

Teacher—"In what ways are a fountain pen and a ball point pen different?"

LEVEL OF CHILD

This type of problem may cause the child excessive difficulty if he is not able to discriminate easily among subtle instances (both positive and negative) of the concept in question.

Example

In discussing the concept of a "knife" the child incorrectly identifies a scissors as a knife. With help, he begins to recognize their difference and so the teacher says, "Now can you think of anything that's the same about a scissors and a knife?" (In shifting the focus from differences to similarities, this question will confuse the child since he is barely able to cope with the question of differences by itself.)

ANALYSIS OF LABEL RELATIVE TO ITS REFERENT

The child can be further helped to comprehend the distinction between the word and its referent if he is led to realize that many labels such as compound words are not arbitrary, but rather bear meaningful (logical) associations to their referents. This is particularly true of words that are used in an analogous fashion.

When Applicable. The child can be led to focus on compound words that are relevant to material with which he is familiar.

Relevant words for the preschool child might be shopping-bag, stomach-ache, eye-glasses, lip-stick, button-hole, etc.[2]

Example

Teacher—"If polish on the floor is called floor polish and polish for your nails is called nail polish, what do you think polish for your shoes is called?"

If the child can be led to discern that many parts of common objects are labeled as if they were parts of the body (e.g., wings of a plane, eye of a needle, tongue of a shoe, skin of a fruit, etc.), he will begin to realize that the underlying referent to the word remains stable, even when the referent is embedded in different physical objects.

Example

Teacher—"What is alike about the legs of a desk and the legs of a person?"

When Not Applicable.

SETTING

If the derivation of the word is not based on a clear perceptual similarity, but rather requires a grasp of language at an abstract and/or metaphorical level.

Example

Teacher—"Yes, your head is a very important part of your body. Now, can you imagine what people mean when they say he is the 'head of the house'?"

---

[2] Adults often undergo a similar experience when they suddenly realize that the components of certain words have a meaning in their own right (e.g., sky-scraper, fear-less, rail-road, high-way, white-house, etc.). This realization is much more striking when one hears these expressions translated into a foreign language. Because foreign languages lack the binding tie between the word and the thing, one has the distance necessary to consider the word apart from its referent. Thus, "honeymoon" automatically calls to mind the referent "blissful vacation after the marriage ceremony"—while the term "lune de ceil" brings to mind the disconcerting feeling "Oh, my goodness, it really is 'honey' and 'moon'."

WORDS IN THE ABSENCE OF THEIR REFERENTS

The magic power of words to be an intimate part of an object curiously seems to reside only in words that have been paired with their referents (e.g., saying *truck* in the presence of the relevant toy). Once the situation is such so that the words are removed from their usual context, the child displays the opposite predisposition—he ignores much of the meaning. For example, many children are shocked when they are led to realize that songs are composed of real words. Before this, the child appears to become so enveloped by the richness of the context (i.e., the melody, the group singing, and the musical instruments) that he cannot achieve the psychological distance needed to understand the words associated with the cues. (A similar lack of recognition occurs when one encounters well-known words embedded in a foreign language. For example, upon hearing "nous regardons la tee vee," a common reaction is to ask "What is the tee vee?" The change in accent and the set to perceive foreign words turn the familiar into the unknown).

The child must begin to understand that words can be meaningful, even in the absence of usual concrete objects or actions. This skill is vital if he is to cope with the demands of dialogue since a high percentage of the words cannot be tied to any tangible reality. Phrases like "it might be," "there are," "if we wait," and "after a while" have no concrete referents, yet they are often critical to understanding the content of any verbal message.

When Applicable. In attempting to foster skill in this area, it is useful to have the child engage in tasks which take words out of their usual context. The hope is that the novelty and delay will impel the child to pause over the words and thus realize that the words have meaning, even when they are apart from their immediate concrete referents.

Example

1. Labeling Object After Removed From View—Teacher—"Look at this picture, don't say anything to me now. Just say the name of the picture to yourself, but after I take it away, I want you to tell me its name."

(In this task, the teacher is leading the child to focus on the words that will be demanded, while preventing him from executing the desired behavior. In a sense, he is dealing with a complex command, involving both activation and inhibition of response.)

2. Delay On Simple Commands—Teacher—"I'm going to ask you to do something. But before you do it, I want you first to repeat the words I am going to ask you to do. Say walk to the door and open it." Child does so. Teacher—"Good. Now do what you just said."

3. Mental Operations on Verbal Sequences—Teacher—"Oh, you know Mary had a little lamb. Well, this time we're going to do it differently—don't sing it now; instead I want you to *say* the words that you just sang before."

When Not Applicable.

SETTING

The use of verbal sequences containing unusual words (including words with no clear perceptual referents) will only confuse the child, since such words have little meaning when used out of context.

Example

Teacher—"Now let's say the words of Old King Cole."

LEVEL OF CHILD

When the child, especially in the initial sessions, is timid, the need for novel restructuring of the familiar will cause him anxiety.

Example

The child has been responding with monosyllabic whispers and teacher says, "Remember the song we heard yesterday. I want you to say it for me now. Don't sing it, just say it."

DEVELOPMENT OF SEQUENTIAL ORDERING

The child's customary view of the world is based upon gestalts. For example, he sees a car as a unified whole, even though it is composed of many discrete parts. The impression of unity extends to the auditory world of early language, for the child perceives the sentence as a totality and not as independent words (e.g., "go to the door" is not perceived as four words, but as unified verbal representation of a single behavioral act). Because he is not accustomed to judging items on the basis of isolated properties, the child experiences difficulty in academic tasks that require such analysis. For example, problems involving concepts such as size, color, texture, and shape can only be dealt with if the child abstracts the individual components of what he experiences as total indivisible objects.

Tasks such as these cause little trouble for well-functioning children since their curiousity impels them to ask many spontaneous *why* and *how* questions—questions whose answers require attention to isolated properties. For example, a question such as "How does the bike go forward?" cannot be answered adequately without focusing on isolated components of the bicycle. In this way, the child's higher level problem solving forces him to make use of his verbal concepts. For the poorly functioning child, however, the situation is fraught with potential difficulty. He may learn to cope with the teacher's demands for learning isolated verbal concepts, but, at the same time, view them as curious anomalies to what he considers the normal (perceptual) scheme of things.

To help the child in this sphere, it is useful to present tasks which require him to dissect seemingly unified situations—situations which, in fact, are composed of interdependent units, for example, a sequence of pictures depicting a story. This task helps the child realize that the analysis of a totality into parts holds for a wider world than he thought. If the child grasps this idea, he will begin to use concepts in a way that goes beyond the coding of apparently arbitrary, discrete properties.

When Applicable. When a phenomenon, whether visual, auditory, or verbal, can be divided into units representing a succession of ideas, the child can be requested to perform certain operations to achieve the correct order.

Example

1. Verbal Material
   Teacher asks child to complete the last word of a sentence such as "Every morning I go to. . . ."
2. Pictorial Material
   Teacher shows child a series of pictures (a child is pouring milk into a glass, drinking the milk, and then there is an almost empty glass). She then says to the child, "Put these pictures in the right order so they tell a story."

When Not Applicable.

SETTING

Although the material of each task must be presented perceptually (e.g., through pictures), perceptual cues alone should not be sufficient as a basis for solution. The task should be organized so that it can be completed correctly only if the child independently applies the relevant concepts. Concepts covering long time spans are particularly vulnerable to misuse for they often contain perceptual cues that give away the answers. Such cues enable the child to solve the problem on a simple level while giving the appearance of more complex problem solving.

Example

Teacher shows a series of cards depicting a seed growing into a plant and says, "Put these in the right order." (The child can succeed on the basis of size and yet look as if he has understood the concept of plant metamorphasis.)

LEVEL OF CHILD

A prerequisite for this technique is that a child have extensive expressive verbalization. A child who can only give single word responses in describing a picture will find it difficult to recognize the interrelatedness among a series of pictures.

Example

Teacher—"Now, what is happening in this picture?" The child responds with monosyllables for a series of pictures. Because the words are relevant, the teacher interprets them as meaning that the child understands what is occurring in the pictures and says, "Now, put these together to tell a story."

CATEGORIES OF EXCLUSION

A well-functioning preschool child was observed in the following scene. He touched a thick window pane that had a crack deep inside it. He looked quizzically at the teacher and asked, "Why doesn't it feel rough?" The importance of this query resides not in its expressed content, but in what lies below the surface. Implicit in the question was the unstated observation that the smoothness of the glass was contrary to what he expected and this fact could and should be explained.

It is here that the weaknesses of the poorly functioning child are critical. The child is so bound to the present that he does not spontaneously search for relationships between the present and nonpresent. Yet an idea of "why isn't it rough?" could not be achieved if the child's conceptual categories were limited to abstractions of the immediately perceived. For instance, in the current illustration, the highest level of abstraction "of the present" could only be a statement such as "This glass is smooth." While such a statement is valid, it does not begin to approach the idea that such smoothness is unexpected. This insight can only be attained if the child recognizes that an object can reasonably have properties other than the ones he is experiencing at any moment (e.g., the cup in front of him is red, but it need not be red; it could just as readily be green).

The technique, categories of exclusion, attempts to achieve this awareness by defining a desired concept not by its presence, but by its relationship to a set of stimuli (e.g., "things that are not circles"). Because the specific object labeled defines what should *not* be done, the child must overcome his almost compelling urge to respond only to key words and instead independently determine an appropriate concept within this frame of reference.

When Applicable.

LIMITATION OF CATEGORY

When it is possible, the child should be asked to combine the label for a concept with more subtle linguistic categories such as prepositions and adverbs ("not," "other than," "besides," "something else," etc.).

Example

The teacher shows the child a group of objects and says, "Please get me something that writes, but is *not* a pen." (A pen must be available to provide a conflicting perceptual pull for the child. If it is lacking, no exclusion problem exists since the child will just pick up anything that writes, thereby seeming to be correct even if he has not understood the concept of "not.")

ALTERNATIVE USES

When the child has offered a solution to a problem where alternative paths could be taken, the teacher can acknowledge the child's response, *explicitly state the conditions where his solution would be inadequate,* and then ask what might be done under these restricted circumstances.

Example

A child may be asked how to keep up his overalls when he had lost a button. He suggests sewing it back on. Teacher says, "That's a great idea, but we have no needle and thread here. So what else might we use?" (If the teacher fails to make the statement, "We have no needle and thread," this technique can easily lead to confusion since the young child will not understand why his legitimate suggestion was rejected.)

When Not Applicable.

SETTING

When the problem refers to open-ended instances where particular objects may be inappropriate, a consideration of such instances offers a wide frame of reference in which the child has no cues by which to guide his search.

Example

Child is drawing with a crayon. Teacher says, "When would you *not* use a crayon?"

LEVEL OF CHILD

Demands for exclusion may be threatening to the timid child since he may interpret the request as a sign of having done something incorrectly.

Example

Teacher—"Draw a line."
Child slowly and timidly does so, looking quite uncomfortable in the process.
Teacher—"Good, now draw something that is not a line."

PROBLEM-SOLVING ABILITIES

Once the child has begun to develop his verbally based skills, he is able to move into the area of more complex problem solving, that is, he can be asked to channel this skill to solve complex why and how questions (e.g., if he can say the sentence such as "turn on the light," he can be asked questions such as "What can we do so that the room won't be so dark.") The section that follows considers techniques which can foster problem solving.

Because these are the most complex problems that can be presented, general competence is needed before any of the problem-solving questions can be posed. Therefore the category, Not Applicable—Level of the Child, will be omitted from this section. In general it can be assumed that these questions should not be attempted if the child is timid, unsure of his knowledge, or poor in appropriate, relevant, expressive verbalization.

Problems, and their solutions, are most meaningful when they are self-initiated. Under this condition, the person recognizes that he does not understand a situation fully and therefore he feels propelled to fill in the gap. This quality is evident in the way well-functioning young children plague their parents with questions such as "But if heavy things sink, why do boats stay on top of the water?"

The absence of this spontaneous questioning in the poorly functioning child places a heavy responsibility on the skills of the teacher. The teacher must not only formulate relevant ideas, but she must compensate for the excitement that the child has failed to generate. This is a difficult task, for questions posed by others can rarely elicit the excitement aroused by questions which are initiated by the child himself (see Isaacs, 1930). These limitations mean that there must be careful structuring of the questions that are formulated for the child.

The teacher is fortunately helped in this effort by a number of subtle, but important, features. One such feature is the compulsion most human beings feel to answer a question once it is posed. For example, even when children do not understand the meaning of question words (i.e., they do not distinguish between the terms *what*, *where*, and *when*), they still recognize the intonation of a question and offer some response. This predisposition gives the teacher a beginning tool for motivating the young child's problem-solving behavior. With the asking of a question, the child is almost inevitably drawn into the dialogue situation.

If, however, the child has been drawn into a dialogue that is beyond his grasp, he will quickly retreat. The teacher will then have fostered more resistance than was present at the start. (Like medicine, education has its own iatrogenic problems.) It is here that the use of previously developed concepts can be most useful. Many problem-solving questions can only be answered by the application of appropriate concepts. For example, a question such as "Why can't you pick up the box?" requires the child to focus on concepts such as size or weight. These questions thus allow the child to put to work concepts which he has previously acquired.

Questions that are formulated to capitalize on knowledge already in the child's repertoire enhance his motivation, for he feels mastery at being able to answer correctly. In addition, he may suddenly see the usefulness of concepts which, until then, have existed as isolated bits of information. For example, the fact that a fork has spaces between the tines matters little when it is simply a statement of reality. It comes to matter, however, when it is the key to answering a question such as "Why didn't the fork hold the soup the way the spoon did?" It is at this point that the feeling of discovery becomes important in the child's learning. His ability to apply already acquired information leads him to feel that he has discovered ideas of major significance. (The element of discovery resides mainly in the child's feelings—for the questions are raised by the teacher and not by the child. In other words, it is a form of guided learning—with the aspect of discovery as a byproduct of a highly structured, intriguing problem. For example, in the fork illustration above, the child probably would never have thought of using a fork for soup and therefore the inadequacy of the fork would never have crossed his mind. The peculiar juxtaposition of objects which is contained in the teacher's question, however, may be sufficient to impel the child to further effort. But almost everything depends upon the adequacy with which the questions are formulated. Unless they are organized so as to capture the child's interest, the teaching effort will be fruitless.)

The following techniques have thus far been developed in the area of problem-solving skills.

RATIONALE FOR REALITY

A vast percentage of the young child's functioning involves sensorimotor components in which he is quite proficient. For example, upon seeing a candle, the child acts to blow it out; upon seeing a fork next to some food, the child uses the utensil for eating; upon encountering a ball, the child plays with it; and so on. Such competency at the sensorimotor level is no assurance, however, that the child understands the logic or reason for the associations.

The lack of understanding becomes evident in situations where the rote response is no longer sufficient. For example, one five-year-old boy asked for a paint brush to mix some dye into water. No paint brush was available and therefore the teacher suggested that he use a fork to achieve the mixing. He adamantly refused on the grounds that "a fork couldn't mix colors." When told to "try it anyway," he was amazed to see that this course of action was possible.

The lack of awareness, which was so glaring in this situation, is not detrimental in many tasks. It may even be essential for the rapid execution of well-learned habits (e.g., it might not be possible to drive a car if one were totally conscious of the exact sequence of actions involved). Lack of awareness becomes a major limitation, however, if the aim is to have the child consciously understand his world. In particular, he must be helped to go beyond simply performing appropriate behaviors and begin to recognize the rationale that makes the behaviors appropriate. He must be made aware of the connections that logically relate events (e.g., handles on cups have a useful function, they just don't happen to exist; tires are round for a purpose, they don't just happen to exist, etc.).

In attempting to foster a recognition of the logic of reality, it is useful to question the qualities of the most commonplace material (e.g., clothes, toys, and furniture) since the child knows these well. The questioning of such accepted phenomena may help him realize that even things he has taken for granted can and should be examined when the situation so demands.

RATIONALE FOR OBSERVATIONS, BEHAVIOR, AND EVENTS

When Applicable.   The rationale for observations can be demanded only when it is possible *to relate one feature or attribute in the environment to another.*

Example

"Why is it so bright in this room?" (This can be related to the sunshine, to the shades not being drawn, etc.)

RATIONALE DESPITE IRRELEVANT INFORMATION

When Applicable.   This technique extends the child's recognition of the relevant by requiring him to justify the relevant in the face of irrelevant (distracting) information.

Example

Child has correctly answered that it "wouldn't matter if the juice were poured into a cup instead of a glass." The teacher may then ask, "Why wouldn't it matter?"

When Not Applicable.

SETTING

When the feature associated with the phenomenon is subtle, undemonstrable, or has no features to which the phenomenon can be related.

Example

"Yes, the chicken's wings are very small; why do you think it has such small wings?" (This characteristic is unrelated to any other demonstrably relevant feature.)

LEVEL OF THE CHILD

It is premature to ask this type of question if it has not first been determined that the child recognizes relevant from irrelevant information.

Example

Child has correctly identified that a handerchief is a pink color and the teacher asks, "Why wouldn't it matter if it were white instead of pink?"

MODELS FOR CAUSE-AND-EFFECT REASONING

During the course of his sensorimotor play, the young child engages in activities which cause changes in the arrangement of his world—he empties cups of water, he molds clay into different shapes, and he constructs objects out of blocks. Despite his skill with the material, the poorly functioning child may be unaware of the changes that he is effecting. He is carried along by the joy of manipulation rather than by a need to understand what is occurring.

This lack of awareness does not interfere with the child's handling of situations in which the action and the effect are closely related in time (e.g., reaching for an object leads to acquisition of the object, dropping of an object leads to its falling, etc.). *It causes serious problems, however, in understanding events that are sequenced over time.* It is here that the well-functioning child's possession of temporal concepts becomes so vital to adaptation. For example, in the absence of these concepts children frequently see no connection between:

1. Ice and water, even when they themselves have filled the ice trays and put them in the refrigerator

2. A seed and the plant that emerges, even when they themselves have planted the seed

3. Flour and dough, even when they themselves have mixed the flour with the other ingredients to form dough

In all these cases, the length of time and the change in appearance are so great that the original product and the final product are seen as totally independent objects. The absence of appropriate verbalization does not automatically mean that the child has not grasped the situation. Nonverbal evidence, however, reinforces the hypothesis that the children have not understood what has occurred. For example, if some change is introduced which interferes with the expected sequence, the poorly functioning child shows a lack of excitement that some unusual thing has taken place (Kohlberg, 1968) (e.g., disconnecting the refrigerator so that ice is not formed; putting water in the oven and taking out ice). His reaction suggests that, regardless of his appropriate sensorimotor adaptation, the child has few conscious expectations of the sequence of events.

The ability to deal with these changes is vital in helping the child to develop an adequate grasp of causality. While a true notion of causality is not possible for the preschool child, he can achieve preliminary steps through problems that might best be termed "demands for rational associations"; that is, the child is required to learn to select out which of the many features in the environment are relevant to a particular result and which are irrelevant.

When Applicable.   When situations exist in which a change can be effected either:

1. In the situation or
2. In the child's knowledge of the situation

Example

Teacher—"These dishes are dirty. What could we do to get them clean?"
Teacher—"If I gave you two boxes—one with marbles and one with feathers—what could you do to find out which kind of material was in which box?"

When Not Applicable.

SETTING

Questions which elicit clichéd responses should be avoided since the child can merely mouth the cliché without any true understanding.

Example

Teacher—"Why does the doctor give you medicine?"

IMAGERY

Critical to cause-and-effect reasoning is the ability to image the outcome of an action. Unless the child can do this, he will be forced to resort to inefficient, undirected trial and error every time he has to figure out the end result of any change. Imaging of events is also essential to almost consciously directed memory where one attempts to select out past experiences that will be relevant to a present situation.

Piaget states that rudimentary imaging is present by the end of the sensorimotor period, for example, if presented with a form board, the child may compare the objects to their respective openings without actually completing the action. Such imagery, however, is bound to situations immediately confronting the child. If internal representation is to adequately serve abstract thinking, the child must be able to deal with situations which are removed in both time and space from his immediate experience.

When Applicable. When the child is confronted with material where there are realistically possible courses of events which are not occurring at the moment.

IMAGERY OF CHANGE OF PLACE

Example

"Where would the doll be if it fell from the table?"

IMAGERY OF COUNTERFACTUAL CONDITION

Example

Teacher—"That's right, the beads did make more noise than the cotton when I shook them. Now, if I take the beads out of the box, and shake the box, what will you hear then?"

When Not Applicable.

SETTING

These questions should not be asked if only one of an item is available (i.e., no duplicates are present) and the suggested action will prevent the item from being restored to its original condition.

Example

Teacher has only one whistle and says, "What will happen if we take out the little ball from inside the whistle?" (This question is valid if two whistles are available. If the child fails the question, the teacher can demonstrate the comparison of the whistle with the ball and without the ball. By contrast, the presence of only one whistle means that the child must remember what the whistle sounded like before the change took place. This places both memory and imagery demands on a child who has already failed an imagery question.)

GENERALIZATION

Perceptual skills have long been emphasized as essential for the child's success in subjects such as reading and writing. Yet children can develop sophisticated perceptual abilities and still be bound to a concrete level of thinking. For example, a child in playing with paints may mix colors and be able to name each of the resulting combinations. Nevertheless, when questioned about the phenomenon, he is often at a loss as to how to grapple with the problem. For example, if asked "What do you think will happen if I put blue and yellow together?" he looks bewildered. It is not simply that he is unable to predict the specific answer "green." Generally, he has no expectation that a different color will emerge. He fails because he does not generalize the rules implicit in the actions he regularly performs and observes.

This level of generalization is qualitatively different from simple perceptual generalization where one recognizes an object even when it appears in a variety of forms (e.g., the child recognizes that pencils of different sizes and colors are still all members of the category pencil). By contrast, the level of generalization referred to above is an instance of problem solving which lays the groundwork for inductive and deductive reasoning. The child must reason about his experiences and determine how and where to extend their meaning (e.g., "if blue and yellow combined make a different color, then perhaps the mixture of other colors will also yield different colors"). This type of thinking may be required even in tasks which seem to involve only perceptual skills. For example, in reading, a child may see a word "low" for the first time in a sentence such as "The chair was too low for Goldilocks." His first choice might be to rhyme "low" with words of similar appearance such as "cow" and "now." Since this will not serve in this situation, the child must deduce that an alternative word family, for example, row, crow, and mow, is applicable.

When Applicable. When a variety of disparate instances can be presented which share some significant characteristic or function, the child can be led to formulate the underlying principle.

Example

Teacher has shown that celery placed in different colored liquids absorbs the color of the liquid. She may then ask "What happens if we put celery in different colored water?"

When Not Applicable.

SETTING

This type of request should not be made if the child has been given an insufficient number of examples from which to draw the expected generalization.

Example

Teacher showed that red liquid colored some flour red. She then says, "Look what happened to the flour when I added red to it. Right, it became red. What will happen to the flour if we add any color to it?"

PERCEPTUAL REPRESENTATION

The discussion of language-based skills has omitted another vital set of higher level skills—that of perceptual representation. While this area has not been discussed at all, those trained in working with young children will be quite familiar with the type of problems that can be posed. Therefore, the comments below are not meant at all to be a complete outline; rather they are intended to highlight the major types of demands that can be asked in this area.

Although language is not critical in this area, it plays a central role in communicating to the child exactly what needs to be done. The possible demands in this sphere can be organized as shown below:

1. Verbal Labeling—the child must execute a figure or sequence appropriate to a particular label (e.g., "draw a circle"). This both helps to enlarge relevant vocabulary and requires the child to tie his actions to verbalization.

2. Reproducing a figure by a model—the child must independently reproduce a figure from a model (e.g., he is shown a square and is asked to reproduce it). This requires analysis of the figure into its component parts.

3. Reproducing a figure after it is withdrawn from view—this technique introduces a memory demand which encourages the child either to use imagery and/or verbal cues to retain the essential features of the absent figure (e.g., child is asked to draw the square after it has been withdrawn from view). (In all cases, the figure that is withdrawn is kept available. It can be shown to the child when necessary.)

4. Reproducing a figure which is presented in a different material—in (2) and (3) above, the child's reproduction, if accurate, will be exactly like the model he is shown (e.g., he is shown a sequence of beads and is given a set of identical beads through which to make an exact copy of the original). In the present technique, the material given to the child differs in some way from the model (e.g., the model is a two-dimensional drawing and he is to reproduce it with three-dimensional sticks).

5. Reproducing a figure of a different material after it is withdrawn from view—this demand combines tasks (3) and (4) in that (a) the reproduction will be different from the original model, and (b) the model will not be present when the child executes the problem (e.g., child is shown a drawing of three circles of different colors which is then withdrawn. He is given a group of colored buttons and is asked to produce a pattern like the drawing he saw).

6. Increased demands to prevent rote performance—the young child's desire for repetition has both advantages as well as disadvantages. Thus, while it leads to mastery of the skill, the repeated practice also may instill the tasks as unthinking rote habits.[3] They may then be a useful part of the child's adaptive repertoire, but they no longer serve to foster cognitive growth. One means around this difficulty is to offer tasks that require the child to interrupt well-established sequenced tasks in order that new information be incorporated into the task. This allows the child to utilize already established skills, but in such a way that rote performance is prevented.

These techniques are illustrated in the following tasks:

A. Simple, Geometric Figures

1. By verbal label—with no model present ("draw a circle")
2. Identical model present (e.g., teacher shows a drawing of a circle and asks child to reproduce it)

---

[3] The disadvantages of such ingrained responses exist on both the perceptual and verbal level. For example, some nine- and ten-year-old children were being questioned about their knowledge of maternal behavior and the process of reproduction. They readily offered the information that female mammals such as cats, dogs, and sheep had to give birth before they could produce milk. They substantiated these statements with principles such as "Mammals feed their young with milk." When asked about cows, several said "No, cows don't have to have babies first. Cows just give milk." When asked how this occurred, the general principle was no longer in evidence. Instead, comments were offered such as "They just eat grass and then they get milk." This response was offered even with the children were aware that "cows are mammals." It was relatively easy to get the children to recognize the inaccuracy of their logic. More important than the correction, however, was the fact that this error occurred at all. It appeared that the deeply ingrained association between "cows and milk" which was stressed from early childhood made the concept of a cow inaccessible to logical implications of its being a member of the category mammal.

3. Identical model shown but withdrawn (e.g., teacher removes the circle and asks child to reproduce it)
4. Model present in different form (e.g., teacher shows a three-dimensional ring and asks child to draw it)
5. Model in different form shown but withdrawn (e.g., teacher removes the ring and asks child to draw it)
6. Increased demands to prevent rote performance ("draw a circle in the air with your finger")

B. *Complex Sequences and Puzzles*

1. By verbal label—("make a row of three red dots and two yellow ones")
2. Identical model present—("make a row like this one")
3. Identical model shown but withdrawn
4. Model present in different form—("see this row of buttons; draw a row like it")
5. Model in different form shown but withdrawn
6. Matching sets of sequences (e.g., "which one of these three rows of buttons is exactly like the row over here")

C. *Complex Figures (face, house, letters of the alphabet)*

1. By verbal label ("draw a picture of a face")
2. Identical model present
3. Identical model shown but withdrawn
4. Model in different form present
5. Model in different form shown but withdrawn
6. Problem in puzzle form ("put these parts together to form a face")
7. Increase demands to prevent rote performance ("draw a face upside down")

D. *Schematic Representation (e.g., map drawing)*

1. By verbal label ("draw a house with a door and a person standing inside"—this type of task is given to focus the child on the various size proportions involved)
2. Identical model present (e.g., child can be asked to reproduce

a simple map such as one diagramming the furniture in the room)

3. Identical model shown but withdrawn
4. Model in different form present (e.g., child must place toy figures in accordance with a simple map drawing)
5. Model in different form shown but withdrawn

E. Motor Sequences

1. By verbal label—(an almost nonexistent category since few tasks in this sphere can be defined by verbal labels, e.g., complex sequences such as riding a bicycle have no easily available verbal descriptions; conversely, most long verbal descriptions [e.g., touch your eyes, run to the door, pick up the pencil, etc.] describe relatively simple motor sequences)
2. By identical model present—(another almost nonexistent category since most sequences by definition are temporarily presented, therefore, they cannot remain available for the child to copy them)
3. Identical model shown but withdrawn—(e.g., Teacher—"Do what I do," and she proceeds to go through a complex series of movements such as using the thumb on one hand to touch every finger on her other hand except her index finger—the child must then reproduce the sequence after the teacher has completed it)
4. Model in different form present—(e.g., teacher shows schematic drawing of a person in various postures—the child is asked to perform the action indicated in the pictures)
5. Model in different form shown but withdrawn—(e.g., child must reproduce sequence in [4] above after the pictures are withdrawn from view)

The following list summarizes the major categories that have been presented:

1. Cognitively Directed Perception.
   A. Selective visual attention.
   B. Attention to nonvisual stimuli.
   C. Development of memory.

    D. Directed dialogue.
    E. Validation of child's response.

2. Concepts.

    A. Verbal concepts.
    B. Relation of word to its referent.
    C. Words in the absence of their referents.
    D. Development of sequential ordering.
    E. Categories of exclusion.

3. Problem-Solving Abilities.

    A. Rationale for reality.
    B. Models for cause-and-effect reasoning.
    C. Imagery.
    D. Generalization.

4. Perceptual Representation.

    A. Simple, geometric figures.
    B. Complex sequences and puzzles.
    C. Complex figures.
    D. Schematic representation.
    E. Motor sequences.

chapter 10

The Problem in Its Setting

The present chapter elaborates on the content of the tutorial lessons—a subject which was first raised in Chapter 5. In particular, it attempts to show how the content interweaves with the types of cognitive demands that can be posed. Five major content areas were defined. These include:
1. Construction of material
2. Transformation of material
3. Storytelling
4. Gross motor games
5. Perceptual analysis

Each of these will be discussed separately.

CONSTRUCTION OF MATERIAL

This area is designed to help the child analyze the complexity that is inherent in common material that he usually takes for granted. This is achieved by having him construct familiar objects such as a doll house, a book, a chair, and a piece of clothing. While such lessons are common in preschools, frequently the situation is so constrained that the correct product is inevitable;

it rarely requires thinking and problem solving. For example, in a lesson on making a book, paper, crayons, and a stapler may be handed out, the child draws some pictures, imitates others stapling the papers together, and then brings home a book. The child, however, could do little else in the circumstances since it was the setting, and not his thinking, that led to this result.

The situation changes markedly if it is structured so that the child is led to solve problems at each point in the sequence. For example, when the teacher hands the child the correct material, she has bypassed any need for him to determine what is needed. This lost opportunity can be recouped if no materials are distributed and the child is asked "If we are going to make a book, what will we need?" An incorrect response is highly likely, but it need not be a deterrent since the problem can be simplified through demands such as "Well, look there's a book on the desk. Open it and feel the pages. What do you think they are made of?"

Each type of material that is available in this sphere lends itself to somewhat different concepts (e.g., building a house leads to a focus on parts of houses such as doors, windows, and roofs, while sewing a dress leads to a focus on cloth, needles, thread, etc.). In addition, the same material can be used to teach the simplest of skills or the most complex thinking. In this sense, the teaching is in accord with the principles of sequenced instruction (Gagne, 1965) in that the questions that can be asked of a child in any lesson vary considerably according to his developmental level. For example, a lesson in the area of *construction of material* might involve the child's building a chair. For this purpose, the following material would be needed.

> Bits of wood already cut into shapes that would serve as the seat, the back, and the legs.
> A simple chair or picture of a simple chair to serve as the model to guide the child's construction.
> Material that would clearly be inappropriate for constructing the chair—such as paper, rocks, shoes, ashtray, and so forth.
> Material for combining the parts—this can be glue, hammer and nails, or strong tape.

If the child is poorly functioning, the questions could be confined to simple demands such as:

Problem	*Cognitive Technique*
1. "What is this called" (referring to the picture of a chair)?	Simple labeling—expressive.
2. "What do we do with chairs?"	Concept by function—expressive.
3. "Take the hammer and bang in this nail."	Simple command—receptive.
4. "Find me a picture of a chair on this page" (referring to a page filled with pictures).	Search behavior.
5. "What other things do you see on the page?"	Categories of exclusion—(simple).
6. "See that chair over in the corner of the room; go over and bring it here so we can see how it is built!"	Simple command—receptive.
7. "Show me the legs on the chair."	Simple labeling—receptive.
8. "Get me some more nails now so we can fix the other legs."	Simple command—receptive.
9. "Oh look, the chair is finished. You say that."	Conversational skills—imitation of sentence.
10. "Show me where we should put the chair so we can have it when you come in tomorrow."	Simple labeling—receptive.

By contrast, in a complex lesson dealing with the same materials, the following types of questions may be asked.

1. "How many legs should we put on the chair?"	Concepts—abstract—expressive.
2. "Why shouldn't we put on just two legs?"	Rationale for behavior—(argument against the inappropriate).
3. "Why is a chair made of wood instead of glass?"	Rationale for construction of reality.
4. "Can you think of anything else that we sit on that is not a chair?"	Categories of exclusion.

Problem	*Cognitive Technique*
5. "Do you think we could hammer the screw in like we hammered in the nail?"	Concepts—function—identification of negative instance (subtle contrast).
6. "If we didn't have nails to hold the chair together, what else could we use?"	Categories of exclusion.
7. "What will make a louder sound—when you bang the hammer on the wood or when you bang it on the foam?"	Concept—auditory—identification of positive instance.
8. "If we wanted to make this chair the same color as the chair in the book, what would we have to do?"	Cause-effect reasoning—(problem solving).
9. "What is the same about our legs and the legs of a chair?"	Relation of word to referent.
10. "Close your eyes, I'm going to put two things in your hand—(a nail and a screw)—you give me the nail."	Attention to nonvisual stimuli.

The differences between the two sets of questions are evident. The first set is confined to simple directions, labeling of common objects, imitation of short sentences, and the association between common objects and their functions; the problems are phrased in simple structures such as "what," "where," "pick up," and "bring over." The second set involves complex problem solving, attention to nonvisual modalities, and the analysis of subtle contrasts; the problems are phrased in complex terms requiring the use of "how," "why," "what if," and "why didn't?" These lessons illustrate how material is used mainly to create a concrete, meaningful setting which will engage the child's interest. The use of the identical material will vary completely according to the child's developmental level.

Lessons comparable to the one of the book can be worked out with the following material:

1. Building a doll house.
2. Sewing a dress.
3. Analyzing the construction of writing implements (pens, crayons, chalk, pencils, etc.).
4. Taking apart a plant to discern the roots, leaves, flowers, and so on.
5. Creating a birthday party to analyze the candles.
6. Analyzing electrical appliances such as a flashlight, lamp, and tape recorder (the essential parts needed for their functioning, the effects each achieves, etc.).
7. Analyzing keys and locks.
8. Analyzing the usefulness of a suitcase, shopping bag, and so forth.
9. Analyzing the usefulness of utensils such as knives, forks, and spoons.

TRANSFORMATION OF MATERIAL

Lessons on construction of material focus on objects which permit themselves to be dissected into parts (e.g., taking the lead out of a pencil, building a chair from bits of wood, etc.). Since the component parts do not lose their identity, it remains possible for the child to recognize the original objects, despite the alterations which they have undergone. By contrast, there is a large class of events which involve changes that are so great that the young child no longer recognizes any similarity between the original object and its final product. This area generally concerns materials which undergo changes in state (e.g., flour to dough, fruit to juice, ice to water, etc.). The basic difficulty arises because the changed object bears little physical similarity to its appearance in its initial state. The child's difficulty is further compounded by the fact that many of these changes are irreversible (e.g., the flour cannot be extracted from the dough). Since the original product cannot be restored, the poorly functioning child receives reinforcement for his beliefs that objects dissappear in totally incomprehensible ways. He does not believe that the substance has been conserved because the change in appearance is too great. The initial and end product appear to him as unrelated items.

For example, water obtained from snow is frequently seen as independent of the snow, even when the child has observed the melting of the snow from beginning to end.

Simple verbal labeling can be a handicap rather than an aid in this sphere, for transformable material often has different labels for the products at the various stages of change (ice to water, water to steam, etc.). The use of different labels can easily be justified. The change in the label added to the change in appearance, however, reinforces the child's view that these are independent objects. Depending upon the child's difficulty, this separation can be carried to unexpected lengths. For example, one child who added green dye to water refused to believe that the substance was still "water." She insisted that "before it was water, now it is green." (This confusion is certainly understandable since the child has never before seen green water. However, it is important as a sign of her need for assistance in the area of transformation. It is also important as a sign of her difficulty in grasping the concept of a mass noun. The fact that she could substitute the adjective "green" for the noun "water" suggests that she treated the word "water" as a label for some indefinite properties of the material, and not as a term which subsumed all the properties of the substance.)

Through careful structuring of materials, the child can be led to discern the relationships between the various states of transformed materials. This area is therefore central in helping the child establish logical order in what had been an area of chaos for him. Because food has great attraction for the young child, transformation of material achieved through cooking is an especially useful area (e.g., cooking eggs, making puddings, squeezing juice, changing ice to water, etc.).

A typical lesson might involve the *making of grapefruit juice.* Questions such as the following could be incorporated into the teaching:

Demand	*Type of Cognitive Technique*
1. "I want to cut this fruit, what could we use?"	Concepts—function—expressive.
2. (Teacher hides the fruit) "Do you remember what color the fruit was?"	Memory (for concept).

Demand	*Type of Cognitive Technique*
3. "What parts of the fruit can we eat?"	Concepts—part-whole relation.
4. "What parts of the fruit can't we eat?"	Categories of exclusion.
5. "Why can't we use the skin of this fruit?"	Rationale for behavior (argument against the inappropriate).
6. "Can you think of any fruits skins we can eat?"	Concepts—function—expressive.
7. "Where did the juice come from?"	Concepts—part-whole relations—receptive.
8. "If both of us want to drink some juice, how many cups will we need?"	Concepts—abstract—expressive.
9. "Why isn't one cup enough?"	Rationale for behavior (argument against the inappropriate).
10. "How is this fruit different from this fruit" (grapefruit vs. orange)?	Relation of word to its referent (similarities and differences).

Aside from lessons with food, a particular valuable group of lessons on transformation is available through the mixing of colors. The aim is not to have the child remember specific combinations (blue and yellow → green, etc.), but to realize that the mixing of different components yields different products. A sample lesson based on food coloring dyes might begin by having the child fill a series of jars with water. He will then be asked to add coloring to the water in accordance with the teacher's directions. As in all lessons, there are opportunities to incorporate ideas that go beyond the immediately available material. For example, the first request in the lesson might be to ask the child to "put two drops of blue in the water." Relevant elaboration at this point might include questions such as "What can we use to mix the blue into the water," "Go to the drawer and find a spoon so we can stir the blue into the water," and "What else did you see in the drawer when you got the spoon." Such questions enrich the lessons since they require the child to deal with a broad range of ideas over and above the immediate content. While such questions are always asked in the actual teaching, they are excluded from the outline below. The aim here is to present the key questions that will offer an overview of the main flow of the lesson. Some of the central questions are:

"Put two drops of blue in this jar of water."

"Put two drops of yellow in this jar of water."

"If we put some of the blue in this (third) jar and add some of the yellow to it, what do you think will happen?" [1]

"What happened?"

"Let's try the same thing with paints, and see if it works. Here, let's put some blue paint on the paper and some yellow paint over it."

"What happened?"

"Let's try the same thing, but with different colors. Let us use red and yellow this time. Put red in this jar and yellow in this."

"Do you think it will turn green this time like it did when we mixed the blue and yellow?"

"What happened?"

"Is this different from what happened when we mixed the yellow and blue?"

This type of lesson can be extended in subsequent sessions to help the child grasp the basis for a written system of representation. Although children frequently use written representation (e.g., they recognize a particular product by the design on the box), they are not aware of any logic in the organization of these

---

[1] A part of each liquid is combined in a third jar in order to retain some of the original material in an untransformed state in the original jars. As indicated in the discussion of duplication of exemplars, this is essential to overcome any difficulties the child has in grasping the change.

cues. Generally, from their point of view, there is no logic! Thus, a picture of a duck on the seal of one phonograph record is the mark which permits him to identify the songs on that record while, on another record, the identifying mark is a group of interlinked circles. This same lack of logic continues when the child is asked to begin formal reading. Suddenly, he is confronted with a wide array of symbols that have no physical similarity to the things they are supposed to represent.

Pictures are frequently called in as the bridge to the child's understanding. This might seem to be a logical choice since the pictures are still written representations, they at least bear some physical resemblance to the objects they depict. Unfortunately, this route is often a poor one. Children have so much skill in picture interpretation that the picture is treated almost as identical to the real object. Very young children typically show this misconception, as is evidenced by their attempts to eat the carrots in a picture or to lift out the ball that they see. The same behavior continues, however, in poorly functioning children of three and four years of age. For example, they may predict that a cup in a picture will hold water as readily as a "real cup." When told to execute the action (e.g., "Okay, let's try and fill it"), they are amazed by the failure of the cup to hold the water; they had treated the picture as the object, not as the representation of the object. Because of these difficulties, realistic pictorial representations are not a sufficient bridge to understanding more complex (seemingly arbitrary) written representation.

A much more practical tool is available through schematic representation where (1) some physical similarity is retained between the object and its representation, but (2) the difference between the two is great enough so that one clearly cannot be confused as identical with the other. These conditions are met in drawings which depict the mixing of colors. The following sequence illustrates the way in which this may be done.

At this point the child's drawing looks like this:

"Let's draw what we just did—first we put in two drops of blue; so you draw two blue dots."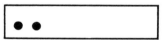

"Then we put two drops of yellow in the other jar; draw that here."

"Now let's make a line over here because I'm going to make a jar on the other side." (The line and the distinctive jar shape are perceptual cues to help the child distinguish between the input and the product of the transformation.)

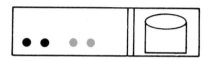

"Okay, what color should you put in the jar when we have mixed blue and yellow together?"

The child can then be led to draw the results of other transformations that he has performed such as yellow-red and blue-red. Ultimately, he can be given a completed set of drawings and asked to carry them out (e.g., the presence of yellow and red dots means that he should mix these two colors). In this way, he is "reading" a set of visual symbols that represent the action he must perform. For example, the chart can "read" as shown below.

These represent the task instructions:

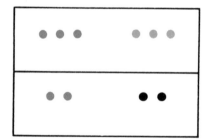

Mix three drops of red and three drops of yellow.

Mix two drops of red and two drops of blue.

If his skill is great enough, the child can be given a series of diagrams which depict both the input and output. One of the diagrams can be incorrect and the child can be asked to determine what is necessary to correct the situation. For example, he can be shown a chart such as the following:

Blue	Red	Purple
Red	Yellow	Orange
Blue	Yellow	Brown

Invariably, after executing the blue-yellow instructions, the young child feels that he has erred in his procedures and he insists on redoing the task. Replication is encouraged in order to show the child that this idea cannot explain the conflict. The teacher can then lead the child to recognize that it is the drawing and not his actions that require reexamination. This experience can be useful in showing the child that the external world (in particular, the world of authority) is not always correct and that he has the power and opportunity to question it when it is incorrect. This awareness can be of great value to the poorly functioning child who often experiences great difficulty in challenging authority.

Other lessons in the area of transformation might include:

1. Comparing a hard-boiled, soft-boiled, and uncooked egg.
2. Cooking pudding.
3. Making chocolate milk.
4. Making juice from oranges, grapefruits, and so forth.
5. Shelling nuts.
6. Changing ice to water and the reverse . . .

STORYTELLING

Another major content area for young children is available through the traditionally used medium of stories. While stories can be highly motivating, the usual means of story presentation is often beyond the capability of the poorly functioning child. As a result, these stories do not achieve the cognitive goals for which they were intended. The difficulties arise, in large measure, because of the sequentially dependent nature of the content. Sequential material is meaningful only if the listener independently supplies the links that will connect the information. The poorly functioning child's difficulty in dealing with implicit meaning makes this linkage most unlikely. For example, a story may have a passage such as—"He tried to climb the tree, but he couldn't. Then he tried to jump the fence, but he couldn't. Then he tried to throw the ball in the basket, but he couldn't. So he was very unhappy and started to cry."

The adult finds the connection between the experience of failure and the subsequent emotion so self-evident that he often cannot believe that the young child sees these as unrelated events. Our experience suggests, however, that this does occur with the result that the children frequently experience the story as a random collection of independent facts. The difficulty can be overcome only if the teacher has a total grasp of the child's comprehension at the moment. This, in turn, can be attained only if she questions him about almost every bit of information that is offered. Thus, books are never read in the traditional way of "telling a story." Instead, the story creates an interesting, unifying background for a series of cognitive demands (e.g., the child may be shown a picture in the story and be asked to interpret the actions depicted, to predict subsequent events, to describe the picture from memory, etc.). Storytelling for other purposes, of course, continues in the classroom.

Prerequisite to all these techniques, however, is the child's ability to tie the word to reality. Even if the story is pure fantasy, the child must be able to envision the image represented by the word (whether it be a "fairy," a "dragon," or a "house of flowers"). The story will be a meaningless series of words if the child does not recognize that the words are supposed to represent objects in the outside world. The principles of demonstrability and verifiability become essential here since difficulties with the verbal realm can be overcome only if the words can be translated into actual experience. Thus, if the child fails to grasp the idea of a story about a bicycle breaking, actual (toy) objects should be present to demonstrate the ideas that the story represents.

The principle of demonstrability may even be greatly expanded here to encompass the technique of dramatic enactment—in other words, bringing the story "to life" for the child by creating it before his eyes. An illustration of storytelling and story dramatization is presented below. While this type of sequence can be used with many stories, "The Three Bears" is used here because it is so widely known. During the course of reading the story, the following types of questions might be asked:

1. The child is shown the picture on the cover and is asked, "What do you think this story is about?"

Concept—label—expressive.

2. "What makes you think that it's a story about animals?"

Rationale for observations.

3. Part of the story is read, followed by "Now Goldilocks is in the house. How do you think she got into the house?"

Cause-effect reasoning—problem-solving strategy.

4. "What did she see when she got in" (showing child the picture)?

Concepts—label—expressive.

5. "She ate from the little bowl—which of these is the little bowl" (showing the child the picture)?

Concepts—abstract—receptive.

6. "Then she lay down on the bed. Why do you think she lay down?"

Rationale for behavior.

7. "How many beds were there in the room?"

Concepts—abstract—expressive.

8. "Do you remember who left   Memory.
   the house before Goldilocks
   came in? Who was it?"

9. "Why did the little bear cry   Rationale for behavior.
   when he looked at the table?"

10. "What do you think Goldi-   Imagery.
    locks said when she saw the
    bears?"

The dramatization of the story in a subsequent lesson may use the following types of questions:

1. "Let's act out the story of   Memory (over previous sessions).
   The Three Bears. What things
   will we need if we are going
   to do that story?"

2. "There are some toy bears on   Selective attention.
   the shelf—go over to it and
   bring them here."

3. "How many bowls do we need   Memory (concepts).
   on the table?"

4. "What thing would Goldi-   Concepts—function—expressive.
   locks need so she could eat
   the food out of the bowl?"

5. "What did she do after she   Memory.
   finished eating?"

6. "Goldilocks fits very nicely on   Concepts—part-whole—identifi-
   that bed. Would the father   cation of negative instance.
   bear be able to sleep on that
   bed?"

7. "Why not?"   Rationale for behavior (argument
                                       against the inappropriate).

8. "When the little bear saw that   Memory.
his food was gone, what did
he do?"

9. "Is Goldilocks a bear?"   Concepts—label—yes-no identification.

10. "What is she?"   Concepts—label—expressive.

It is not necessary to enumerate the precise lessons that can be offered in this sphere since many children's books lend themselves readily to this teaching. The chief criteria for the appropriateness of material in this sphere are:

1. There should be the sequential development of a verifiable theme (thus, stories which on one page tell about a duck, on the following page about a dog, on the next about a cat, etc., are to be discouraged, for they contain almost no relationship from one page to the other).[2]
2. There should be clear, interpretable pictures which demonstrate key points in the story.
3. The story should include characters (both animal and human) who experience emotions with which the child can identify, and who perform actions that are familiar to the child.

Given these criteria as a base, there are almost no limits to the imagination that may be brought to bear in discussing any story. For example, one particularly enticing lesson concerns the dramatization of Humpty Dumpty. First, the child is led to discern that the picture of Humpty Dumpty is a picture of an egg with facial features drawn on it. The lesson then proceeds to make a facsimile Humpty Dumpty with a real egg (e.g., eyes, a nose, and a mouth are drawn on the shell). Then each sentence in the poem is dissected and enacted. For example, the statement "Humpty Dumpty sat on a wall" leads to the construction of a

---

[2] This type of book may be useful in developing skills of perceptual analysis since the child may be led to analyze the content of the pictures, to draw certain objects that are shown, and so forth. Although books are used, such material does not develop an understanding of the verbal content of stories.

wall (from building blocks); then "Humpty Dumpty had a great fall" leads to dropping the egg from the top of the wall. At this point, the statement "and they couldn't put Humpty Dumpty together again" assumes a vividness it never before contained in the simple reading of the poem. The children try everything they know in an effort to restore the egg. (One little boy even patiently attempted to stick the pieces together with tape.) When all these varied and industrious efforts fail, the children conclude, and understand, that "the men couldn't put Humpty together again."

GROSS MOTOR GAMES

Gross motor games (e.g., simplified versions of bowling, soccer, etc.) offer another excellent motivational setting for work with young children, particularly with boys who prefer active motor involvement. These games, with their overriding physical involvement, are usually seen as an area that is apart from "thinking." By bringing them into the cognitive sphere, therefore they have the added advantage of showing the child that almost any activity he performs can be subjected to analysis (when he so desires). Many of the usual nursery school games can be used for this purpose (see Redler and Kephart, 1960). The general format is to have the child start playing the game and then interlace the activity with cognitive demands (e.g., after the child knocks down some "bowling pins" he can be asked to determine how many fell, he can be directed to pick them up in a particular sequence, etc.). Because of the varied number of games that can be played, almost any cognitive technique can legitimately be posed in this sphere.

A sample lesson in this area which can appeal even to the most withdrawn child might proceed in the following way. Large patterns of different shapes and colors (e.g., green triangles, red circles, etc.) can be given to the child. Then he can be asked:

1. "See the spots on the floor   Concepts—simple—receptive.
   (teacher has marked the floor
   at various points) put one of
   these on top of each spot on
   the floor."

2. "Which paper on the floor is the same shape as this one" (referring to a triangle in the book)?

Selective attention.

3. "I want you to walk so that you touch only the papers that are blue."

Concepts—abstract—receptive.

4. "Walk on all the papers that you didn't walk on before."

Categories of exclusion.

5. "This time you tell me which ones to walk on."

Conversational skills (directions to others).

6. "How many forms did you put down on the floor?"

Concepts—abstract—expressive.

7. "If we take all the papers away, how many will we have left?"

Concepts—abstract—expressive.

8. "Can you find me anything else in this room that is the same color as this one?"

Selective attention.

9. "Now try and jump from the green triangle to the blue square."

Concepts—multiple—receptive.

10. "Which ones of the shapes on the floor have points?"

Concepts—abstract—receptive.

As in the transformation lessons, this type of material can be extended to help the child use a written symbol system. For example, in a modified version of bowling (e.g., involving three to four pins) the following ideas might be raised:

"Oh great, you knocked down all the pins that time. I have an idea. Let's keep score so we can remember how many pins each of us knocks down."

Teacher brings over a blackboard and shows the child how to mark down one line for each pin knocked down.

"Now you knocked down three pins. So let's make three marks."

"Okay, I knocked down two pins, so let's make two marks."

"Oh, but there's a problem. How will we know which of these marks are for the ones you knocked down and which are for the ones I knocked down?"

The teacher can then lead the child to use some sort of code to represent the two players' scores. For example, the child's "side" can be represented by the drawing of a small boy and the teacher's "side" by the drawing of an adult.

In addition to these ideas, the lesson is interlaced with physical activity (e.g., "Okay, it's your turn—roll the ball") and other forms of cognitive demands (e.g., "This time roll the ball so that it moves very slowly"). These demands give the variety and motivation necessary to keep the child's interest alive.

PERCEPTUAL ANALYSIS

The final content that will be considered is that of perceptual analysis. This area requires the child to analyze complex perceptual material so that instead of seeing it as indivisible gestalts, he becomes aware that it has component parts. Included in this area are many of the games traditionally associated with preschool education such as Lotto, drawing, and pattern reproduction. By their very nature, these materials do not lend themselves to many problem-solving questions. For example, if a child has completed a puzzle, it is meaningless to ask many questions demanding his rationale for behavior (e.g., "Why did you put this piece here?"). While some problem-solving questions can be used, in the main this area lends itself to detailed development of language-directed preception, concepts, and complex pictorial representation (e.g., constructing a puzzle).

As is indicated in Chapter 9, nonverbal representation includes both complex pictorial representation (e.g., reproducing a sequence of beads of a certain color pattern) and complex motor sequencing (e.g., reproducing a sequence of actions). While verbal cues can be an aid in this type of representation, the dominant form of mediation appears to be that of imagery. For example, one four-year-old child who had both poor receptive and expressive verbalization was able to reproduce sequences of blocks (e.g., a stack of blocks in the order of red, blue, and green) even when the model was withdrawn from view. It is most unlikely that this child used verbal cues (e.g., "red, blue, green") to retain the sequence, since he did not even know the names of colors. It is much more likely that he retained the information in the form of a visual image. This child was typical of the group of children with poor language skills whom we have found do well on pictorial representation. Conversely, we have also found children with a high degree of language skills who do badly in this sphere.[3] These observations tend to confirm Olson's thesis (1970) that the media of language and drawing make different demands and yield different information.

Skill on complex pictorial representation appears to be one of the nonlinguistic areas that is highly relevant to cognitive competence. For example, performance on tests like block design correlate well with school performance. If the child is to have competence in the total cognitive sphere, he must be helped to develop skills in this area as well.

A lesson in this area might revolve about constructing a schematic human figure from Cuisinaire rods. The central demand could include the following:

1. "Let's make a person from these sticks. First I'll make the head here." (The teacher does this to establish some perceptual cues by which the child can guide his subsequent behavior.)

   This will be represented as:

2. "Now what part of the body is under the head?"

---

[3] This lack of correlation is in accordance with the hemispheric differentiation that exists in the brain. Language-based functions are located in the dominant hemisphere while complex spatial analysis is localized in the nondominant hemisphere of the brain (Gazzaniga and Sperry, 1967).

3. "Look here at my shoulders—get a big stick that we can put across for shoulders."

4. "What part of your body comes down from your shoulders?"

5. "What can you do with your arms?"

6. "What part of the body did we leave out."

7. "How many legs do we need?"

8. "What part of your body is at the bottom of your legs?"

9. "Now, let's put the pieces back in the box. First give me the part of the body that is between the head and shoulders."

10. "Now give me the part of the body we use for walking."

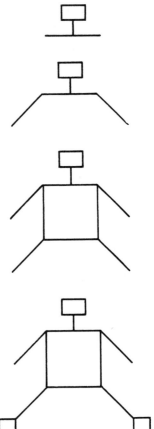

The aim of this type of lesson is not to teach the child how to reproduce a schematic human figure, but rather to present a situation in which the child is systematically led to analyze material that he would have accepted as an indivisible gestalt.

A wide variety of lessons can be presented in the area of perceptual analysis. Some of these are:

1. Reproducing visual sequences (e.g., having the child reproduce patterns such as two blue buttons, one red button, one yellow button)
2. Lotto

3. Playing with paper dolls (e.g., dressing them appropriately according to certain kinds of weather)
4. Training in sound discrimination (e.g., identifying sounds of various objects)
5. Puzzles (e.g., putting together a picture of an automobile which has been cut into several pieces)
6. Drawing patterns (e.g., drawing a striped shirt)
7. Reading a simple diagram (e.g., the child may be asked to put blocks back in a box according to a simple diagram outlining the key colors or shapes)
8. Analyzing the pictures in story books (e.g., look on this page and find me the yellow dog with the pink hat, now the pink dog with the yellow hat, etc.)
9. Single board games (e.g., the child must move a toy figure to the color on the board that is the same color as the card he just selected, etc.)
10. Verbally guided puzzles (e.g., "see these spaces" referring to openings for a triangle, circle, and square—"fill them in with the right forms, but make sure every form is a different color")

Because each of the areas tends to foster different ideas and material, together they may be seen as the precursor of the curriculum given to the school-age child. Thus transformation and construction cover what is frequently termed science for the preschool child; storytelling and perceptual analysis are highly related to the language arts (storytelling deals with the comprehension of verbal material, while perceptual analysis deals with the skills needed for learning a written symbol system). The gross motor games reflect a more open area which can be used for a wide variety of purposes, depending upon the way the lesson is organized (e.g., a lesson focused on scoring a game is useful for understanding written coding, while a lesson focused on shapes and colors can be useful for perceptual analysis).

It is helpful if the lessons are not seen as representing firm categories; any lesson can easily shift across areas. For example, in a lesson on cooking, it might be useful to introduce drawing (e.g., drawing a fried egg) to help the child focus on the different parts of an object. In addition, some lessons do not fit easily into any category. Thus, introductory lessons with timid children frequently are based upon undemanding, nonthreatening situations such as the doll play traditionally associated with play therapy. While it is possible to use aspects of such lessons for cognitive development (e.g., "let's fill the pan with water, where did you put the doll's clothes?" etc.), the lesson does not appear to fit into any of the defined categories. Thus, rather than viewing the categories as rigid areas, they can be seen as flexible frameworks in which to cover almost any idea that can be meaningfully raised with a young child.

chapter 11

Teacher-Child Interaction Codified

Chapter 8 delineated a system wherein the teacher-child interaction could be quantified. The scales for this purpose have only been sketched in outline form thus far. The present chapter is directed toward a fuller explanation of this work.

Included in this section are:

1. The scales designed to assess the teacher's response to the child
2. The child's response to the cognitive demand
3. Illustrations of the way dialogue can be coded with these scales

THE TEACHER'S RESPONSE TO THE CHILD'S RESPONSE

Many of the behaviors cited here are analogous to scales already available; they have, however, been modified so as to be relevant to the young child. For example, one scale for coding teacher behavior recognizes the importance of her quest for feedback about the child's comprehension. For this purpose, it measures the teacher's use of questions such as "do you understand" (Aschner et al., 1965). Requests for feedback are also useful with the preschool child since here too the teacher must determine what the child understands of the lesson. The request for the preschool child, however, can never be phrased in the form "do you understand?" The young child may not even understand that he has failed to grasp essential elements of the teaching. Feedback has to be achieved through more indirect means such as that exemplified in the simplification technique, "Makes child clarify statement or action." Thus, if the child cannot clarify his response the teacher possesses a strong sign that he is having difficulty with the material. All the ratings below are designed specifically with the preschool child in mind.

In general, the coding is self-explanatory. Where doubt may exist, examples have been supplied to guide the reader.

I. TEACHER'S RESPONSE WHEN CHILD IS CORRECT (CORRECT INCLUDES WELL-FORMULATED QUESTIONS FROM THE CHILD REQUESTING COGNITIVE INFORMATION)

A	*B*
1. Praises.	1. Fails to praise a novel or well-formulated idea or question of child (even though idea may be acknowledged.
2. Acknowledges child's response (either explicitly or implicitly) by continuing to make appropriate demands relative to subject being discussed . . .	2. Ignores child's response (or a central part of his response).
3. Uses word or phrase introduced by child in continuing appropriate demands . . .	3. Accepts and/or praises an incomplete response.
4. Elaborates a statement made by child . . .	4. Makes child explain, elaborate, or justify nonexplainable fact ("tell me how you know it's a line").
5. Gives rationale related to the idea or material being dis-	5. Simplifies question before giving child a chance to respond.

cussed (including rationale for
a demand).

6. Uses humor . . .

II. TEACHER'S RESPONSE WHEN CHILD IS INCORRECT

A	*B*
1. Praises effort when effort was obviously involved.	1. Praises effort when no effort was involved.
2. Acknowledges (either implicitly or explicitly) child's incorrect response and perseveres appropriately.	2. Disregards child's incorrect response (e.g., by failure to persevere on problem originally posed).
3. Explains misinterpretation to child (including use of incorrect word used by child).	3. Fails to recognize misinterpretation or error of child (e.g., that child has distorted meaning of original question).
4. Gives rationale for introducing material.	4. Rejects child's suggestion without giving reason why.
	5. Uses incorrect label or incorrect idea introduced by child.
	6. Introduces questions dealing with nonverifiable material.
	7. Condemns child ("that isn't what you learned").

III. TEACHER'S RESPONSE WHEN CHILD FAILS TO RESPOND

A	*B*
1. Perseveres on task by using a simplification technique.	1. Fails to persevere (e.g., supplies answer didactically, drops question).

2. Encourages child ("it's very hard, but maybe you can try").

    2. Interprets inner feelings of child ("I know you feel afraid, but don't worry, I'm here to help you").

3. Gives rationale for material.

    3. Introduces demands or questions dealing with nonverifiable material.

    4. Condemns child or lectures him with implied threat ("when you grow up, you'll need this in school and then what will you do?").

    5. Praises effort.

IV. TEACHER'S RESPONSE WHEN CHILD'S RESPONSE IS UN-CLEAR, IRRELEVANT, AMBIGUOUS, OR NOT TOTALLY SUITABLE

A	*B*
1. Praises child's effort when effort was involved	1. Praises effort when no effort was involved (including clear acceptance of the irrelevancy as acceptable behavior).
2. Continues to make appropriate demands relative to subject being discussed (including introduction of verifiable material; adapting child's words to lesson).	2. Responds to the irrelevancy by abandoning original line of questioning to follow the irrelevancy.
3. Explains misinterpretation to child.	3. Fails to understand child's misinterpretation.
4. Gives rationale related to idea or material being discussed.	4. Rejects child's suggestion without giving reason why.
5. Indicates to child that response is inappropriate.	5. Makes child explain or elaborate a nonexplainable fact.

6. Introduces questions dealing with nonverifiable material.

7. Accepts without further demand evasive or ambiguous statement by child.

8. Fails to give rationale—or gives poor rationale to child.

V. TEACHER'S RESPONSE WHEN CHILD REQUESTS HELP (NOT INCLUDING WELL-FORMULATED QUESTIONS REQUESTING COGNITIVE INFORMATION)

A	*B*
1. Acknowledges child's response.	1. Ignores child's response.
2. Uses word used by child—(thereby also implicitly acknowledging his response).	2. Condemns child ("I thought you could do that").
3. Encourages child.	3. Introduces questions dealing with nonverifiable material.
	4. Gives inadequate explanation.

VI. TEACHER'S RESPONSE WHEN CHILD IS CONFRONTED WITH NEW INFORMATION, NEW SITUATION, OR NEW DIRECTIONS IN LESSON (THIS CATEGORY EXCLUDES RESPONSES OR COMMENTS THAT CHILD MAKES WHEN NO REQUEST HAS BEEN MADE OF HIM—THE LATTER ARE SCORED UNDER OTHER CATEGORIES [1])

A	B
1. Gives rationale related to idea or material being discussed . . .	1. States obvious about a unique occurrence or incomplete explanation rather than explain-

---

[1] For example, if child has made a spontaneous irrelevant comment, the teacher's reaction would be scored under teacher's response when child is irrelevant.

ing the reason for the unusual circumstances ("yes, that's a bicycle with wings").

2. Gives child choice of action (e.g., "which game would you like to play?") . . .

2. Gives rationale to child without sufficient explanation (including sole reliance on didactic teaching when such teaching need not be the only source of child's learning).

3. Makes appropriate demands relative to subject being discussed . . .

3. Introduces questions dealing with nonverifiable material.

4. Uses humor . . .

4. Allows child free, undirected reign to proceed with the material.

5. Structures situation so that child must use information that he has been offered . . .

THE CHILD'S RESPONSE

As described earlier, in line with the cognitive emphasis of the tutorial program, the child's behavior is scored on only a single category—the correctness of his behavior in meeting the problem that was set before him.

1. Correct.

    a . Verbal—only a verbal response is possible—but it is totally adequate.
    b . Verbal—when verbal is not essential.
    c . Nonverbal.
    d . Partially completes task.
    e . Answers relevantly—but not entirely correctly.
    f . Spontaneous observation of significant properties.
    g . Indicates phenomenon or observation contrary to expectation.
    h . Elaborates spontaneously and relevantly.

    i . Indicates he knows how to seek information from relevant sources.

    j . Asks a question indicative of thought or requesting information.

    k . Behavior indicates that he anticipates question or dialogue that is forthcoming.

    l . Extension of task—not against instructions, but also not limiting self to instructions.

    m. Indicates desire to achieve task independently.

    n . Changes an incorrect response because it has been questioned.

2. Incorrect.

    a . Perseverates a response he gave before.

    b . Rotely repeats teacher's statement or action.

    c . Speaks incoherently.

    d . Completes task omitting some central element of the task demanded.

    e . Changes a correct response because it has been questioned.

    f . Makes errors based upon position or random alternation.

    g . Fails to grasp consensually validated meaning of language.

    h . Includes irrelevant details in the response.

    i . Gives incorrect response indicative of thinking.

    j . Executes a response contrary to instruction (generally includes situations where delay or inhibition is required).

    k . No discernible error pattern—but response is incorrect (generally includes a broad range of undefined responses that are produced simply because a response has been requested) . . .

3. No Response.

    a . Silence.

    b . "Don't know" or shakes head.

    c . Shrugs.

    d . Indicates—or corroborates—a lack of comprehension.

    e . Negativistic.

    f . Acknowledges that teacher has made a statement (by nodding).

    g . Acquiesces to teacher's idea, statement, or question.

    h . "Don't know" accompanied by well-formulated explanation or statement . . .

4. Irrelevant.

   a . Response is tangentially relevant—but it is really a rote association to one part of the situation.
   b . Short, irrelevant verbalization unrelated to task.
   c . Lengthy, irrelevant verbalization unrelated to task.
   d . Uses question for evasion.
   e . Directs the teacher.
   f . Distracted to some other feature in situation . . .

5. Asks for guidance.

6. Questionable.

   a . Ambiguous answer.
   b . Nonverifiable patter.

7. Behavior when No Requests Have Been Made. (In general, this
category is similar to the groupings above—but it reflects the child's
spontaneous behavior when no request has been made of him)

   a . Relevant comments or behavior about the material.
   b . Relevant questions about material.
   c . Requests information.
   d . Irrelevant comments.
   e . Irrelevant questions.
   f . Incorrect comments.
   g . Questionable . . .

These scales, plus the coding of the cognitive and simplification
techniques, are used below to analyze the sample interviews with
Julie that were presented in Chapter 3.

TABLE 3

Dialogue	Child's Response	Teacher's Behavior		
		Cognitive Process Demanded[2]	Simpli- fication Used	Response to Child's Response
Session 1.				
Teacher—Do you re- member what we did when you were here yesterday?		Memory		Not applicable (first question)
Julie— Yes	6a			
Teacher—What did we do?		Memory	9	IV A2
Julie— I don't know.	3b			
Teacher—Let's see if I can help you.				III A3
Is there anything on this table that we worked with the last time (a limited variety of materials is present)?		Memory	7a	III A1
Julie— (Points to black- board.)	1c			
Teacher—That's just point- ing. Tell me what we did.		Directed dialogue		I A5 I A2
Julie— We did—we did a square.	1a			

[2] The classification is in broad categories. As indicated in Chapter 9, much finer differen- tiations are possible and they should be made if one wishes to define more precisely the areas in which the child experiences difficulty. These finer differentiations were used in the analysis of the dialogues in Chapter 8 where it was stated that the teacher trained in the tutorial program used thirteen types of problems while the other teacher used only five types.

[3] See Chapter 4 for listing of the Simplification Techniques.

	Dialogue	Child's Response	Teacher's Behavior		
			Cognitive Process Demanded	Simplification Used	Response to Child's Response
Teacher—Right. What did we do with the square?			Memory		I A1 I A2
Julie— (Hesitates.)		3a			
Teacher—Think about it for a minute.			Memory		III A1
Julie— We took it off (child refers to erasing).		1a			
Teacher—Good. Now, what did we use to take it off?			Memory		I A1
Julie— I don't know.		3b			
Teacher—(Brings blackboard forward) All right—what would you do if you had a square on here and you wanted to get rid of it? How could you get it off?			Cause-effect	6	III A1
Julie— Maybe we could use paper.		1a			
Teacher—Why could we use paper? What would it do?			Rationale Cause-effect	13	I A3 I B5
Julie— It could take it off. It could rub it off.		1a			

Dialogue	Child's Response	Teacher's Behavior		
		Cognitive Process Demanded	Simpli- fication Used	Response to Child's Response
Teacher—Fine. Now, remember what we did? We didn't use paper to take off the square. Do you remember what it was we *did* use?		Memory		I A1 I A5 I A2
Julie— A sponge.	1a			
Teacher—Very good. Would you get the sponge for me and wet it? Get a paper towel and wet that too. Wet them both.		Words in absence of referents		I A1 I A2
Julie— (Goes to sink in room and reaches not for the re- quested items, but for the soap.)	4f			
Teacher—(Follows child over to sink) Do we need the soap?		Concepts (Identi- fication of nega- tive instances)	13	IV A5
Julie— No (takes sponge and pieces of paper toweling and starts to return to seat).	1a 1d			
Teacher—Do you re- member what I asked you to do with the paper and sponge?		Memory	13	I A2

| | | Teacher's Behavior | | |
Dialogue	Child's Response	Cognitive Process Demanded	Simpli- fication Used	Response to Child's Response
Julie— Uh huh. Wet them.	1a			
*Teacher—*Fine. Then, do that.		Concepts (receptive)		I A1 I A2
Julie— (Wets toweling and sponge) They are full of water.	1c 1f			
*Teacher—*Do you need all that water?		Concepts (identifi- cation of negative)		I B1 I A3
Julie— (Shakes head to indicate "No.")	1c			
*Teacher—*What could you do to get rid of the water that you don't need?		Cause- effect		I A2
Julie— (Squeezes water from both sponge and paper.)	1c			
*Teacher—*What did you do?		Directed dialogue		I A2
Julie— The water comes out.	1d			
*Teacher—*That's fine, Julie. You really didn't need all that water (they return to the table).				I B3 I A5
*Teacher—*I'd like you to draw something for me on the blackboard.		Perceptual represen- tation (unde- fined)		VI A3

		Teacher's Behavior		
Dialogue	*Child's Response*	*Cognitive Process Demanded*	*Simpli-fication Used*	*Response to Child's Response*
Julie— What color?	5			
Teacher—What color would you like to use?		Concepts (attribute)		V A1
Julie— Green (and selects green crayon).	1a 1c			
Teacher—Green is fine. Draw some green lines for me.		Perceptual represen- tation (simple)		I A3 I A2
Julie— I'll make some big ones (she proceeds to draw).	1b			
Teacher—Okay, we can work with big ones. Oh! Those are very big lines. What will happen if you wipe the sponge on those lines?		Imagery		I A3 I A3 I A2
Julie— I don't know.	3b			
Teacher—Think about it Julie. If you put this sponge over your lines and wipe them, what will happen?		Imagery	3	III A1
Julie— (Moves sponge over drawing.)	2j			
Teacher—What's happen-ing to the lines Julie?		Directed dialogue	13	II A2

Teacher's Behavior

Dialogue	Child's Response	Cognitive Process Demanded	Simplification Used	Response to Child's Response
Julie— (With surprise) They're not there anymore.	1a			
Teacher—(Holds sponge down to prevent child from lifting it) If I lift up the sponge, what color is going to be on the sponge?		Imagery		I A2
Julie— White.	4a			
*Teacher—*Why white?		Rationale	9	IV A2
Julie— Green.	1n			
*Teacher—*Tell me why you said green? Why do you think it will be green?		Rationale		I A3
Julie— 'Cause I wipe it off.	1a			
*Teacher—*What did you wipe off?		Concepts (attribute)		I A2
Julie— The green color.	1a			
*Teacher—*Let's see if you're right. (Lifts sponge) Green! You're right. Very good.				I A5
				I A1

| | | Teacher's Behavior | | |
Dialogue	Child's Response	Cognitive Process Demanded	Simpli- fication Used	Response to Child's Response

Session 2

As Julie entered, she looked at the flowers. The teacher noticed this and said:

Dialogue	Child's Response	Cognitive Process Demanded	Simplification Used	Response to Child's Response
Teacher—Have you seen the flowers?		Concepts (Identifi- cation of positive instance)		VI A3
Julie— I saw a beautiful flower outside.	4a			
Teacher—A beautiful flower? What color was it?		Concepts	Fails to simplify	IV B2 IV B6
Julie— I don't know. It is a beautiful flower.	3h	Concepts (Identifi- cation of negative instance)	Fails to simplify	III B3
Teacher—Did you put it in the ground?				
Julie— I picked it up.	4a			
Teacher—You picked it up? What kind was it?		Concepts		IV B2 IV B6
Julie— I don't know.	3b			
Teacher—Was it little and yellow? Maybe it was a dandelion? Did you plant the flower? Was it a seed and now it's a flower?		Concepts Concepts Concepts Concepts (All identi- fication of negative instance)	Fails to simplify	III B3 III B3 III B3 III B3

| | | Teacher's Behavior | | |
Dialogue	*Child's Response*	*Cognitive Process Demanded*	*Simpli- fication Used*	*Response to Child's Response*
Julie— (Nods.)	3g			
Teacher—Why don't you draw a picture of the flower and then we can see what color it is?		Perceptual representation (complex figures)	6	III B3
Julie— I'd like to do any color flower.	4a			
Teacher—I'd love to have a drawing of it.		No request	Fails to simplify	IV B1
Julie— I'm gonna make a beautiful flower (child proceeds to draw).	7a			
Teacher—Good.				VI B4
Julie— What's this (the child is referring to the design from the table which comes through her drawing)?	7b			
Teacher—That's the table- cloth coming up; the pattern.				VI B2

After an interchange about flowers conducted while the child was drawing, the teacher said:

Teacher—Do you know how many flowers you have there now?		Concepts		VI A3

	Dialogue	Child's Response	Teacher's Behavior		
			Cognitive Process Demanded	*Simpli- fication Used*	*Response to Child's Response*
Julie—	Three. I'm five years old.	1a 4a			
Teacher—	You're five years old? Maybe you could make flowers for how old you are! Do you know how many more you would need?		Concepts		IV B2 IV A4 IV A2
Julie—	Five.	2a			
Teacher—	Five *altogether.* And how many do you have there?		Concepts	8a 6	II A3 II A2
Julie—	I'll make one more. What kind of brown is this? It's a tree.	4a 4d 4b			
Teacher—	Oh, that's pretty Julie. That's very, very nice.			Fails to simplify	IV B1
Julie—	I bet it's time to wake up now.	7d			
Teacher—	What time do you get up?		Concepts		IV B2
Julie—	I get up five o'clock.	4a			
Teacher—	In the morning? (Incredulously) Do you really		Concepts (Identifi- cation of		IV B3

| | | | Teacher's Behavior | | |
Dialogue	Child's Response	Cognitive Process Demanded	Simplification Used	Response to Child's Response
wake up at five o'clock in the morning?		negative instance)		
Julie— I do.	6b			
*Teacher—*And what time do you come to school?		Concepts		
Julie— I don't know what time—nighttime?	3b 5			
*Teacher—*No.	6a			V B4
Julie— I think so. I got a clock. I'm tired.	4a 4a			

IN CONCLUSION

Having discussed a number of different issues in the exposition of the tutorial program, it now seems fruitful to step back and gain an overview of the work. In common with any teaching model, the tutorial program encompasses a variety of theoretical and practical issues, including:

1. The child's entering characteristics
2. The subject matter
3. The type of instruction
4. The amount of instruction and its place in the total curriculum
5. The objectives of instruction (De Cecco, 1968)

Although these areas are interrelated, for purposes of explication they must be considered separately—and that is the manner in which the tutorial program has been presented. Thus, Chapter 1 is basically concerned with the children's initial level of function-

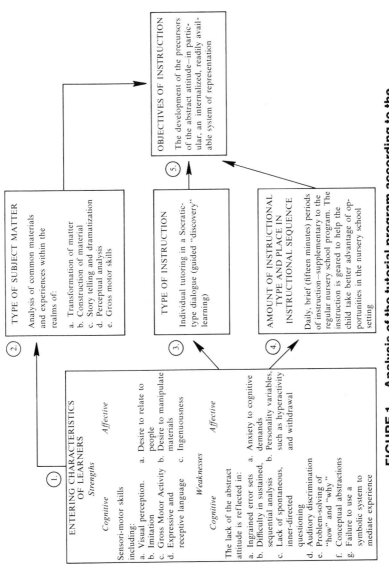

FIGURE 1. Analysis of the tutorial program according to the parameters of teaching models.

① ENTERING CHARACTERISTICS OF LEARNERS

Strengths

Cognitive

Sensori-motor skills including:
a. Visual perception.
b. Imitation
c. Gross Motor Activity
d. Expressive and receptive language

Affective

a. Desire to relate to people
b. Desire to manipulate materials
c. Ingenuousness

Weaknesses

Cognitive

The lack of the abstract attitude is reflected in:
a. Ingrained error sets
b. Difficulty in sustained, sequential analysis
c. Lack of spontaneous, inner-directed questioning
d. Auditory discrimination
e. Problem-solving of "how" and "why"
f. Conceptual abstractions
g. Failure to use a symbolic system to mediate experience

Affective

a. Anxiety to cognitive demands
b. Personality variables, such as hyperactivity and withdrawal

② TYPE OF SUBJECT MATTER

Analysis of common materials and experiences within the realms of:

a. Transformation of matter
b. Construction of material
c. Story telling and dramatization
d. Perceptual analysis
e. Gross motor skills

③ TYPE OF INSTRUCTION

Individual tutoring in a Socratic-type dialogue (guided "discovery" learning)

④ AMOUNT OF INSTRUCTIONAL TYPE AND PLACE IN INSTRUCTIONAL SEQUENCE

Daily, brief (fifteen minutes) periods of instruction—supplementary to the regular nursery school program. The instruction is geared to help the child take better advantage of opportunities in the nursery school setting

⑤ OBJECTIVES OF INSTRUCTION

The development of the precursors of the abstract attitude—in particular, an internalized, readily available system of representation

301

ing, while Chapter 2 is largely concerned with the subject matter. At this juncture, however, it seems valuable to consider the inter-relationships among these factors. Accordingly, the program is represented diagrammatically within a framework outlined by Cronbach (1966) and elaborated by Shulman (1970).

While a number of models could be used, this particular one has been selected because it so aptly mirrors the sequence with which the tutorial program developed. In many teaching programs, the basic goal is to transmit the body of knowledge accumulated by the society. This goal places the logical starting point of program development at the content to be taught (e.g., the particular aspects of mathematics, English, science, etc., that one wishes the student to acquire). The entering characteristics of the learner arise only secondarily insofar as they affect the way in which the content will be taught (e.g., slow learners may have to be taught in a more detailed, specific fashion than would fast learners).

The tutorial program is guided by a different set of consid-erations which leads to a reversal of priorities. Primary attention is directed toward the student's entering characteristics, for they are the chief reason for establishing the program. The poorly functioning child requires attention precisely because of his wide-spread academic failure. The goal is not to teach traditional subject matter, but rather to alter the child's mode of intellectual function-ing so that general learning is facilitated. Content arises only insofar as it may foster changes in overall level of functioning.

The first step, therefore, is devoted toward defining the factors that underlay children's scholastic difficulties. On the basis of their almost uniformly poor test performance, it is hypothesized that the children have failed to develop the "abstract attitude"—the mental attitude or set that impels well-functioning young children to think about the why and how of their world. The weakness in the abstract attitude has significant affective, as well as cognitive, consequences. Because of their thinking difficulties, the children are led to feel vulnerable in cognitively demanding situations. As a result, they attempt to avoid such demands. The irony of this situation is that poorly functioning children gear their activities to avoid those situations that compensatory education is precisely designed to offer.

Fortunately, though, the children have many strengths. These have not been stressed in the book, largely because the focus has consistently been on the areas that needed help. The children's strengths, however, have been implicit (e.g., as in the dialogues presented) and the program would have been impossible without them. These behaviors include well-established perceptual-motor skills, many skills of language, and a wide variety of social skills vital for meaningful teacher-child interaction. These skills serve as vital building blocks in the development of other abilities. In themselves, however, they are not sufficient to enable the child to take advantage of most programs of compensatory education.

Given this picture of the children's entering characteristics, the method and the aims of the instruction follow naturally. The aims of the teaching are to develop the precursors of abstract thinking so that the child will have an internalized, readily available symbolic system. It was hypothesized that this can best be obtained through altering the structure of the teaching situation. The traditional group-based instruction must be supplemented, since its built-in constraints prevent the teacher from reaching those children who most need help.

These considerations are reflected in the middle set of boxes in Figure 1. First, the tutorial setting is selected since it is the situation in which (1) the abstract attitude is most readily acquired and (2) the teacher has the opportunity needed to diagnose and treat the child's difficulties. Second, the medium of instruction is a Socratic-type dialogue since it affords the sustained, interchange needed to pursue an idea. The child then sees events not in isolated fragments, but as part of a meaningful framework. This dialogue also permits the teacher to work with the child to overcome the wrong responses that are the inevitable accompaniment of learning. Third, the instruction is given daily, but involves brief periods of time (i.e., fifteen to twenty minutes). Frequent lessons give the child the opportunity for repeated practice of cognitive skills; the short duration of the lesson allows the child to work without being fatigued or bored.

The subject matter is embedded in the material of common, everyday life. In this respect, the tutorial program differs least from more traditional preschool programs. There is little reason to change this aspect of the curriculum, for such materials are the natural medium of instruction for the young child. In addition, available materials are well designed and attractive. They are, however, used differently from the way they are generally used in preschool instruction. Their purpose is, first, to create a motivational context which will permit the various cognitive problems to be raised in a meaningful way and, second, to lead the child to examine the commonplace materials of his world so that he appreciates their hitherto hidden richness and complexity.

Within this setting questions are posed to the child—not solely in the expectation that they will be answered; rather, they also function as widespread scanning systems which will expose his areas of difficulty. Difficulty here does not refer to the absence of particular information, but to the presence of systematic error patterns which interfere with the child's ability to learn. Once an error is identified, the problem is systematically reduced until the child can overcome the factors that are interfering with his functioning.

The tutorial system represents only one possible teaching model and, as such, it can be challenged at each point—this includes the hypothesized deficit, the suggested treatment, and the effectiveness of the teaching. Each point of dissent with the model will critically influence the method of intervention chosen. For example, there could be agreement as to the nature of the deficit, but disagreement as to the essential role of the tutorial dialogue. Such an interpretation would permit the use of group-based instruction as a reasonable means of fostering the desired skills.

These issues can only be settled by long-term research which will determine the validity of the tutorial program relative to other methods of instruction. At this stage of our knowledge, it would be foolhardy to state that the tutorial program is the only solution for the poorly functioning child. A variety of programs must be devised to systematically test out hypotheses in each of the major spheres of teaching models (i.e., the level of the child, the method of instruction, the performance assessment, etc.).

Although these problems are serious, perhaps the greatest doubts about the program do not concern its validity, but its practicality. These doubts revolve around the issues of economics and training. Both tend to start with the statements such as "That's fine for an experimental research program. . . ." At this point, the statements diverge—the argument about economics proceeds:

"But how on earth can we afford tutorial education for all the children who need it?"

It is evident that the program is costly, but the expense is far less than is conjured up by the extravagance implicit in the word tutorial. The daily program is confined to very limited time periods (i.e., fifteen minutes) and therefore it is possible for a teacher to see seven children in a half-day program.[1] Also, tutorial education need not be without end. For example, teaching in small groups may prove sufficient even after a few months when the children begin to improve in their functioning. Any possible reductions must be highly speculative and could only be assessed in the actual running of the program over a long period of time. Implementation, however, is not the central economic issue. As education has developed, we have come to recognize the vital role that can be played by highly trained specialists in areas such as speech, reading, music, and art. If the formulation of cognitive difficulties presented here is correct, then the tutorial teacher can be accepted in much the same light as other specialists.

Even when the economics are not seen as insurmountable, the issue of training generally is. Here we come to the second major doubt about the tutorial program. The teaching is based upon a carefully controlled situation in which the teacher must be finely attuned to each child's functioning and totally aware of how material must be structured to foster his performance. With such stringent demands placed upon the teacher, observers are led to comment "If the teacher has to watch her every word and gesture, the situation is hopeless. We will never have teachers with this much skill." The situation is extremely complex—and it will do no good to deny its complexity. The task is difficult, but it is not impossible. With careful supervision and sensitive personnel selection, teachers can be trained to achieve a high level of proficiency in these techniques. The issue seems to be one of whether we are willing to make the commitment to the major innovations that such a program necessitates.

---

[1] Although the teacher could theoretically work with fourteen children a day, the demanding nature of the tutorial interchange makes this a rather unfeasable goal. If a full-time teacher were employed, it would be preferable to limit her tutorial teaching to half of her time and then have her perform other teaching duties in the remaining half of her time.

The necessity for innovation has clearly been acknowledged by all concerned with quality education. Frequently, though, the basic situation has not been altered. This is not to deny that changes are made—but they are often not central to the problem. They involve such things as teacher-pupil ratio, more equipment, longer hours, and better classrooms. Such changes, although costly and well meaning, may be totally irrelevant to the child, for they do nothing to ensure that the new organization will actually deal with the difficulties he experiences.

In many ways, education is in an analogous position to the apocryphal man who is out searching for a lost item under a street lamp. A passerby stops and asks, "What are you looking for?" The man replies, "My wallet." The passerby then continues, "Where did you lose it?" The man replies, "On the other street." Flustered, the passerby asks, "Then why are you looking here?" The man assuredly replied, "Because it's dark on the other street and here I can see."

It may well be easier to see—and to effect—changes in external factors of organization which involve shifting of classrooms, the introduction of equipment, and the alteration in hours. But education for poorly functioning children will become effective only if we can develop techniques that allow us to reach their minds. For this goal, education must evolve into an intricate, sophisticated science.

Education may be unwilling or, perhaps more fairly, unable to achieve this end. Tremendous responsibility has been placed upon the school to somehow correct all the wrongs of society. As a result, it has become a convenient whipping boy for every child who fails. It may be that the institution of the school cannot offer the kind of care and instruction that the disadvantaged child requires if he is to learn. If this is the case, then we must develop other kinds of social institutions which may be capable of fulfilling this function. Bettelheim (1969) argued as much in suggesting the possibility of a kibbutz-type environment for children from backgrounds of poverty. On the other hand, if the school and training institutions for school wish to adapt, the effort will have to be enormous. Whether the tutorial program is ultimately selected for these purposes is not at issue. Whichever programs are selected, they will almost certainly require a type of skill and precision that is rarely demanded of education. The task of reorienting education so that it becomes intricate enough to cope with the problems of poorly functioning children will obviously be long and complex. If the school wishes to pursue the goal of education for all citizens, however, it must be prepared to cope with this degree of difficulty.

epilogue

As stated in the Preface, this book was written a decade ago and had as its focus the *functions,* or the *uses,* of the language that occurred when teachers and children communicated with one another. The orientation of most research at that time, however, was quite different. Largely because of Chomsky's seminal work in transformational grammar, language development research concentrated on the structure of children's verbal productions. As a result, there was a paucity of concepts for presenting a full and coherent account of language from a communication viewpoint. Marked strides have been made since that time and it seems appropriate to discuss the ways in which the ideas in the book would vary had the writing occurred in 1982 rather than 1972.

To do this I will highlight the major themes in the book and briefly discuss the role I feel they ought to play in current models of classroom communication.

1. The abstract attitude: Of all the themes, the concept of the abstract attitude would probably not appear if the writing had taken place today. Its deletion is not to be interpreted as meaning that I believe the concept to be "wrong." The concept of the abstract attitude, like that of intelligence, seems to capture behaviors that are "real" and important. For example, there clearly are differences

among children in the ways in which they seek information, organize ideas, and feel compelled to solve disequilibria. The term "abstract attitude" seems an apt way to capture this self-initiated search for meaning.

Its seeming power, however, remains at the level of intuition. When pressed to define actual, measurable behaviors that represent this aspect of intellectual activity, one finds the concept seriously lacking. It seems incapable of being raised to the level of objectivity necessary if we are to add light, rather than heat, to the issues at hand.

2. The language of dialogue: By contrast, the "language of dialogue" represents an issue that would be considerably expanded. For many years, research on children's language has concentrated on language at the level of *the word* and *the sentence*. These efforts are clearly reflected in the classroom where language at the level of *the word* is translated into an emphasis on verbal concepts (i.e., teaching sizes, names, colors, numbers, etc.) and language at the level of *the sentence* is translated into an emphasis on children offering expanded utterances (e.g., having them report the events over the weekend in a "show and tell" session).

Once a dialogue framework is adopted, a focus on either words or sentences is insufficient. Instead, one must move beyond these units and consider the relationships *among utterances*. For example, from a structural perspective, there is nothing awry with the sentence "My daddy is going to buy me a balloon tomorrow." However, if it is offered as a reply to the question "What did you see at the zoo yesterday?", the sentence seems strange and inappropriate.

The need for an expanded frame of reference becomes far greater when one considers not only two-step interchanges such as the one above, but also the long sequences that can and ought to occur in productive dialogues. This book contains numerous references to the idea that dialogue contains sequentially organized, independent utterances. The full significance of this idea, however, is only now beginning to be realized and the coming decade is likely to be marked by major developments in this realm.

Hopefully, a consequence of this development will be clear and explicit rules not only as to the parameters that characterize dialogue but also the parameters that determine whether or not a dialogue is productive. Productivity in dialogue has been a long sought goal of schooling. Indeed, the whole teaching process is designed with the aim of achieving a productive or effective interchange. The attainment of productivity, however, has been hampered by the tendency to confine the analysis of language to units lower than the level of sustained discourse. For instance, the "zoo-balloon" illustration above has some of the characteristics of a non-productive dialogue; a key factor determining this non-productivity is the inappropriateness of the response relative to the question that has been posed. Yet the issue of inappropriateness is one that rarely appears when focusing on words or sentences — it is an issue that cannot be ignored when considering sequenced interaction.

Appropriateness is in large measure governed by the issue of topic, the content of the conversation that is taking place. This issue has occupied little space in the current book but is one which deserves extensive elaboration. This elaboration is particularly important in any consideration of school language because classroom conversation is commonly marked by distortions in appropriateness. This point is perhaps best appreciated by comparing non-school and school dialogue. For example, if one were discussing the financial crisis in the world (the topic), any number of issues might be raised — e.g., the cause of the crisis, possible solutions, the countries which will fare best, etc. At the same time, many issues will almost certainly not be raised — e.g., the various colors of the paper money in different countries, the various sizes of the bills, the different lettering on the bills, etc. In other words, many ideas, although associated, are in fact irrelevant to a particular discussion once the topic has been selected. Further, the issues avoided when discussing one topic might be exactly the issues that ought to be raised if a different topic were being considered. In other words, the content of conversation is highly variable, depending upon the goal and topic of the discussion.

Unfortunately, in much school dialogue with young children the constraints of topic have not yet been sufficiently recognized. Regardless of the topic (e.g., making a cake, retelling a visit to the zoo, reporting in a show and tell exercise), the same set of concepts is raised: the children are asked for the *size, shape, color* and *number* of whatever content is under discussion. In essence, they are being taught a single repetitive script which may actually give them misleading information as to the nature of productive, topic-relevant dialogue. As the parameters of dialogue become increasingly well defined, there are likely to be dramatic and exciting changes in the nature of school discourse.

3. The role of questions: One of the most interesting consequences of a communication approach to language is the way in which it changes our perception of questions. This alteration occurs on a number of levels. First, in many cases, adults are unaware of the extent to which they ask questions of children and make evaluations of children's language based on the questions they have asked. For instance, in reports it is typical to state "John knows his colors, he knows his prepositions, he knows his numbers," etc. Children, like adults, do not walk about spouting colors or prepositions or numbers. Rather, they offer this type of information *when they are asked questions by the adult.* In other words, implied in the statement "John knows his colors" is the clause "when he is asked them by his teacher or therapist." Recognition of the adult's role is vital since it moves us from seeing language as a set of skills *within the child* to a set of behaviors occurring in an *interaction between* adult and child.

There is yet another way in which a communication approach alters our perception of questions. For a considerable length of time, questions have automatically been considered a "good" in teaching. Indeed, the general principle has been that the higher the level of the question, the better is the teaching. This approach, which essentially views questions as "stimuli for thinking," overlooks their communicative aspects. Questions are initiations from one person which demand comprehension and relevant responses from a second person. As questions take on higher and higher levels, the demands on the other person correspondingly increase. Questions then become triggers not for intellectual growth but for failure and shame.

The theme of question-induced failure is present throughout the book. However, the reader has been offered only a schematic framework for ascertaining the complexity of any question. (This is presented in Chapter 9, where a variety of question types is discussed, e.g., demands for memory, imitation, labeling, rationalization, etc.) Subsequent to the writing of this volume,

Sue Rose, Laura Berlin, and I have developed a simplified system which allows one to place any question at one of four levels of complexity. Limitations of space do not permit outlining the four levels here but readers who are interested may refer to Blank, M., Rose, S.A., and Berlin, L.J., *The Language of Learning* and *The Preschool Language Assessment Instrument,* New York, Grune & Stratton, 1978. These materials allow one not only to ascertain the complexity of a question, but also to determine a child's ability to deal with the four level continuum. Once an assessment is made, the teacher can then match the questions to the children's level and thereby conduct a conversation whereby the child is led through a sustained dialogue that is within his realm of comprehension.

4. The wrong response: Many observers have commented on the fact that teachers often ask questions to which they expect a particular response. Any response which fails to meet their expectations is then judged as wrong. The following is an illustration of this phenomenon. In an effort to stimulate conversation, a teacher asked a little boy who was holding a ball, "Do you like to play ball?" The child replied "No" (which happened to be the case). The teacher answered "You don't?" stating her response in such a way as to indicate disbelief and a disinclination to accept the child's response. This type of interaction is clearly unfortunate since it conveys many undesirable messages to the child. The negative consequences of this interaction, however, extend well beyond the effects they have on the child. Specifically, they have led many to state that there is no such thing as a wrong response — any utterance that the child offers is deemed to be a valid representation of his views and feelings.

On one level this view is legitimate and were I to be writing Chapter 4 today, it would probably have been labeled *The Quality of the Response* rather than *The Wrong Response.* There is a tone of harshness about the phrase The Wrong Response which makes it appear as though the child were being indicted simply for expressing his ideas when he was asked to do so. At another level, however, the term The Wrong Response is useful. It captures the uncontrollable, disconcerting effect that such responses have on conversation. For example, when a teacher asks a child for the name of an object (e.g., a cup) and the child replies with the wrong response (e.g., "drink" or "red" or "coffee"), an uncomfortable pause occurs in the conversation — a pause that leaves both the child and the teacher feeling vulnerable and uncomfortable. And yet the pause is almost beyond control. Regardless of the permissiveness of the teacher, a cup is not "drink," or "red," or "coffee"; it is a cup and the adult invariably conveys the idea that the response is somehow unacceptable, i.e., wrong.

Thus, while the term The Wrong Response may be less than optimal, the concept is nevertheless useful for both diagnosis and teaching. On the one hand, the quality of the child's response allows one to gain much greater insight into the child's level of understanding. Indeed, this aspect is a central feature of Piaget's clinical interview with young children. On the other hand, once identified, the wrong response can be treated so as to lead the child to higher levels of understanding. To this end, the simplification techniques (described in Chapter 4) are and continue to be an invaluable aid.

5. Poorly functioning children: The reader may have noticed that this epilogue contains no mention of "poorly functioning children." Since this concept played such a major role in the original text, it seems necessary to elaborate on the reasons for its exclusion at this time.

The initial inclusion of the term requires little explanation. The program described here, like other intervention programs of the time, was designed to enhance the performance of children who were failing, or who were likely to fail, in school. The term "poorly functioning children" served as useful shorthand for referring to this wide and varied group.

In both my program and those of others, the focus on these children was accompanied by a significant, but generally unstated, assumption that the school experience for well functioning children was profitable and productive. After all, the children were, by definition, performing effectively in the classroom and neither the teachers nor the children could be said to experience the failure and frustration that were such a part of the daily school life of poorly functioning children.

While the failure of non-achieving children was sad and painful, from the point of view of educational planning, it was in some ways helpful. The students' inability to deal effectively with classroom demands clearly revealed the inadequacy of the teaching encounters prepared for them and, accordingly, the need for alternative approaches. Following this line of reasoning, the success of well functioning children may be seen to have served an obfusticating role *vis à vis* educational planning. Since the children seemed to be functioning effectively, there was little pressure either to examine or alter the experiences with which they were provided.

However, years of classroom observation have led me to have considerable doubt about the language curricula for all children in the early years of schooling. The weaknesses in the curricula are understandable in light of the limited knowledge about discourse that has been available until now. Nevertheless, the fact remains that most language experiences in the classroom expose the children to interchanges which do little to serve the avowed goals of education.

In elaborating on this point, I will return to the example cited earlier (in 2 above) on the rigid format of much dialogue for young children. Observation of almost any classroom over the course of a year will reveal literally hundreds of repetitions of the same set of questions about *size, shape, color,* and *number.* There seems no way in which this repetition can be given an educational justification. When asked of poorly functioning children, the failure rate is and tends to remain high. Thus the repetition seems to serve little purpose other than to repeatedly expose the children to failure. When asked of well functioning children, the failure rate is admittedly low. The presence of success is clearly preferable to that of failure but one is still left to ponder the question: what can be gained by endlessly repeating the same set of questions day in and day out? If a child knows the colors *red, green, blue,* and *yellow* in the first, second, and third weeks of school, he is unlikely to forget them by the fifteenth or thirtieth week. Yet the questions continue to be asked.

As a result of these and similar observations, I now feel that most of the issues discussed in the original text and in this section (i.e., the language of dialogue, the role of questions, etc.) are applicable not simply to poorly functioning children but to all children. We are at a point where we are beginning to understand the nature and quality of productive dialogue and with this understanding conversations in classrooms ought to change dramatically. The likelihood of such change, however, is far from certain. Educational practices are determined not only by advances in knowledge, but also, and perhaps in greater measure, by a variety of economic, social, and political pressures. If these pressures can be contained, the coming period is likely to be exciting and the benefits great. Hopefully, this will be the case!

References

Anastasi, A. *Psychological Testing.* New York: Macmillan, 1961.

Aschner, M. J.; Perry, J. M.; Jenne, W.; Gallagher, J. J.; Afsar, S. S.; and Farr, H. *Aschner-Gallagher System for Classifying Thought in the Context of Classroom Verbal Interaction.* Chicago: University of Illinois Institute for Research on Exceptional Children, 1965.

Ausubel, D. *Educational Psychology: A Cognitive View.* New York: Holt, Rinehart & Winston, 1968.

Bandura, A., and Walters, R. H. *Social Learning and Personality Development.* New York: Holt, Rinehart & Winston, 1963.

Bangs, T. E. *Language and Learning Disorders of the Preacademic Child.* New York: Appleton-Century Crofts, Educational Division, 1968.

Baratz, S. S., and Baratz, J. C. "Early Childhood Intervention. The Social Science Base of Institutional Racism." *Harvard Educational Review* vol. 40, no. 1 (1970): 28-50.

Baratz, J. C., and Shuy, R. W., editors. *Teaching Black Children to Read.* Washington: Center for Applied Linguistics, 1969.

Bereiter, C. "Genetics and Educability: Educational Implication of the Jensen Debate." In *Disadvantaged Child*, edited by J. Hellmuth, Vol. 3. New York: Brunner/Mazel, 1970.

Bereiter, C., and Englemann, S. *Teaching Disadvantaged Children in the Preschool.* Englewood Cliffs, New Jersey: Prentice-Hall, 1966.

Bernstein, B. "Social Class and Linguistic Development: A Theory of Social Learning." In *Education, Economy and Society*, edited by A. H. Halsey, J. Flond, and C. A. Anderson. New York: Free Press of Glencoe, 1961.

Bettelheim, B. *The Children of the Dream.* New York: Macmillan, 1969.

Biber, B., and Franklin, M. "The Relevance of Developmental and Psychodynamic Concepts to the Education of the Preschool Child." *Journal of the American Academy of Child Psychiatry,* 6 (1967).

Birch, H., and Belmont, L. "Auditory-Visual Integration in Normal and Retarded Readers." *American Journal of Orthopsychiatry* 34 (1964): 852-61.

Bitterman, M. E. "The Evolution of Intelligence." *Scientific American* 212 (1965): 92-100.

Blank, M. "Cognitive Processes in Auditory Discrimination in Normal and Retarded Readers." *Child Development* 39 (1968a): 1091-101.

_____ "Effect of Stimulus Characteristics on Dimensional Shifting in Kindergarten Children." *Journal of Comparative and Physiological Psychology* 64 (1967): 522-25.

_____ "Experimental Approaches to Concept Development in Young Children." In *Development in Learning,* edited by E. A. Lunzer. London: Staples Press, 1968b.

_____ "The Treatment of Personality Variables in a Preschool Cognitive Program." In *Preschool Program for the Disadvantaged,* edited by J. Stanley. Baltimore: John Hopkins Press, 1972b.

_____ "The Wrong Response: Is It to Be Ignored, Prevented, or Treated?" In *Preschool in Action,* edited by R. K. Parker. Boston: Allyn and Bacon, Inc., 1972a.

Blank, M., and Bridger, W. "Cross-Modal Transfer in Nursery School Children." *Journal of Comparative and Physiological Psychology,* 58 (1964): 277-82.

_____ "Perceptual Abilities and Conceptual Deficiencies in Retarded Readers." In *Psychopathology of Mental Development,* edited by J. Zubin, p. 401-12. New York: Grune & Stratton, 1967.

_____ "Deficiencies in Verbal Labeling in Retarded Readers." *American Journal of Orthopsychiatry* 36 (1966): 840-47.

Blank, M., and Frank, S. "Story Recall in Kindergarten Children: Effect of Method of Presentation on Psycholinguistic Performance." *Child Development* 42 (1971): 299-312.

Blank, M., and Solomon, F. "A Tutorial Language Program to Develop Abstract Thinking in Socially Disadvantaged Preschool Children." *Child Development* 39 (1968): 379-89.

_____. "How Shall the Disadvantaged Child Be Taught?" *Child Development* 40 (1969): 47-61.

Blank, M.; Altman, D.; and Bridger, W. "Cross-Modal Transfer of Form Discrimination in Preschool Children." *Psychonomic Science* 10 (1968): 51-52.

Blank, M.; Higgins, T.; and Bridger, W. "Stimulus Complexity and Intramodal Reaction Time in Retarded Readers." *Journal of Educational Psychology* 62 (1971): 117-22.

Blank, M.; Koltuv, M.; and Wood, M. "Individual Teaching for Disadvantaged Kindergarten Children: A Comparison of Two Methods." *Journal of Special Education,* 6 (1972): 207-19

Blank, M.; Weider, S.; and Bridger, W. "Verbal Deficiencies in Abstract Thinking in Early Reading Retardation." *American Journal of Orthopsychiatry* 38 (1968): 823-34.

Brown, R. *Words and Things.* Glencoe, Illinois: The Free Press, 1958.

Brown, R., and Bellugi, V. "Three Processes in the Child's Acquisition of Syntax." *Harvard Educational Review* 34 (1964): 133-51.

Bruner, J. S. "Going beyond the Information Given." In *Contemporary Approaches to Cognition,* edited by J. S. Bruner et al. Cambridge: Harvard University Press, 1957.

_____. "On Cognitive Growth." In *Studies in Cognitive Growth,* edited by J. S. Bruner; R. R. Olver, and P. M. Greenfield. New York: John Wiley, 1966.

Bruner, J. S.; Goodnow, J. J.; and Austin, G. A. *A Study of Thinking.* New York: John Wiley, 1956.

Chomsky, N. "The General Properties of Language." In *Brain Mechanisms Underlying Speech and Language,* edited by C. H. Millikan and F. Darley. New York: Grune & Stratton, 1967.

_____. *Syntactic Structures.* The Hague: Mouton, 1957.

Chukovsky, K. *From Two to Five,* translated and edited by M. Morton. Berkeley: University of California Press, 1963.

Cole, M.. and Bruner, J. S. "Cultural Differences and Inferences about Psychological Processes." *American Psychologist* 25 (1971): 867-76.

Coleman, J. S. et al. *Equality of Educational Opportunity.* Washington, D.C.: Government Printing Office, 1966.

Cronbach, L. J. "The Logic of Experiments on Discovery." In *Learning by Discovery: A Critical Appraisal,* edited by L. S. Shulman and E. R. Keisler. Chicago: Rand McNally, 1966.

DeCecco, J. P. *The Psychology of Learning and Instruction: Educational Psychology.* Englewood Cliffs, New Jersey: Prentice-Hall, 1968.

De Hirsch, K.; Jansky, J.; and Langford, W. *Predicting Reading Failure.* New York: Harper and Row, 1966.

Deutsch, C. P. "Learning in the Disadvantaged." In *Analyses of Concept Learning,* edited by H. J. Klausmeuer and C. W. Harris. New York: Academic Press, 1966.

Deutsch, C. P., and Deutsch, M. "Brief Reflections on the Theory of Early Childhood Enrichment Programs." In *The Disadvantaged Child: Studies in the Social Environment and the Learning Process,* edited by M. Deutsch et al. New York: Basic Books, 1967.

De Vries, A. K. "The Utrecht Language and Thought Program." Gronengen: Walters Noordhoff, 1972.

Dewey, J. *The Child and the Curriculum.* Chicago: University of Chicago Press, 1902.

_____. *The School and Society*. Chicago: University of Chicago Press, 1900.

Eastman, P. D. *Are You My Mother?* New York: Random House, Beginner Books, 1960.

Erikson, E. H. *Childhood and Society*. New York: Norton, 1950.

Ervin, S. M., and Miller, W. R. "Language Development." In *Child Psychology, 62nd Yearbook, National Society for the Study of Education Part I*. Chicago: University of Chicago Press, 1963.

Frankenstein, C. *Impaired Intelligence: Pathology and Rehabilitation*. London: Gordon & Breach, 1970.

_____. *The Roots of the Ego*. Baltimore: Williams & Wilkins, 1966.

Freud, S. *The Basic Writings of Sigmund Freud*. New York: Random House, 1938.

Furth, H. G. *Piaget and Knowledge: Theoretical Foundations*. Englewood Cliffs, New Jersey: Prentice-Hall, 1969.

Gagné, R. M. *The Conditions of Learning*. New York: Holt Rinehart & Winston, 1965.

Gahagan, D. M., and Gahagan, G. A. "Talk Reform: Exploration in Language in the Primary School: Primary Socialization, Language, and Educational." Volume 3 of Sociological Research Unit, Monograph Series directed by B. Bernstein. London: Routledge & Kegan Paul, 1971.

Gazzaniga, M. S., and Sperry, R. W. "Language after Section of the Cerebral Commissures." *Brain* 90 (1967): 131-48.

Gesell, A.; Thompson, H.; and Amatruda, C. S. *The Psychology of Early Growth*. New York: Macmillan, 1938.

Goldstein, K. "Functional Disturbances in Brain Damage." In *American Handbook of Psychiatry*, edited by S. Arieti. New York: Basic Books, 1959.

Gordon, I. J. "Intellectual Stimulation for Infants and Toddlers." Paper presented at the Society for Research in Child Development, Santa Monica, California, March, 1969.

Gotkin, L. S.; Caudle, F.; Cans, H.; Saggessee, V.; and Schoenfeld, L. "Effects of Two Types of Feedback on Training and Posttest Performance in a Visual Discrimination Task." Unpublished manuscript from Institute for Developmental Studies, New York, 1968.

Gray, S. W., and Klaus, R. A. "An Experimental Preschool Program for Culturally Deprived Preschool Children." *Child Development* 36 (1965): 887-98.

Harlow, H. F. "Learning Set and Error Theory." In *Psychology: A Study of a Science. Volume 2: General Systematic Formulations, Learning and Special Processes*, edited by S. Koch. New York: McGraw-Hill, 1959.

Hebb, D. O. *A Textbook of Psychology*. Philadelphia: Saunders, 1966.

Heider, E. R.; Cazden, C. B.; and Brown, R. "Social Class Differences in the Effectiveness and Style of Children's Coding Ability." Report for Project Literacy, 1968.

Hertzig, M.; Birch, H.; Thomas, A.; and Mendez, O. Class and Ethnic Differences in the Responsiveness of Preschool Children to Cognitive Demands." *Monographs of the Society for Research in Child Development* 33 (1969): 1-69.

Hess, R. D., and Shipman, V. C. "Maternal Influences upon Early Learning: The Cognitive Environment of Urban Preschool Children." In *Early Education,* edited by R. D. Hess and R. M. Bear. Chicago: Aldine, 1966.

Hetzer, H. *Kindheit und Armut Psychologische Methoden in Amutsforschung and Armutsbekampfung.* Leipzig: Verlag Von S. Hirzel, 1929.

Holt, J. C. *How Children Fail.* New York: Pitman, 1964.

Honig, A. S.; Caldwell, B. M.; and Tannenbaum, J. "Patterns of Information Processing Used by and with Young Children in a Nursery School Setting." *Child Development* 41 (1970): 1045-65.

Houston, S. H. "A Reexamination of Some Assumptions about the Language of the Disadvantaged Child." *Child Development* 41 (1970): 947-63.

Hunt, J. McV. *Intelligence and Experience.* New York: Ronald Press, 1961.

Huttenlocher, J. "Some Effects of Negative Instances on the Formation of Simple Concepts." *Psychological Reports* 11 (1962): 35-42.

Illich, I. *Deschooling Society.* New York: Harper and Row, 1971.

Isaacs, S. *Intellectual Growth in Young Children.* London: G. Routledge, 1930.

John, V. P. "The Intellectual Development of Slum Children: Some Preliminary Findings." *American Journal of Orthopsychiatry* 33 (1963): 813-22.

John, V. P., and Goldstein, L. S. "The Social Context of Language Acquisition." *Merrill Palmer Quarterly of Behavior and Development* 10 (1964): 265-75.

Kagan, J.; Moss, H. A.; and Sigel, I. E. "Psychological Significance of Styles of Conceptualization." In *Basic Cognitive Processes in Children,* edited by J. C. Wright and J. Kagan. *Monographs of the Society for Research in Child Development* 28 (1963): 73-118.

Kamii, C. "An Application of Piaget's Theory to the Conceptualization of a Preschool Curriculum." In *Preschool in Action* edited by R. K. Parker. Boston: Allyn & Bacon Inc., 1972.

Karnes, M. B.; Teska, J. A.; and Hodgins, A. S. "The Effects of Our Programs of Classroom Intervention on the Intellectual and Language Development of Four-year-old Disadvantaged Children." *American Journal of Orthopsychiatry* 40 (1970): 58-76.

Kohlberg, L. "Early Education: A Cognitive Development View." *Child Development* 39 (1968): 1013-62.

Kohler, W. *The Mentality of Apes.* New York: Harcourt, Brace, Jovanovich, 1925.

Kohnstamm, G. A. "An Evaluation of Part of Piaget's Theory." *Acta Psychologica* 21 (1963): 313-56.

Krauss, R. *A Hole Is to Dig.* New York: Harper and Row, 1952.

Labov, W.; Cohen, P.; and Robbins, C. "A Preliminary Study of the Structure of English Used by Negro and Puerto Rican Speakers in New York City."

Final Report, Cooperative Research Project No. 3091. Washington, D.C.: U.S. Office of Education, 1965.

Labov, W. "The Logic of Nonstandard English." In *Monograph Series on Languages and Linguistics,* edited by J. E. Alatis. (1969).

Langer, J. "Disequilibrium as a Source of Development in Trends and Issues. In *Developmental Psychology,* edited by P. Mussen, J. Langer, and M. Covington. New York: Holt, Rinehart & Winston, 1969.

Langer, S. K. *Philosophy in a New Key.* New York: Mentor Books, 1949.

Levenstein, P. "Cognitive Growth in Preschoolers through Verbal Interaction with Mothers." *American Journal of Orthopsychiatry* 40 (1970): 426-32.

Lewis, M. M. *Infant Speech.* New York: Harcourt, Brace, Jovanovich, 1936.

Lewis, O. *La Vida: A Puerto Rican Family in the Culture of Poverty. San Juan and New York.* New York: Random House, 1966.

Lindamood, C. G., and Lindamood, P. C. *Lindamood Auditory Conceptualization Test Preliminary Manual.* Boston: Teaching Resources Corp, 1971.

Lombard, A. D. "Home Instruction Program for Preschool Youngsters." *Interim Report.* Hebrew University Center for Research in the Education of the Disadvantaged, 1971.

Luria, A. R. "The Role of Language in the Formation of Temporary Connection." In *Psychology in the Soviet Union,* edited by S. B. Simon. Stamford: Stamford Press, 1957.

Luria, A. R., and Yudovich, F. I. *Speech and the Development of Mental Processes in the Child.* London: Staples Press, 1959.

MacNamara, J. "Cognitive Basis of Language Learning in Infants." *Psychological Review* 79 (1972): 1-13.

Mandler, G. "From Association to Structure." *Psychological Review* 9 (1962): 415-27.

Mattick, I. Adaptation of Nursery School Techniques to Deprived Children: Some Notes on the Experiences of Teaching Children of Multi-Problem Families in a Therapeutically-Oriented Nursery School. *Journal of the American Academy of Child Psychiatry* 4 (1965): 670-700.

McNeill, D. "Developmental Psycholinguistics." In *The Genesis of Language: A Psycholinguistic Study,* edited by F. Smith and G. Miller. Cambridge: Massachusetts Institute of Technology Press, 1966.

Milner, A. D., and Bryant, P. E. "Cross-Modal Matching by Young Children." *Journal of Comparative Physiological Psychology* 71 (1970): 453-58.

Moffett, J. *Teaching the Universe of Discourse.* Boston: Houghton Mifflin, 1968.

Montessori, M. *The Montessori Method.* New York: F. A. Stokes, 1912.

Myklebust, H. R. *The Psychology of Deafness.* New York: Grune & Stratton, 1960.

Olson, D. R. "Language and Thought: Aspects of a Cognitive Theory of Semantics." *Psychological Review* 77 (1970a): 257-73.

Olson, D. R. *Cognitive Development. The Child's Acquisition of Diagonality.* New York: Academic Press, 1970b.

Ortar, G., and Carman, H. "An Analysis of Mothers' Speech as a Factor in the Development of Children's Intelligence." Jerusalem: unpublished manuscript, 1969.

Osser, H. "Language Development." In: *Psychology and the Education Process,* edited by G. Lesser. Glenview: Scott Foresman, in press.

Peal, E., and Lambert, W. "The Relation of Bilingualism to Intelligence." *Psychological Monographs* 76 (1962): 123.

Piaget, J. *The Origins of Intelligence in Children.* New York: International Universities Press, 1952.

_____. *The Psychology of Intelligence,* translated by M. Piercy and D. E. Berlyne. London: Routledge Kegan Paul, 1947.

Radler, D. H., and Kephart, N. *Success through Play: How to Prepare Your Child for School Achievement and Enjoy It.* New York: Harper and Row, 1960.

Rosenthal, R., and Jacobson, L. *Pygmalian in the Classroom.* New York: Holt, Rinehart & Winston, 1968.

Schaefer, E. "Home Tutoring, Maternal Behavior, and Infant Intellectual Development." Paper presented at meeting of the American Psychological Association, 1969.

Shulman, L. S. "Psychology." In *Mathematics Education Sixty Ninth Yearbook of the National Society for the Study of Education,* edited by E. Begle. 1970.

Sigel, I. E., and Hooper, R. H., editors. *Logical Thinking in Children.* New York: Holt, Rinehart & Winston, 1968.

Sigel, I. E.; Anderson, L. M.; and Shapiro, H. "Categorization Behavior of Lower and Middle-Class Negro Preschool Children: Differences in Dealing with Representation of Familiar Objects." *Journal of Negro Education.* (1966): 218-29.

Silberman, C. E. *Crisis in Black and White.* New York: Random House, 1964.

_____. *Crisis in the Classroom: The Remaking of American Education.* New York: Random House, 1970.

Simon, A., and Boyer, E., editors. "Mirrors for Behavior: An Anthology of Classroom Observation Instruments." *Classroom Interaction Newsletter* 3 (1968): 00-00.

Slobin, D. I. "Abstracts of Soviet Studies of Child Language." *The Genesis of Language: A Psycholinguistic Approach,* edited by F. Smith and G. Miller. Cambridge: Massachusetts Institute of Technology Press, 1966.

Smilansky, M. *Intellectual Advancement of Culturally Disadvantaged Children.* New York: John Wiley, 1967.

Smith, F., and Miller, G. *The Genesis of Language: A Psycholinguistic Study.* Cambridge: Massachusetts Institute of Technology Press, 1966.

Spitz, R. A. "Hospitalism: An Inquiry into the Genesis of Psychiatric Conditions in Early Childhood." *Psychoanalytic Study of the Child* 1 (1945): 53-74.

Stamback, M. "Le probleme du Rythme dans le Development de L'enfant et dans les Dyslexies D'evolution." *Enfance* 4 (1951): 480-502.

Stern, C. "Labeling and Variety in Concept Identification with Young Children." *Journal of Educational Psychology* 56 (1965): 235-40.

Valentine, C. A. "Deficit Difference and Bicultural Model of Afro-American Behavior." *Harvard Educational Review* 41 (1971): 137-57.

Vygotsky, L. S. *Thought and Language,* Translated and edited by E. Kaufmann and G. Voltar. New York: John Wiley, 1962.

Weikart, D. P. "Preschool Programs: Preliminary Findings." *Journal of Special Education* 1 (1967): 163-81.

Weikart, D. P., and Weigerink, R. "Initial Results of a Comparative Preschool Curriculum Project." Paper presented at the meeting of the American Psychological Association, San Francisco, September, 1968.

Weir, R. H. *Language in the Crib.* The Hague: Mouton & Co., 1962.

Wepman, J. M. "Auditory Discrimination, Speech, and Reading." *Elementary School Journal* 60 (1960): 325-33.

Werner, H. *Comparative Psychology of Mental Development.* New York: International Universities Press, 1957.

Werner, H., and Kaplan, B. *Symbol Formation.* New York: John Wiley, 1963.

Whorf, B. L. *Language, Thought, and Reality.* Cambridge: Massachusetts Institute of Technology Press, 1956.

Witkin, H. A. et al. *Personality through Perception.* New York: Harper and Row, 1954.

Wittrock, M. C.; Keislar, E.; and Stern, C. Verbal Cues in Concept Identification." *Journal of Educational Psychology* 55 (1964): 195-200.

Wolff, J. L. "Concept-Shift and Discrimination-Reversal Learning in Humans." *Psychological Bulletin* 68 (1967): 369-408.

Author Index